HEALTH CARE ISSUES, COSTS AND ACCESS

# HEALTH INSURANCE INDUSTRY MARKET STRUCTURE: COVERAGE AND COST ISSUES

# Health Care Issues, Costs and Access

Additional books in this series can be found on Nova's website under the Series tab.

Additional E-books in this series can be found on Nova's website under the E-book tab.

# Economic Issues, Problems and Perspectives

Additional books in this series can be found on Nova's website under the Series tab.

Additional E-books in this series can be found on Nova's website under the E-books tab.

HEALTH CARE ISSUES, COSTS AND ACCESS

# HEALTH INSURANCE INDUSTRY MARKET STRUCTURE: COVERAGE AND COST ISSUES

BRENT C. JENNER
EDITOR

Nova Science Publishers, Inc.
*New York*

For permission to use material from this book please contact us:
Telephone 631-231-7269; Fax 631-231-8175
Web Site: http://www.novapublishers.com



**LIBRARY OF CONGRESS CATALOGING-IN-PUBLICATION DATA**

Health insurance industry market structure : coverage and cost issues /
editor, Brent C. Jenner.
p. ; cm.
Includes bibliographical references and index.
ISBN 978-1-61761-289-3 (hardcover)
1. Health insurance. I. Jenner, Brent C.
[DNLM: 1. Insurance, Health--economics--United States. W 275 AA1]
HG9396.H418 2010
368.38'200973--dc22

2010028639

*Published by Nova Science Publishers, Inc. † New York*

# CONTENTS

# PREFACE

This book discusses how the current health insurance market structure affects the two policy goals of expanding health insurance coverage and containing health care costs. Concerns about concentration in health insurance markets are linked to wider concerns about the cost, quality, and availability of health care. The market structure of the health insurance and hospital industries may have contributed to rising health care costs and deteriorating access to affordable health insurance and health care. Many features of the health insurance market and the ways it links to other parts of the health care system can hinder competition, lead to concentrated markets, and produce inefficient outcomes.

Chapter 1- This chapter discusses how the current health insurance market structure affects the two policy goals of expanding health insurance coverage and containing health care costs. Concerns about concentration in health insurance markets are linked to wider concerns about the cost, quality, and availability of health care. The market structure of the health insurance and hospital industries may have contributed to rising health care costs and deteriorating access to affordable health insurance and health care. Many features of the health insurance market and the ways it links to other parts of the health care system can hinder competition, lead to concentrated markets, and produce inefficient outcomes. Health insurers are intermediaries in the transaction of the provision of health care between patients and providers: reimbursing providers on behalf of patients, exercising some control over the number and types of services covered, and negotiating contracts with providers on the payments for health services. Consequently, policies affecting health insurers will likely affect the other parts of the health care sector.

Chapter 2- People buy insurance to protect themselves against the possibility of financial loss in the future. Such losses may be due to a motor vehicle collision, natural disaster, or other circumstance. For patients, financial losses may result from the use of health care services. Health insurance then provides protection against the possibility of financial loss due to high health care expenses. Also, people do not know ahead of time exactly what their health care expenses will be, so paying for health insurance on a regular basis helps smooth out their out-of-pocket spending.

While health coverage continues to be mostly a private enterprise in this country, government plays an increasingly significant role. Especially during the latter half of the 20th century, the government both initiated and responded to dynamics in medicine, the economy, and the workplace through legislation and public policies. For example, the Internal Revenue System clarified that employer contributions to employee health benefits are exempt from taxation, which encouraged the growth of employment-based health coverage. Given the frequent introduction of legislation aimed at modifying or building on the current health insurance system, understanding the potential impact of such proposals requires a working knowledge of how health insurance is designed, provided, purchased, and regulated. This chapter provides background information about these topics.

Chapter 3- Health care providers and members of Congress have raised concerns that consolidation in the private health insurance industry may be resulting in less competitive markets and contributing to rising health insurance rates paid by consumers and employers. However, measuring the extent of changes in market competition over time or the effects of changes is challenging. In particular, reliable, longitudinal data to measure concentration, that is, the number of competitors and their relative market share, are only available on health maintenance organizations (HMO) but not on preferred provider organizations (PPO) or other insurance products that may comprise the market.[1] Further, data on health insurers are not available at all geographic levels. Despite these challenges, researchers have used the data available to study competition in health insurance markets, typically using one of two measures of competition: (1) HMO market concentration or (2) the number of HMOs in a market.[2] Researchers acknowledge that market concentration and the number of competitors are not perfect measures of competition in private health insurance markets and that there are limits to the conclusions to be drawn from studies that rely on the available data.[3] You asked us to review research completed on competition in the private health insurance industry. This chapter summarizes the findings of peer-reviewed research on concentration in private health insurance markets and the relationship between the level of competition and other variables, such as premium prices and provider reimbursement rates.

Chapter 4- As a follow-up to our 2005 and 2002 reports on the competitiveness of the small group health insurance market, you requested updated information on each state and the District of Columbia.[1] Specifically, this chapter provides information from states and the District of Columbia (hereafter referred to as a state) on the number of carriers licensed in the small group market, the largest carriers, and their market share.[2]

To obtain this information, the author sent an electronic survey to the office responsible for regulating insurance, health plans, or both in all 51 states. After following up with nonresponding states by e-mail and telephone, all but 1 state completed the survey. Of the 50 states that responded, however, 3 were unable to provide the requested information on small group carriers and their market share. For the remaining 47 states, not all had the information needed to answer all of the questions. For example, 44 states reported the largest carrier and 39 states provided market share data. Also, the 47 states varied in how they defined the size of a small group. Most—33—defined a small group as 2 to 50 employees; 12 defined a small group as 1 to 50 employees; and 2 had another definition. Finally, states generally reported information as of December 2007, though 6 states were able to provide 2008 numbers, and 3 states were limited to data from 2006. The author did not independently validate the information provided by the states. However, in the survey, the author asked states to describe the source of the information reported and provide clarifying information about the numbers reported. As a result of this information, the author excluded some states' responses from certain market share analysis, e.g., if the state had no way of separating data on small group health insurance from data on all group health insurance. The author performed our work from December 2008 through February 2009 in accordance with all sections of GAO's Quality Assurance Framework that are relevant to our objectives. The framework requires that the author plan and perform the engagement to obtain sufficient and appropriate evidence to meet our stated objectives and to discuss any limitations in our work. The author believe that the information and data obtained, and the analysis conducted, provide a reasonable basis for any findings and conclusions. Because the author did not evaluate the policies or operations of any federal agency to develop the information presented in this chapter, the author did not seek comments from any agency.

Chapter 5- Health care spending is one of the most rapidly growing portions of the federal budget. Projections suggest if the rapid growth in health care costs is not curtailed, governments at all levels will face an uncomfortable choice between significant cuts in other spending priorities or major tax increases. This chapter examines the economic justification for government intervention and involvement in health care markets.

Many analysts claim market-oriented policies, in certain instances, could lower costs and enhance efficiency in health care. This chapter discusses the Invisible Hand Theorem, which states that when certain assumptions hold, market outcomes will be efficient. These assumptions require that no one has an informational advantage over another, that no spillover effects exist in consumption or production, that no one exerts market power, and that no scale economies exist in production.

Many characteristics of health care markets fail to satisfy the assumptions of the Invisible Hand Theorem. Moreover, fundamental characteristics of health care (such as informational asymmetries between patients and health care professionals and between payers and providers, as well as ethical and distributional concerns) complicate efforts to expand the use of market or market-like incentives in health care.

In: Health Insurance Industry Market...
Editors: Brent C. Jenner
ISBN: 978-1-61761-289-3


*Chapter 1*

# THE MARKET STRUCTURE OF THE HEALTH INSURANCE INDUSTRY

***D. Andrew Austin and Thomas L. Hungerford***

## SUMMARY

In March 2010, after more than a year of legislative deliberation, Congress passed a pair of measures designed to reform the U.S. health care system and address the twin challenges of constraining rapid growth of health care costs and expanding access to high-quality health care. On March 21, the House passed the Patient Protection and Affordable Care Act (H.R. 3590), which the Senate had approved on Christmas Eve, as well as the Health Care and Education Reconciliation Act of 2010 (H.R. 4872). President Obama signed the first measure (P.L. 111-148) on March 23 and the second on March 30 (P.L. 111-152). On November 2, 2009, the House Judiciary Committee reported out the Health Insurance Industry Antitrust Enforcement Act of 2009 (H.R. 3596), which would limit antitrust exemptions provided by the McCarran-Ferguson Act (P.L. 79-15).

This chapter discusses how the current health insurance market structure affects the two policy goals of expanding health insurance coverage and containing health care costs. Concerns about concentration in health insurance markets are linked to wider concerns about the cost, quality, and availability of health care. The market structure of the health insurance and hospital industries may have contributed to rising health care costs and deteriorating access to affordable health insurance and health care. Many features of the health insurance market and the ways it links to other parts of the health care system can hinder competition, lead to concentrated markets, and produce inefficient outcomes. Health insurers are intermediaries in the transaction of the provision of health care between patients and providers: reimbursing providers on behalf of patients, exercising some control over the number and types of services covered, and negotiating contracts with providers on the payments for health services. Consequently, policies affecting health insurers will likely affect the other parts of the health care sector.

The market structure of the U.S. health insurance industry not only reflects the nature of health care, but also its origins in the 1930s and its evolution in succeeding decades. Before World War II, many commercial insurers doubted that hospital or medical costs were an insurable risk. But after the rapid spread of Blue Cross plans in the mid-1930s, several commercial insurers began to offer health coverage. By the 1950s, commercial health insurers had become potent competitors and began to cut into Blue Cross's market share in many regions, changing the competitive environment of the health insurance market.

Evidence suggests that health insurance markets are highly concentrated in many local areas. Many large firms that offer health insurance benefits to their employees have self-insured, which may put some competitive pressure on insurers, although this is unlikely to improve market conditions for other consumers. The exercise of market power by firms in concentrated markets generally leads to higher prices and reduced output—high premiums and limited access to health insurance—combined with high profits. Many other characteristics of the health insurance markets, however, also contribute to rising costs and limited access to affordable health insurance. Rising health care costs, in particular, play a key role in rising health insurance costs.

Complex interactions among health insurance, health care providers, employers, pharmaceutical manufacturers, tax policy, and the medical technology industry have helped increase health costs over time. Reducing the growth trajectory of health care costs may require policies that affect these interactions. Policies focused only on health insurance sector reform may yield some results, but are unlikely to solve larger cost growth and limited access problems. This chapter will be updated as events warrant.

# INTRODUCTION

In March 2010, after more than a year of legislative deliberation, Congress passed a pair of measures designed to reform the U.S. health care system and address the twin challenges of constraining rapid growth of health care costs and expanding access to high-quality health care. On March 21, the House passed the Patient Protection and Affordable Care Act (H.R. 3590), which the Senate had approved on Christmas Eve, as well as the Health Care and Education Reconciliation Act of 2010 (H.R. 4872).[1] President Obama signed the first measure (P.L. 111-148) on March 23 and the second on March 30 (P.L. 111-152).

Other health reform proposals were also put forth, such as the Healthy Americans Act (S. 391), introduced by Senators Ron Wyden and Robert Bennett, and the Empowering Patients First Act (H.R. 3400), introduced by Representative Tom Price. On November 2, 2009, the House Judiciary Committee reported out the Health Insurance Industry Antitrust Enforcement Act of 2009 (H.R. 3596), which would limit antitrust exemptions provided by the McCarran-Ferguson Act (P.L. 79-15).[2]

Health care costs in the United States, which have risen rapidly in real terms in the last few decades, have strained state and federal budgets. Future growth in health care costs is projected to threaten the fiscal position of state and federal governments unless major policy changes occur. Additionally, for many Americans, the lack of health insurance coverage complicates access to health care. According to the U.S. Census Bureau, 46.3 million or 15.4% of the people in the United States lack health insurance coverage.[3] Furthermore, even families with health insurance may become vulnerable to the financial burdens of a serious health condition or illness either because of the narrowness of plan benefits or the unpredictability of decisions about what care is covered. Increases in health insurance premiums, according to some research, has degraded access to health care.[4]

Health insurance markets are often highly concentrated with one insurer accounting for over 50% of the market. Concerns about concentration in health insurance markets are linked to wider concerns about the cost, quality, and availability of health care. The market structure of the health insurance and hospital industries may have played a role in rising health care costs and in limiting access to affordable health insurance and health care. Some argue market concentration has led to higher health care prices.[5] Higher prices for health care or health care insurance may then make health care less affordable and thus less accessible for some families. Consumers in the individual and small group markets typically face particularly challenging conditions.

Others, however, contend that health insurers with strong bargaining leverage might help constrain health providers' ability to raise prices, and that the benefit of lower premiums resulting from that ability to bargain may be passed along to consumers. Some industry analysts have described competition among major health insurers as robust, and some pricing trends indicate that competition has strongly affected insurers' market strategies.[6] Moreover, some contend that economies of scale along with state and federal regulation have contributed to the rising levels of concentration in health insurance markets.

The Obama Administration has made reform of the American health insurance and health care system a top policy priority. Several congressional proposals aim to broaden access to health care by increasing the number of Americans with health insurance coverage, by lowering the cost of insurance faced by individuals, by providing stronger incentives for individuals to acquire health insurance, and by restructuring parts of the health insurance market. Some of these health reform proposals also contain measures intended to slow the growth of health care costs, although some policy analysts are uncertain whether current proposals are likely to accomplish that goal.[7] Some argue that a more fundamental reform of the health care sector and the health insurance market would be needed to change the projected trajectory of health care costs.

This chapter discusses whether or not the current health insurance market structure hinders the U.S. health system's ability to reach the policy goals of expanding health insurance coverage and containing health care costs. The report describes the forces that have shaped the health insurance industry, including its historical evolution, characteristics of health care and health insurance, determinants of supply and demand for health insurance, and the nature of competition among health insurers. Reasons for high market concentration are discussed, along with profitability measures for the industry. Finally, options for Congress regarding the health insurance industry are analyzed.

## How the Health Insurance Industry Developed

The market structure of the modern U.S. health insurance industry not only reflects the complexities and uncertainties of health care, but also its origins in the 1930s and its evolution in succeeding decades. Private insurers had offered accident, burial, and sickness policies in the latter half of the 19$^{th}$

century, and some railroad, mining, and timber firms began to offer workplace health benefits.[8] As population shifted from rural agricultural regions to industrialized urban centers, workers were exposed to risks of occupational accidents, but had less support from extended family networks that provided informal insurance benefits. Many workers obtained accident or sickness policies through fraternal organizations, labor unions, or private insurers. These policies were usually indemnity plans, that would pay a set cash amount in the event of a serious accident or health emergency.[9] Social surveys at the turn of century spotlighted the link between industrial accidents and poverty, leading Progressive-era reformers and labor unions to push for compulsory social insurance, which helped lead to workers' compensation programs.[10]

## How the "Blues" Began

The modern health insurance industry in the United States was spurred by the onset of the Great Depression. In 1929, the Baylor University Hospital in Dallas created a pre-paid hospitalization benefit plan for school teachers after a hospital executive discovered that unpaid bills accumulated by local educators were a large burden on hospital finances as well as on the teachers themselves.[11] Unlike earlier health insurance policies, subscribers were entitled to hospital care and services rather than a cash indemnity. While the plan did not cover physician bills, it did improve enrollees' ability to pay those charges.

The Baylor Plan was soon extended to other groups. Other hospitals in Dallas quickly followed suit with their own group hospitalization plans as a means of ensuring a steady revenue source in difficult economic times.[12] For individuals, these plans offered a way to obtain hospital care at a reasonable and predictable cost. In 1932, local hospitals in Sacramento, CA, created a joint plan for group hospitalization benefits, and in 1933, hospitals in Essex County, New Jersey, offered a similar plan. Community-based plans in St. Paul, MN, Washington, DC, and Cleveland were created soon afterwards. The Blue Cross emblem, first used by the St. Paul plan, was widely adopted by other prepaid hospital benefit plans adhering to American Hospital Association (AHA) guidelines.

The AHA's 1933 guidelines required prepaid group hospitalization plans using the Blue Cross symbol to stress the public welfare, limit benefits to hospital charges, organize as a non-profit, and run on a sound economic basis.[13] While many of the early group hospitalization plans were organized by community leaders, voluntary hospitals controlled Blue Cross because they provided the key resources in most cases and because they were responsible for underwriting the policies.[14] Through the 1930s, the number of Blue Cross plans grew and enrollments expanded. By 1937, 1 million subscribers were covered, and by 1939, 25 states had passed legislation to enable hospitalization plans. Many state laws deemed Blue Cross plans charitable community organizations that were exempted from certain insurance regulations and taxes.[15]

The health insurance market in the United States, according to many historians, was originally structured to avoid competition among providers.[16] The earliest plans tied benefits to a single sponsoring hospital; each hospital plan competed with others. Groups or individuals with the option to negotiate with specific hospitals might have been able to exert bargaining power. Hospital and professional groups, however, soon pushed for joint plans that required "free choice of physicians and hospital," rather than plans offered by individual hospitals. Joint plans dampened incentives for local hospitals to compete on the basis of price or generosity of plan benefits. The American Hospital Association strongly favored joint plans that allowed a subscriber to obtain care from any licensed local hospital and viewed single-hospital plans as a threat to the economic stability of community hospitals. Furthermore, in 1937, the AHA required Blue Cross plans to have exclusive territories so that they would not compete against each other.[17]

Hospital and physician groups' opposition to competition in health care and health insurance dovetailed with more general criticism of "destructive competition" that was widespread in the early 1930s. Some business leaders and New Deal policymakers viewed heightened competition as the cause of sharp cuts in wages, which in their view reduced consumer buying power and drove price deflation and market instability during the early years of the Great Depression.[18] Most economists believe measures to reduce market competition imposed during the Great Depression actually retarded economic recovery.[19] Competition in health insurance markets, however, raises issues that do not apply in most markets. If health insurers adopt different underwriting standards, competition can make pooling risks more difficult, an issue discussed in more detail below.

Insurance coverage of physician services lagged behind the growth of Blue Cross hospital plans due to opposition from the American Medical Association (AMA) and restrictive state laws.[20] In several states, however, medical societies set up prepaid service plans to preempt proposed state or federal plans, which evolved into Blue Shield plans. In most states, Blue

Shield was absorbed into Blue Cross plans, although some retained separate governing boards.

Blue Cross plans accelerated their growth during World War II and extended to almost all states by 1946.[21] Wartime wage and price controls authorized in October 1942 excluded "reasonable" insurance and pension benefits.[22] As industries struggled to expand war production, many employers used health insurance and other fringe benefits to attract new workers. In the late 1940s, the National Labor Relations Board (NLRB) successfully sued employers that refused to bargain collectively over fringe benefits, opening the way for unions to negotiate with employers over health insurance, which further helped boost enrollments in health insurance plans.[23]

## Tax Advantages for Employer-Provided Health Insurance Benefits

Prior to 1954, no explicit statutory provision excluded health insurance benefits from federal income taxation.[24] The IRS, however, had indicated in 1943 that group health insurance premiums paid by a firm for its employees would be considered an "ordinary and necessary" business expense rather than as taxable income received by the employee.[25] A major overhaul of the Internal Revenue Code of 1954 included Section 106, which explicitly excluded employer contributions for health insurance from employees' taxable income. The tax exclusion for employer-provided health care made health insurance cheaper than non-tax-advantaged forms of consumption for individuals. One study found that health insurance coverage following the 1954 tax changes expanded more rapidly among employees with higher incomes, who generally had marginal tax rates, which could indicate that the tax exclusion led workers to demand more extensive or generous plans.[26] Other factors, such as rising income levels, competition for workers, and rising medical costs, also spurred growth in employer-provided health benefits.

## Commercial Insurers Enter

Before World War II, many commercial insurers doubted that hospital or medical costs were an insurable risk. Insurers traditionally considered a risk insurable only if the potential losses were definite, measurable and not subject to control by the insured.[27] The financial risks linked to illness or injury, however, could vary depending on the judgment of medical personnel, and behavior of the insured could affect the probability of ill health in many ways. After the rapid spread of Blue Cross plans in the mid-1930s, however, several commercial insurers began to offer similar health coverage. By the 1950s, commercial health insurers had become potent competitors and began to cut into Blue Cross's market share in many parts of the country. The large-scale entry of commercial insurers into the health insurance market changed the competitive environment in two ways. First, Blue Cross organizations, which had been sheltered from competition by exclusive territory and free-choice-of-hospital rules, were now engaged in headto-head competition with commercial rivals.

Second, the commercial health insurers were not bound to set premiums using the Blue Cross community rating principle, which linked premiums to average claims costs across a geographic area rather than to the claims experience of particular groups or individuals. Therefore, commercial insurers using an "experience rating" approach were able to underbid Blue Cross for firms that employed healthier-than-average individuals, which on average were cheaper to insure. The loss of healthier groups then raised average costs among remaining groups, which hampered Blue Cross organizations' ability to compete with commercial insurers on price.[28] Competition from commercial insurers compelled Blue Cross to adopt experience rating in the 1950s, although most Blue Cross plans continued to support efforts to broaden risk pools.[29] The shift toward experience rating changed the nature of competition in the health insurance market. Insurers could cut costs by shifting risks to others, by recruiting firms whose employees and their families were healthier than average, rather than finding more efficient ways of managing risks for a given pool of subscribers.

## Introduction of Medicare and Medicaid

By the late 1950s, health insurance benefits had become a standard part of compensation packages among most major employers.[30] In 1959, Congress created the Federal Employees' Health Benefit Plan (FEHBP), which provided Blue Cross and Blue Shield benefits to federal workers across the country.[31] During the late 1950s, hospital costs rose sharply in many parts of the United States due to new hospital construction, the increasing capital intensity of inpatient care, the replacement of flat-rate per diem reimbursement for hospitals with retrospective fullcost payment, and the spread of health insurance benefits that increased patients' ability to pay. Those cost increases led many Blue Cross affiliates to request large premium increases, which raised public concern and resistance from many state insurance regulators. These pressures, according to some historians, led Blue Cross affiliates and voluntary hospitals to push states to enact certificate of need (CON) regulations in the mid-1960s to deflect more stringent cost control measures while raising barriers to entry to newer and proprietary hospitals.[32]

While Blue Cross/Blue Shield and commercial insurance plans covered a large portion of employees and their dependents at the end of the 1950s, many low-income and elderly people had trouble obtaining affordable health insurance or paying for health care. Congress in the 1950s began to provide federal aid to states that chose to cover health care costs of these groups. Social Security was extended to pay providers to cover certain medical costs incurred by aged, blind, and disabled beneficiaries starting in 1950.[33] The Kerr-Mills Act of 1960 (P.L. 86-778), a forerunner of Medicaid, supported state programs that paid providers for health care of the "aged, blind, or permanently and totally disabled," as well as low-income elderly individuals.[34] State governments, subject to certain federal requirements, retained substantial discretion over benefit levels and income limits, which were typically linked to welfare assistance programs.[35] By 1965, 40 states had implemented Kerr-Mills programs, and three more had authorized plans. Less than 2% of the elderly, however, were covered by Kerr-Mills programs in 1965.[36]

In 1965, the Johnson Administration worked with Ways and Means Committee Chairman Wilbur Mills to create the Medicare program, which provided health insurance for nearly all Americans over age 65.[37] Medicare combined a compulsory hospital insurance program (Part A) with a voluntary physician services plan (Part B). [38] While some had worried that Medicare would displace private insurers, Blue Cross organizations became fiscal intermediaries for Medicare, responsible for issuing payments to providers and other back office operations. Medicaid, created in the same 1965 act, is a means-tested program financed by federal and state funds. Each state designs and administers its own program under federal rules. Over time, Medicaid eligibility standards and federal requirements have become more complex.[39]

Private health insurance companies play an important role in several federal health programs. Many insurers run Medicare Advantage (Part C) and prescription drug benefit plans (Part D), and some help provide CHIP (Childrens' Health Insurance Program, previously known as SCHIP) benefits.

## The Rise of Managed Care

In some parts of the country, plans combining insurance with the direct provision of health care evolved into important players in local markets despite the strong opposition of the AHA and AMA.[40] A health plan designed for southern California construction workers in the mid-1930s eventually became the Kaiser Health Plan. Some physicians set up group practices and clinics in the 1920s and 1930s.[41] Many health care cooperatives were formed by employers, employee groups, and the federal governments during the 1 930s and 1 940s.[42] While some of these plans prospered locally or regionally, they did not achieve national reach until the 1970s.

In 1971, President Nixon announced a program to encourage prepaid group plans that joined insurance and care functions as a way to constrain the growth of medical care costs, which had risen sharply in the years following the startup of the Medicare and Medicaid programs, and to enhance competition in the health insurance market. Advocates claimed that health maintenance organizations (HMOs), which integrate health care and health insurance functions, would have a financial motive to promote wellness and would lack incentives to overprovide care. The Health Maintenance Organization Act of 1973 (P.L. 93-222) provided new grants, loans and loan guarantees to expand the number of HMOs, which then only numbered about 30, so that 90% of the country would have access to HMOs in 10 years.[43]

While this ambitious goal was not reached in the 1970s, by the late 1980s policymakers and businesses began to view greater use of managed care organizations such as HMOs and similar organizations as a key strategy for controlling health care costs.[44] In the mid-1990s, the broader use of more restrictive forms of managed care (such as stringent gatekeeper, second medical opinion, and pre-approval requirements) sparked strong consumer resistance, which forced an industry retreat from some of those strategies.[45] Networks of providers, known as preferred provider organizations (PPOs), grew rapidly in the late 1980s and early 1990s. PPOs, often owned by hospital systems and other providers, typically contract with insurers or self-insured firms and offer discounted fee-for-service (FFS) rates. PPO enrollees who receive care outside of the network typically must obtain plan approval or pay more. Thus, a PPO plans provided patients with more flexibility than staff-model HMOs, which generally did not cover care provided outside of the HMO.[46] As various types of managed care plans such as HMOs and PPOs became widespread, more employers offered choices among competing health plans to let workers willing to pay higher premiums avoid restrictive plans.

## Blurring Distinctions between "Blues" and Commercial Insurers

By the 1980s, health researchers and policymakers had begun to view the differences between Blue Cross/Blue Shield insurers, which were organized as non-profit organizations, and for-profit commercial health insurers as having narrowed.[47] The Internal Revenue Service regulations had regarded Blue Cross organizations as tax exempt community service organizations since their inception in the 1930s.[48] The Tax Reform Act of 1986 (P.L. 99-5 14) removed Blue Cross/Blue Shield plans' tax exemption because Congress believed that "exempt charitable and social welfare organizations that engage in insurance activities are engaged in an activity whose nature and scope is inherently commercial rather than charitable," and that "the tax-exempt status of organizations engaged in insurance activities provided an unfair competitive advantage."[49] The 1986 act retained some limited tax advantages to reflect Blue Cross/Blue Shield plans' provision of community-rated health insurance, especially in the individual and small-group markets.[50]

In the 1990s, many health insurers struggled with rising health care costs and sharper criticism of industry practices. Blue Cross/Blue Shield of West Virginia went bankrupt and several other Blue Cross/Blue Shield affiliates faced serious financial difficulties.[51] In 1994, Blue Cross/Blue Shield guidelines were amended to let affiliates reorganize as for-profit insurers, leading the way for more than a dozen Blue Cross/Blue Shield affiliates to convert to for-profit status.[52] Other Blue Cross/Blue Shield insurers bought other insurers, merged, or restructured in other ways. At the same time, private insurers acquired HMOs and other managed care organizations. Consolidations reduced both the number of commercial and Blue Cross/Blue Shield organizations, leading to the emergence of a small number of very large insurers with strong market positions across the country.[53] For example, the commercial insurer Anthem acquired Blue Cross/Blue Shield affiliates located in Colorado, Connecticut, Indiana, Kentucky, Maine, Missouri, Nevada, New Hampshire, Ohio, Virginia, and Wisconsin. In 2004, Anthem bought WellPoint Inc., which had acquired Blue Cross/Blue Shield plans in California, Georgia, and New York, and now operates under the WellPoint name.[54] **Table 1** lists the top 30 health insurers ranked by total medical enrollment at the end of 2008. Commercial health plan enrollments for fully insured health plans in 2007 totaled 168.2 million enrollees.[55]

**Table 1. Top 30 Health Insurance Companies Ranked By Total Medical Enrollment**

| Company | Total Medical Enrollment (2008) |
|---|---|
| UnitedHealth Group, Inc. | 32,702,445 |
| WellPoint, Inc. | 30,622,381 |
| Aetna, Inc. | 16,318,625 |
| Health Care Service Corporation | 12,218,623 |
| CIGNA HealthCare, Inc. | 9,922,135 |
| Kaiser Permanente | 8,532,951 |
| Humana, Inc. | 8,486,913 |
| Health Net, Inc. | 6,180,395 |
| Highmark, Inc. | 5,182,186 |
| Blue Cross Blue Shield of Michigan | 5,011,359 |
| Coventry Health Care, Inc. | 4,762,000 |
| EmblemHealth, Inc. | 4,035,710 |
| Medical Mutual of Ohio | 3,929,677 |
| WellCare Group of Companies | 3,537,777 |
| Independence Blue Cross | 3,480,168 |
| Horizon Healthcare Services, Inc. | 3,149,279 |
| CareFirst, Inc. | 3,044,880 |
| Blue Cross Blue Shield of North Carolina | 2,789,587 |
| Regence Group, The | 2,545,973 |
| Blue Cross Blue Shield of Minnesota | 2,483,968 |
| Lifetime Healthcare Companies | 1,797,053 |
| Wellmark, Inc. | 1,745,372 |
| Premera, Inc. | 1,720,057 |
| AMERIGROUP Corporation, Inc. | 1,549,000 |
| Molina Healthcare, Inc. | 1,313,211 |
| Centene Corporation | 1,275,829 |
| MVP Health Care Preferred Care | 931,844 |
| CareSource, Inc. | 678,654 |
| Group Health Cooperative | 566,156 |
| University of Pittsburgh Medical Center (UPMC) | 514,377 |

Source: Atlantic Information Service, *Directory of Health Plans: 2009* (Washington, DC: Atlantic Information Service, 2009).

Notes: Membership data represent health plan enrollments in managed care companies offering commercial and certain public-sector (government) programs. Fully funded (insured) and self-insured (administrative services only [ASO]) enrollments are both included. Enrollments are for the fourth quarter of 2008. Parent company enrollment include enrollments of regional subsidiaries. These data exclude ancillary health insurance programs such as for dental, chiropractic, and vision benefits.

In the 1990s, proponents of "consumer-directed" health care proposed measures intended to make consumers more sensitive to medical care costs. In 1996, Congress enacted legislation to create Archer Medical Savings Accounts (MSAs), which were superseded in 2003 when Congress passed legislation to allow consumers with high-deductible health insurance plans to set up Health Savings Accounts (HSAs) that allow people to pay for out-of-pocket expenses through a tax-advantaged medical savings account.[56] By early 2009, HSA-qualified high-deductible plans covered an estimated 8 million consumers.[57]

## DESCRIPTION OF THE HEALTH INSURANCE MARKET

Individuals and families typically buy insurance to avoid risks by paying a known premium in order to receive benefits if an adverse event were to occur during the insurance policy's term. Most individuals are willing to pay an insurer to assume the bulk of financial risks associated with unpredictable health outcomes of uncertain severity. Health insurance is a method of pooling risks so that the financial burden of medical care is distributed among many people. Some insured people will become sick or injured and incur significant medical expenses. Most people, however, will remain relatively healthy, thus incurring little or no medical expenses.[58] While it is difficult to predict who will incur high expenses, the average medical expense among a large group of people is more predictable. Insurance pools the medical expenses of the insured, who pay for the expenses through their premiums. In essence, money is shifted from those who remain healthy to those who become sick or injured.

The health insurance market is tightly interrelated with other parts of the health care system. Consequently, many parties play a role in the health insurance market. Health insurers are intermediaries in the transaction of the provision of health care between patients and providers— health insurers are a third-party who reimburse providers on behalf of patients.[59] Health insurers not only reimburse providers, but also typically have some control over the number and types of services covered and negotiate contracts with providers on the payments for health services— most health insurance plans are managed care plans (HMOs, PPOs) rather than indemnity or traditional health insurance plans that provide unlimited reimbursement for a fixed premium.[60] Other parties involved in the health insurance market include employers (most private health insurance is obtained through an employer), federal, state and local governments, and health care providers. The federal government directly provides health insurance through Medicare. The Department of Veterans

Affairs (VA) health system provides health care benefits, and military health systems provide both health insurance and health care benefits. States and the federal government share responsibility for Medicaid and private health insurance industry regulation.

The health insurance market has many features that push it far from the economic benchmark of perfect competition. Perfectly competitive markets, according to economic theory, allocate goods and services efficiently if certain conditions are met. Markets allocate goods and services efficiently when the social cost of the resources (e.g., labor, buildings, machinery, raw materials) used to make the last unit sold equals the social benefit of consuming that unit.[61] Conditions required to ensure the efficiency of competitive markets include the following:

- many buyers and sellers—each participant is small in relation to the market and cannot affect the price through its own actions;
- neither consumption nor production generates spillover benefits or costs;
- free entry and exit from the market—new firms can open up shop and existing firms can costlessly leave the market as conditions change;
- symmetric information—all market participants know the same things so that no one has an informational advantage over others;
- no transaction costs—the buyers and sellers incur no additional cost in making the transaction, and the complexity of decisions has no effect on choices; and
- firms maximize profits and consumers maximize well-being.

Competitive markets may allocate goods inefficiently if those conditions are not met. Most of these conditions often fail to hold in the health insurance market. Departures from these conditions can hinder markets and lead to inefficient outcomes. Reforms are most likely to be effective, according to some economists, when they are tied to underlying structural causes of poor market performance. [62] The lack of symmetric information plays a particularly important role in the health insurance market; most consumers rely heavily on the specialized knowledge and expertise of intermediaries such as insurers, employers, labor unions, physicians, and others.

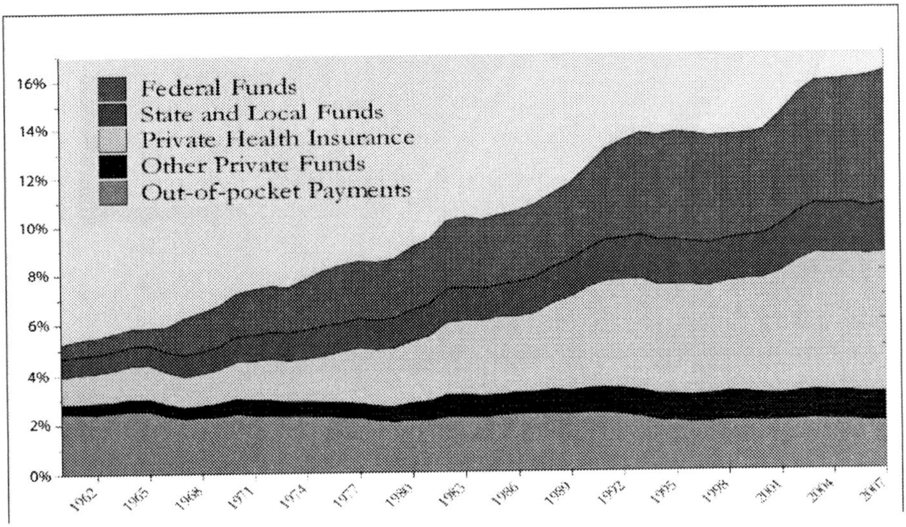


Source: CMS, Office of the Actuary.
Notes: Category definitions are available at http://www.cms.hhs.gov/NationalHealthExpendData/downloads/quickref.pdf.
Figure 1. National Health Expenditures By Source of Payment As a Percentage of GDP

## Intermediaries Play Key Roles in Health Care

Quality of health care is hard to evaluate. Consequently, consumers typically set up relationships with various intermediaries in advance. This can provide benefits as well as limit consumer choice. [63] Health insurers (public and private) make the bulk of health care payments. As **Figure 1** shows, national health expenditures paid through federal, state and local, and private insurance as a proportion of gross domestic product (GDP) have increased since 1960, while the proportion paid by consumers out of pocket has slightly decreased. In other words, over the past 40 years consumer out-of-pocket spending in real (i.e., inflation-adjusted) terms has grown slightly more slowly than the U.S. economy, while health expenditures paid through other sources have grown faster than the U.S. economy.

How insurers design health care networks influences how consumers use health care. Consumers typically choose a primary physician who selects tests and treatments and makes referrals to medical specialists. Employers negotiate with insurers on behalf of their workers, and labor unions negotiate with employers over health benefits on behalf of their members. Health insurers, in turn, negotiate contracts with providers and handle payments for individual services. A primary physician's admitting privileges typically determine where his patient goes for non-emergency hospital care. Patients must go through a physician to obtain most medical tests and pharmaceuticals. Health care consumers typically rely on these intermediaries instead of interacting directly with other parts of the health care system. This heavy reliance on intermediaries is a key characteristic of the current health care market.

Consumers benefit from the specialized expertise of intermediaries, such as employers, insurers, and physicians, as they navigate the health care system. Consumers also may benefit from the bargaining power of their employer or health insurer, in much the same way as they may benefit from the market power of a very large retailer (such as Walmart or Costco) when they buy ordinary consumer goods. Intermediaries may also help patients navigate the fragmented and complex structure of the U.S. health care system.[64] Patients may depend on physicians and health insurers to intermediate with a highly diverse array of health care providers, such as imaging centers, specialized surgery centers, public health clinics, hospice organizations, home health care providers, nursing homes, as well as other health care providers.

Using intermediaries such as health insurers protects consumers from financial risks linked to serious medical problems, but also insulates consumers from information about costs and prices for specific health care goods and services. When a third-party, such as a private insurer or a government, pays for the bulk of health care costs, consumers may demand more care and providers may wish to supply more care. Links among intermediaries and providers can also limit consumers' choices. For example, a person's job may limit her health insurance choices, and another person's choice of physician may limit choices among hospitals.

Some families and individuals lacking these intermediaries must navigate the health insurance and health care system themselves, which may be a serious challenge. People without health insurance coverage are not only vulnerable to the financial risks accompanying serious medical problems, but may also pay higher prices for care because they lack the bargaining leverage of insurers. Hospitals and physicians have charged individuals who pay their own bills far more than they charge insurance companies and public health programs.[65] Generous tax advantages for employer-sponsored plans do not help those who buy health insurance in the individual market. Those without a regular primary care physician may struggle to find an appropriate care setting.

Finally, how intermediaries interact has important consequences in the health care market. For instance, employers and health insurers, which both intermediate on behalf of individuals, interact through negotiations over insurance benefits packages. Politicians can also act as intermediaries for their constituents by helping determine reimbursement rates for public insurance programs and by changing the regulatory environment facing health insurers.[66] The interaction of intermediaries in the health care market can improve or impede efficiency, cost control, and quality of service.

## Demand for Health Insurance

Demand for health insurance, according to economic theory, depends on a person's attitudes towards risk, the variability of medical expenses, the effectiveness of health care covered by insurance, income, and the level of premiums. In a simplified case, an insurance policy is characterized by the premiums charged, medical services covered, and cost sharing (deductibles, coinsurance, and copayments).[67] The insurance premium equals the expected benefits the insurance company will pay out, which equals the average price of medical care multiplied by the average quantity of medical care provided, plus a loading fee to cover administrative expenses and profits.[68] The loading fee acts as a "price" of insurance: other things equal, higher loading fees reduce demand for insurance coverage.

The average price of medical care may depend on the complexity of services, the relative bargaining power of providers and insurers, and the cost structure of the providers. The average quantity depends on consumers' demand for health care, providers' willingness to supply care at prevailing prices, and managed care controls of the insurer. The size of the load factor depends on the insurers' administrative costs, costs of capital, and the ability of insurers to pass along higher premiums to employers and consumers.

In this simple example, providers gain when medical care prices are higher and when quantities are higher, so long as prices exceed their unit costs and so long as prices do not reduce demand too much. Consumers within a given plan benefit when quantities are higher (so long as the benefits of health care exceed out-of-pocket costs and non-monetary costs such as pain and inconvenience) and when prices are lower, so long as providers are willing to supply care. Higher cost-sharing rates and stricter managed care requirements may lead to higher out-of-pocket costs, but lower premiums. Insurers gain when the load factor and cost-sharing rates rise, so long as these do not reduce demand for health insurance too much. If competitive pressure is high, so that employers and consumers can resist higher premiums, insurers will face pressure to lower load factor, cost-sharing rates, prices, and quantities. Factors affecting competition in the health care market are discussed below.

**Table 2. Sources of Health Insurance Coverage, 2008**

| | Age Group | | | All Ages |
|---|---|---|---|---|
| | Under 19 | Under 65 | 65+ | |
| Population (millions) | 78.7 | 263.7 | 37.8 | 301.5 |
| Type of Insurance | | | | |
| Employment-based | 60.0% | 63.3% | 35.5% | 59.8% |
| Private Nongroup | 5.1% | 6.3% | 26.7% | 8.9% |
| Medicare | 0.8% | 2.9% | 93.4% | 14.3% |
| Medicaid or Other Public | 29.7% | 14.9% | 9.1% | 14.1% |
| Military or Veterans' Coverage | 3.0% | 3.3% | 7.5% | 3.8% |
| Uninsured (percent) | 10.3% | 17.3% | 1.7% | 15.4% |
| Uninsured (millions) | 8.1 | 45.7 | 0.6 | 46.3 |

Source: CRS analysis of data from the March 2009 Current Population Survey (CPS), taken from CRS Report 96-891, *Health Insurance Coverage: Characteristics of the Insured and Uninsured in 2008*, by Chris L. Peterson, Table 1, which presents a more detailed breakdown of these data.

Notes: Percentages may total to more than 100 because people may have more than one source of coverage. Employer-based category includes group health insurance through current or former employer or union and all coverage from outside the home (published Census Bureau figures are slightly lower due to the exclusion of certain people with outside coverage). Medicaid and Other Public category includes Children's Health Insurance Program (CHIP) and other state programs for low-income individuals and excludes military and veterans' coverage.

### *Sources of Health Insurance Coverage*

Employer-sponsored health insurance covers the majority of the nonelderly U.S. population (see **Table 2**). Individuals, in general, pay only a fraction of the total premiums of employer-sponsored plans, while employers pay the balance. Research has found, however, that employers generally pass their share of the financial burden onto the employees through reduced compensation.[69]

### *What People Know Differs: Information Problems in Insurance Markets*

When market participants do not share the same information, so that some have information advantages over others, markets may fail to generate efficient outcomes. Insurance analysts have long focused on two basic concepts of information asymmetry: *adverse selection*, which occurs when some have risk characteristics hidden from others, and *moral hazard*, which occurs when insurance status alters behavior. Information asymmetries between a consumer and an intermediary (principal-agent problems) can also create inefficiencies. These concepts are discussed below. Other, more complex information problems affect insurance markets as well.

### Adverse Selection

Differences in what buyers of insurance and insurers know is a central problem in the health insurance market. Buyers of insurance may know more about individual health risk factors than the insurance company.[70] Therefore, an insurer may be unable to distinguish a less healthy applicant, who derives a greater benefit from more generous insurance plans, from healthier applicants. Consequently, the insurance company could offer an insurance plan that would break even if it covered a representative sample of buyers in the market, but would bankrupt the insurer if it attracted a subset of the population with very high health care needs. This is known as adverse selection, a problem that could be especially severe in the individually purchased health insurance market. Adverse selection can force insurers to charge very high premiums, which then can drive healthier buyers out of the voluntary insurance market. Three decades of research suggest that adverse selection is quantitatively large.[71]

Firms typically pay a large portion of the costs of employer-sponsored health insurance plans, which economic research suggests is passed along to employees via lower wages and salaries.[72] Substantial tax advantages and employer cost-sharing of premiums supports high health plan participation, which allows the insurer to attract a group of individuals who are healthy enough to work and who participate in the plan for reasons other than buying health insurance. This reduces the extent of adverse selection, although it also makes employees less sensitive to health insurance costs. Firms' ability to self-insure, however, may raise other adverse selection issues.

Group plans typically charge the same premiums to individuals with differing characteristics (e.g., sex, age, and other health risk factors). This contrasts with risk-rated premiums where younger, healthier individuals are charged lower rates due to their lower expected claims. When premiums are not adjusted for individual characteristics and when consumers can opt in or out of insurance plans, risk pools can splinter, leading to an "adverse selection death spiral." If the proportion of older, sicker individuals increases in the insurance pool, the rates charged will increase in response to the higher costs (claims). Some of the younger, healthier individuals will respond by dropping coverage (either dropping health coverage altogether or moving to a less expensive plan). This could cause costs to rise further, leading to higher rates and, consequently, more younger, healthier individuals dropping their coverage in the plan. In the extreme, only older, sicker individuals will be left in the plan. Studies have documented that an adverse selection death spiral can occur when an employer offers a choice of health insurance plans.[73] Other researchers find that a common premium need not result in a death spiral.[74]

The splintering of health insurance pools into narrower risk categories in the small group and individual insurance markets has raised congressional concern about the availability and affordability of coverage for individuals who lack employer-sponsored health insurance coverage and who are ineligible for public insurance programs. Individual mandates that would require more people to obtain health insurance coverage, according to proponents, could mitigate some adverse selection risks.

## Cancellation, Renewal, and Incentives

The insurance benefit of a policy is reduced if the insurance carrier can cancel it when adverse events occur or are anticipated. Similarly, if insurers can change conditions and premiums for a policy renewal once an adverse event occurs, which would make renewal unaffordable or unattractive for the enrollee, then insurance plans become a less effective means of spreading risks. Conversely, insurers suffer losses due to adverse selection if uninsured individuals can enroll once they anticipate an adverse event. For this reason, some group health insurance plans have limited open enrollment seasons for large group insurance and impose preexisting conditions limits on individual or small-group insurance. In the individual health insurance market, the lack of guaranteed renewal at average-risk rates can limit effective risk pooling.

When individuals can switch insurers, insurers may lack sufficient incentives to make long-term investments in an individuals' health. For example, an insurer may hesitate to cover wellness benefits that lower health costs in future years if enrollees can switch plans in coming months.

## Moral Hazard

Moral hazard, which occurs when insurance status changes behavior, is another problem in the health insurance market.[75] Moral hazard occurs if an insured individual consumes more medical services than she would have had she been uninsured. For example, having health insurance could induce someone to seek medical care for minor conditions (e.g., a sore throat), choose a high- amenity health care setting (e.g., a more hotel-like hospital), or neglect his health (e.g., by eating fatty foods). Consequently, moral hazard leads the insurer to pay providers more for an insured person's medical services than that person would have paid out of his own pocket had he not been insured.[76] Of course, non-monetary costs, such as the pain and inconvenience of obtaining unnecessary medical care, may help limit moral hazard among patients.

Insurers typically react to moral hazard by raising premiums to cover the costs of additional services and by limiting care, either directly (e.g., through prior approval requirements) or through cost-sharing measures such as copayments and deductibles. Research has shown that the extent of cost-sharing does have a significant impact on health care spending.[77] The lack of transparency in the pricing of medical services contributes to this problem—most people do not know the cost of medical services (both what the provider normally charges and what the insurance company reimburses the provider).[78]

## The Principal-Agent Problem

A patient (here, a *principal*), as noted above, typically relies on a physician (an *agent*) for care and advice. The physician, or other intermediary, might face incentives to act to further their own interests, rather than those of the patient, by providing a higher quantity or lower quality of care than would be appropriate for a patient.[79]

When someone uses an intermediary (agent) with special knowledge or expertise, the principal often has trouble evaluating or monitoring the quality or appropriateness of the agent's work. When the aims of the principal and agent do not fully coincide, payment and incentive systems may mitigate conflicts of interests. Professional standards and professional organizations may also help mitigate those conflicts. Fixed fees and a system of professional standards and licensing may be seen as one response to the principal-agent problem between patients and physicians.

While that arrangement may avoid some problems, it may not solve others. In fee-for-service (FFS) arrangements, physicians and other providers may face financial incentives to provide more care than would best suit the patient's interests. When insurance pays most of the costs associated with health care, providers have little financial incentive to control costs and may overprovide health care services. One study randomly selected doctors into a salary group and a fee-for-service group during a nine-month study.[80] The results show that doctors in the fee-forservice group scheduled more office visits than salaried doctors and almost all of the difference was due to the fee-for-service doctors seeing well patients rather than sick patients. Defensive medicine, in which physicians or other providers order tests that may reduce the probability of medical malpractice litigation but which provide limited therapeutic benefits to the patient, presents a similar problem.[81]

## Information Problems and the Structure of Health Care Finance

Responses to adverse selection, moral hazard, and principal-agent problems affect the structure of the health financing system. Health insurers, as noted above, use coinsurance and pre-approval requirements to limit potential moral hazard among patients. Health insurers concerned about moral hazard and principal-agent problems among providers design incentive systems to limit overprovision of care. For example, the rapid transition to managed care in the 1990s might be seen as an attempt to control costs due to moral hazard. In addition, research and development (R&D) decisions made by medical technology and pharmaceutical firms may be indirectly guided by how health insurance coverage affects choices of providers and patients. Reforms that change the health financing system without taking into account potential moral hazards that previous structures and practices were designed to mitigate could encounter unanticipated problems.

### *Price Effects*

How price affects the demand for health insurance is an important piece of information given the extent of current tax subsidies for health insurance, proposals to change this tax treatment, and proposals to further subsidize the purchase of health insurance. Consumers' price sensitivity is usually measured in terms of price elasticity. A price elasticity is the percentage change in market demand for a good resulting from a 1% increase in its price. Many older studies (published before 1995) estimated price elasticities for health insurance that are quite large, ranging from -1.0 to - 2.0; that is, a 1% increase in price would lead to a 1% to 2% reduction in the number of people buying health insurance.[82] This suggests that a small price reduction could lead to moderately large increases in health insurance coverage. With improved data and empirical methods, more recent studies find elasticities in the range of 0.0

to -0.1.[83] This research, however, applies to workers who are offered group health insurance; workers who are not offered employer- sponsored insurance (about three-quarters of the uninsured) might react differently to price changes.[84] One study examining the group of uninsured not offered employer-sponsored insurance estimates an elasticity in the range of -0.3 to -0.4.[85] Lastly, a recent study using time- series data estimates a price elasticity in the range of -0.2 to -0.3.[86] Overall, the recent studies estimate that a 1% increase in price would lead to a 0% to 0.4% reduction in participation in health insurance. These recent results suggest that subsidies, by themselves, would have to be quite large to increase health insurance coverage. Moreover, cost-effective targeting health insurance subsidies to this group (employees not offered health insurance) is difficult, which could increase the public costs of such subsidy programs.[87]

### *Tax Benefits*

Health insurance is subsidized through the tax system in several ways. First, workers pay no income or payroll tax on the portion of the health insurance premium paid by the employer on behalf of covered workers. The Joint Committee on Taxation (JCT) estimates the federal government forgoes about $230 billion annually in tax revenue because of this exclusion.[88] Second, the self-employed may deduct the full amount paid for health insurance and long-term care insurance, which JCT estimated led to a revenue loss of $4.4 billion in 2008. Third, some taxpayers may deduct their own contributions to health savings accounts, which leads to an estimated revenue loss of $500 million in 2008.[89]

## Supply of Health Insurance

The basic tasks of insurers are to bear risks, which are pooled to reduce overall risks, and to administer plans, by paying claims, providing customer support, and negotiating with providers.

### *Risk-Sharing*

While the medical expenses of an insured group may be somewhat predictable, a group's expenses could be extraordinarily high or low. This variability, however, declines as the number of people in the insured pool increases.[90] Insurance risk is inversely related to group size. In other words, according to the law of large numbers, average expenses for larger and larger groups will become less and less variable—and thus less risky.[91] Some experts believe that a financially sound health insurer would need a minimum insurance pool size of about 25,000 policies, which would cover about 50,000 individuals, along with appropriate surplus or stabilization funds.[92] Even very large employer pools, such as the Federal Employee Health Benefit (FEHP) program, can experience year-to-year random fluctuations in expenses. Many individual and small-group insurance pools, by contrast, are much smaller. Higher expense variability and adverse selection risks may explain, in part, why premiums in the individual and small-group market are high relative to large-group premiums.

### *Administration*

The administrative tasks of insurance companies include underwriting, processing claims, making payments to providers, and negotiating agreements with providers. The main components of this production process are people, computers, and buildings. These costs are covered by the loading fees, which are included in premiums charged by the insurance company. Insurance companies also earn a return on investments. Premiums are usually collected at the beginning of the policy period, but claims are paid throughout the policy period or afterwards. Because of this timing difference, the insurance companies hold and invest premiums until needed to pay claims. The lag between premium collection and claims payments, however, may be shorter than for some other types of insurance.

### *Types of Health Plans*

The predominant type of health insurance plan has changed dramatically over the past 25 years. Over 90% of the privately insured were covered by an indemnity or traditional "unmanaged" health insurance plan in 1980; now the share is less than 10%.[93] Today, most people covered by private insurance are covered by some kind of managed care plan ranging from a managed indemnity plan (e.g., PPOs, where the insurers negotiate fees with providers) to a staff HMO (the insurer and the provider are the same, and patients see physicians who are on salary). With managed care, the health insurers and the providers are vertically integrated to some extent.[94]

Most major health insurers offer administrative service only (ASO) support to self-insured plans, which in some ways resembles a specialized type of outsourcing. The characteristics of the ASO market differ in some important ways from more traditional health plans that combine risk- bearing and administration, which is discussed in more detail below.

**Table 3. Percentage of Private-Sector Establishments Offering Health Insurance That Self-Insure At Least One Plan**

| | Total | Fewer than 100 Employees | 100-499 Employees | 500 or More Employees |
|---|---|---|---|---|
| All Firms | 34.2% | 13.1% | 29.2% | 81.8% |
| Number of Locations | | | | |
| 1 location only | 13.6% | 13.3% | 24.1% | 38.8% |
| 2 or more locations | 63.5% | 11.0% | 30.3% | 82.0% |
| Industry group** | | | | |
| Agriculture, fishing, forestry | 15.1% | 12.1% | 12.5% | 71.9% |
| Mining and manufacturing | 25.5% | 9.9% | 41.6% | 84.8% |
| Construction | 17.5% | 14.6% | 39.1% | 76.2% |
| Utilities and transportation | 41.5% | 9.3% | 26.7% | 87.3% |
| Wholesale trade | 28.8% | 9.3% | 42.9% | 86.1% |
| Financial services and real estate | 46.5% | 10.5% | 29.7% | 85.5% |
| Retail trade | 53.7% | 12.6% | 31.3% | 89.4% |
| Professional services | 26.3% | 14.3% | 23.2% | 74.6% |
| Other services | 31.4% | 14.9% | 24.2% | 71.2% |
| Ownership | | | | |
| For profit, incorporated | 37.6% | 12.9% | 31.7% | 84.1% |
| For profit, unincorporated | 25.0% | 11.8% | 28.2% | 78.3% |
| Nonprofit | 23.1% | 17.2% | 20.9% | 50.8% |
| Unionization | | | | |
| No union employees | 27.9% | 12.4% | 27.6% | 77.6% |
| Has union employees | 72.5% | 32.4% | 44.3% | 92.3% |
| Low wage employees | | | | |
| 50% or more low wage | 43.0% | 13.8% | 25.3% | 80.7% |
| Less than 50% low wage | 31.3% | 12.9% | 31.1% | 82.4% |

Source: Agency for Healthcare Research and Quality, Center for Financing, Access and Cost Trends. 2008 Medical Expenditure Panel Survey-Insurance Component., available at http://www.meps.ahrq.gov/mepsweb/ data_stats/summ_tables/insr/national/series_1 /2008/tia2a.htm

Notes: See *Technical Notes* for the Insurance Component of the Medical Expenditure Panel Survey, available at http://meps.ahrq.gov/mepsweb/survey

### *Types of Insurance Companies*

Health insurers are a diverse group of organizations. Health insurers may be commercial insurance firms, for-profit or non-for-profit Blue Cross/Blue Shield plans, or HMO-type organizations such as Kaiser Permanente. Established health insurance companies can be either non-profit organizations or for-profit companies.

These non-profit organizations have limited tax advantages and often face less state regulation (depending on the state) than their for-profit rivals. The "Blues" (Blue Cross/Blue Shield) have been the most prominent example of non-profit health insurers, although Blue Cross/Blue Shield organizations have been allowed to convert to for-profit status since 1994. These organizations were originally organized on a state or substate level, which may have prevented them from taking advantage of possible economies of scale that larger multi-state insurers can capture.[95] Many Blue Cross/Blue Shield plans are now part of large national insurers, such as WellPoint.

Employers that self-insure take on some or all of the functions of an insurance company, such as bearing risk and paying the claims of its employees. Self-insuring employers mostly contract with an established insurance company for administrative services. The Employee Retirement and Income Security Act of 1974 (ERISA, P.L. 93-406) provides some advantages to large multi-state firms that self-insure by preempting state regulation and establishing federal standards, which ensures that the firm's employee benefits are subject to the same benefit law across all states. ERISA, which exempts firms from certain benefit mandates and premium taxes, also benefits firms that operate in a single state.

For-profit insurers play an increasingly prominent role in the health insurance market. Many offer a wide variety of plans tailored for different firms or market segments. These insurers have an obligation to their shareholders to maximize profits. Many operate in several states or nationwide and often offer other lines of insurance, such as life or disability coverage.

### *Role of Employers*

Most private health insurance is offered through employers. With employer-sponsored plans, employers may simply offer health benefit plans through an insurance company for a negotiated price and bear no insurance risk. At the other extreme, the employer may self-insure and handle the plan itself, thus bearing all of the insurance risk and the administrative burden of the plan. Often the extent of employer involvement depends on the number of employees. Research has found that 80% of large employers (500 or more employees) choose to self-insure rather than purchase coverage from a health insurer.[96] **Table 3** presents data on characteristics of establishments offering health insurance that have chosen to self-insure at least one health plan.

Additionally, choice of insurance options also differs by firm size. Among small firms (fewer than 200 employees) offering health benefits, 86% offer only one plan to their employees. Among very large firms (5,000 or more employees), 72% offer two or more plan choices to their employees.[97] Research evidence suggests that plan choice is associated with higher levels of employer- sponsored health coverage and health care satisfaction.[98]

Health insurance premiums have increased dramatically over the past nine years. Between 1999 and 2008, the average worker contribution for employer-sponsored health insurance increased by 80% in real (inflation-adjusted) terms while the employer's contribution increased by 83%.[99] Nonetheless, evidence suggests that employer's health insurance decisions are fairly unresponsive to price with estimated elasticities in the range of -0.1 to -0.25.[100] As noted above, employer cost sharing, which covers about 75% of premiums on average, along with the large tax exemption for employer-provided health insurance, helps insulate employees from the price of health insurance.

### *Regulation of Health Insurers*

Health insurance is primarily regulated at the state level, although some federal standards apply. Regulation seeks to promote a variety of social goals including assuring the financial solvency of insurance companies, protecting consumers from insurance fraud, and ensuring promised benefits are paid. While all states require insurers to be solvent and pay claims, state regulations pertaining to health insurance access, minimum acceptable ratings, and covered benefits vary.[101] Large employers that self-insure are exempt from many state regulations under ERISA. State laws still apply to these firms for issues involving the "business of insurance." Longstanding debates and litigation continue, however, over the scope of the ERISA preemption.[102]

Federal standards were generally set in two pieces of legislation.[103] The Consolidated Omnibus Budget Reconciliation Act of 1985 (COBRA, P.L. 99-272) gives workers who lost their jobs a right to pay for continued job-based coverage of their dependents and themselves under certain circumstances.[104] The Health Insurance Portability and Accountability Act of 1996 (HIPAA, P.L. 104-191) improved access to health insurance by restricting exclusions for pre-existing conditions and prohibiting discrimination against certain people with medical needs and limited the use of preexisting condition restrictions. HIPAA, however, does not guarantee that consumers can renew their policies at rates that reflect pool characteristics, which some contend limits the act's effectiveness.[105] Moreover, while HIPAA can help ensure continuity and portability of insurance coverage when a person changes from employer-provided group insurance to individual coverage, HIPAA does not cover certain other transitions.[106]

# MARKET CONCENTRATION AMONG HEALTH INSURANCE

The health insurance market, according to many researchers, is highly concentrated in much of the United States. If large health insurers in highly concentrated markets exercised market power when selling insurance, prices would be distorted and an inefficiently low level of health insurance coverage would be provided. In simple economic models, firms with market power in product markets raise prices above and reduce output below competitive levels.[107] Firms that exercise market power when buying from suppliers (i.e., hiring labor and buying inputs) can lower payments and reduce output below competitive levels. [108] Firms' profitability depends on market interactions with both consumers and suppliers. For instance, a firm with a market position relative to its suppliers may be forced to pass along savings by strong competitive forces in the consumer market. A buyer that exercises market power to lower supplier prices below competitive levels, however, reduces economic efficiency, whether or not gains are retained by the firm or passed onto consumers.

## Measures of Market Concentration

Measures of market concentration are intended to reflect the potential for firms within a specific market to exercise market power by raising prices. Market concentration is typically measured by analyzing market shares of firms that supply a specific good or service within a particular geographic area. Factors other than market share may also affect a firm's ability to exercise market power. A firm with a strong brand, obtained through successful advertising and marketing or through a reputation for higher quality and reliability, may possess more market power than indicated by concentration measures based on market share data. Potential entry by new firms, or by firms in related markets, may constrain firms from exerting market power.

Two common measures are N-firm concentration ratios and the Hirschman-Herfindahl index (HHI), which are based on market shares of firms that sell products competing within a geographic area. An N-firm concentration ratio (CR) is the simple sum of the market shares of the top N firms. For example, a CR-3 is just the total market share of the top three firms in a market. The Hirschman-Herfindahl index is calculated by summing the squares of the percentage market share of all firms in the market. For instance, the HHI for an market with two firms with equal market shares would be $50^2 + 50^2 = 5000$. A market with 100 firms with equal market shares would have a HHI of $100.1^2 = 100$. Thus, a higher HHI indicates a greater degree of market concentration. The HHI measure has the advantage of reflecting the market shares of all firms in the market and is commonly used in antitrust and merger analysis.

## DOJ-FTC Merger Guidelines

The U.S. Department of Justice (DOJ) first incorporated the HHI into its horizontal merger guidelines in 1982.[109] The guidelines included detailed requirements for defining product markets and geographic market areas. The merger guidelines have been revised several times by the Department of Justice and Federal Trade Commission since 1982, most recently in 1997.[110]

The merger guidelines were intended to provide a clearer indication of which corporate mergers or acquisitions the U.S. Department of Justice or Federal Trade Commission would be likely to oppose by specifying HHI thresholds. Markets with an HHI below 1,000 were deemed "unconcentrated," those with an HHI between 1,000 and 1,800 were deemed "moderately concentrated," and those with an HHI above 1,800 were deemed "highly concentrated." The guidelines stated that mergers in unconcentrated or moderately concentrated markets were unlikely to face federal opposition unless the merger significantly raised the HHI.[111]

The 1982 merger guidelines reflected new research that suggested that economies of scale and economies of scope (that is, efficiencies made possible by combining related lines of business within one firm) could play important roles in shaping market structure and in serving consumers. Moreover, some industrial organization researchers argued that the success of leading firms, who might possess superior management or better technologies, could lead to high levels of market concentration, but still benefit consumers.[112] For these reasons, industrial organization economists note that an industry concentrated due to forces that promoted economic efficiency (e.g., a firm with a superior technology) could easily resemble an industry that was concentrated because of anticompetitive consolidation strategies. The 1982 merger guidelines and subsequent updates reflected those views and allowed a wider role for "efficiency defenses" in antitrust policy.[113]

Concentration measures are sensitive to how a market is defined in terms of product lines and geographic area. If a market is defined to include a broader variety of products, more firms will be counted as competing in the market, which tends to lower measured market concentration. Similarly, if the geographic area of a market is large, more firms will be included, which will tend to produce lower measures of market concentration. For example, Coca Cola, responding to a Federal Trade Commission (FTC) antitrust challenge to carbonated soft drink producers, argued that the relevant market should include all beverages, including coffee, tea, and milk, and the geographic scope of the market extended throughout the United States.[114] Market concentration computed using that market definition was sharply lower compared with measures that defined the relevant market as carbonated soft drinks within local metropolitan areas. Thus, defining markets by product category and by geographic area so that they reflect a reasonable set of alternatives available to consumers is crucial to obtaining a valid measure of market concentration.[115]

## Market Concentration among Health Insurers

Health insurance markets in most parts of the country, according to data published by the American Medical Association (AMA) and others, are highly concentrated.[116] In 2007, according to the AMA, 295 out of 314 metropolitan statistical areas (MSAs) had HHIs over 1800 for the combined HMO and PPO market, a range that the DOJ/FTC merger guidelines deem "highly concentrated" (that is, if the AMA market and product definitions are accepted). The percentages for the HMO and PPO markets considered separately were higher. The Government Accountability Office (GAO) found that in 2004, markets for private small group health insurance coverage were highly concentrated in most states.[117]

The AMA market share statistics underlying the concentration measures are based on commercial health insurance data on enrollments in managed care organizations. Those enrolled in public insurance plans such as Medicare and the State Children's Health Insurance Plan are excluded. In addition, some enrolled in self-insured employer plans are also excluded.[118] Because some might consider that HMO plans and PPO type plans belong to distinct market segments, the AMA report calculates concentration statistics for the HMO market, the PPO market, and the combined HMO and PPO market. If most consumers view HMO and PPO plans as substitutes competing in the same market segment, then the market will be more competitive than if the market for each type of plan were considered separately. Differences between HMO and PPO plans have blurred over the last two decades to the point that a significant minority of consumers do not know which type of plan they have.[119] This suggests that HMO and PPO plans no longer occupy distinct market segments.

Counting employees in fully or partially self-insured employer plans as enrollees of health insurers who administer such plans, however, could arguably overstate the effective market shares of those insurers if the market for administrative services to self-insured firms was more competitive than the standard commercial insurance market. Industry analysts note that many large employers have responded to rising premiums by shifting to self-insured plans.[120] The bulk of administrative service only (ASO) contracts with self-insured firms are held by large health insurers. Some evidence, discussed below, suggests that profit margins on ASO contracts are lower than on standard commercial health plans. Of course, firms with ASO contracts bear risks and some administrative costs that would be borne by insurance companies in a standard plan.

Market share data collected on the consumer side of the health insurance market might not reflect important factors that affect the potential for health insurers to exert market power on the supply side of the market. Many health care providers and health insurers are deeply involved in public health insurance programs such as Medicare Advantage (MA), Medicare drug benefit plans, the State Childrens' Health Insurance Program (CHIP; formerly known as SCHIP), and Medicaid. Most hospitals derive a large share of their revenues from Medicare Part A. A few health care providers derive significant shares of their revenue from self-paying individuals. To the extent that providers and insurers can enter or leave specific market segments, concentration measures based on consumer shares in the private health insurance market may underestimate the competitiveness of the supply side.

## Market Concentration and Market Power

Market concentration, as noted above, might not translate into the ability to use market power to raise prices or lower output or quality for several reasons.[121] First, concentration measures may be computed in ways that overlook the range of alternatives available to consumers and employers. Second, potential entrants may curb incumbent firms' ability to raise prices. For instance, other types of insurers with extensive contacts with firms could potentially enter the health insurance business, and some firms may choose to offer health insurance benefits through self-insured plans. Market concentration could be overestimated in areas where employer self-insured plans not included in AMA data have significant enrollments.

Third, firms in concentrated industries might choose not to exercise what market power they may possess, perhaps because their governance and organizational structure is designed to pursue other goals. For instance, some contend that non-profit health insurers act differently than for- profit insurers and may choose not to exercise their market power. [122] On the other hand, others have expressed skepticism that non-profit and for-profit health care providers and insurers act in substantially different ways.[123]

Whether market concentration allows firms to enhance profitability by exercising market power has fueled controversy among economists and industry analysts. Many economists have pointed to strong correlations between market concentration levels and elevated profit levels across industries.[124] Those correlations led some economists to argue that market concentration enables firms to exercise market power through enhanced pricing power. While prices elevated above competitive levels increase firms' profitability, they reduce economic efficiency by reducing output levels below optimal levels. Others point out that other factors, such as successful innovation, could both promote economic efficiency and market concentration.

Several recent studies have examined the effects of market concentration in the health insurance market. One study found evidence that private health insurers charge higher premiums to more profitable firms, indicating that health insurers have exercised market power. Furthermore, this effect was estimated to be stronger where health insurance markets were more concentrated.[125] A related study estimated that the increase in health insurance market concentration between 1998 and 2006 led to a 2% average increase in inflation-adjusted premiums over that period, after controlling for many employee and employer characteristics. Moreover, the study found that increased market concentration was linked to lower job and earnings growth for physicians, but higher job and earnings growth for nurses. [126] That finding supports claims of some provider groups that assert many health insurers exert their market power to lower prices paid to providers below efficient levels.[127] The exertion of insurer market power, however, could affect various provider types in different ways. Another recent study found that hospitals in areas where health insurance markets were more concentrated provided more inpatient days of service, which the authors contend shows that concentration among health insurers enhances provider efficiency.[128] Finally, one health economist contends that some health insurers with a dominant market position use high physician reimbursement rates to deter entry by potential rivals.[129]

Many economists who studied the effects of industrial structure in the 1960s and 1970s viewed market structure as a primary determinant of firm behavior, including pricing and output policies. Firms' choices, in this view, in turn determined the performance of the industry as a whole, as reflected in market prices and aggregate output, the rate of technical progress, and the success in meeting consumer needs while minimizing production costs.[130] In this view, market concentration led to higher output prices and profits, as well as lower output levels and product quality.

More recently, economists who study the structure of industries and markets emphasize deeper causes of market concentration, while allowing a role for historical factors in some types of industries. [131] More modern theories of market competition have focused on cost structures such as economies of scale and the intensity of competition as influencing market structures. For example, industries with strong economies of scale, such as those that manage networks, will tend to be highly concentrated because larger firms can reduce costs more than smaller firms.[132] In other industries in which branding strategies can be effective, market structure may reflect leading firms' past strategic choices. Other economists note that regulation and legislative barriers to entry, which might also reflect policy responses structural factors such as economies of scale, can also promote highly concentrated market structures. Factors that may affect market concentration are discussed in more detail in the following section.

## Possible Causes of Concentration in the Health Insurance Market

The causes of market concentration in the health insurance market are complex, and reflect historical elements as well as forces related to the special characteristics of health insurance and health care. Historically, the original structure of Blue Cross plans was designed to avoid competition by requiring exclusive territories and barring plans linked to specific hospitals. Those requirements may have been aimed at supporting community rating policies and broadly based risk pools, which may have benefited many consumers. Regulators and policymakers at times have also made decisions that were intended to avoid splintering of risk pools, which may have tended to encourage higher levels of market concentration. As commercial insurers and managed care strategies became more prominent, market forces along with merger and acquisition strategies have helped reshape the health insurance market. Some insurers may have engineered mergers and acquisitions to enhance their market power; the success of that strategy depends on underlying factors that determine the structure of the market.

The nature of employment-based health benefits and the market structure of health care providers may strongly affect the structure of the health insurance market. In addition, state and federal regulations and tax policy have helped shape the health insurance market. Moreover, the federal government's involvement in health markets through Medicare, Medicaid, and other programs has profoundly affected U.S. health care markets, and may have important indirect effects on the private health insurance market. Federal antitrust policy has affected the market structure of many industries, but at times federal enforcement agencies have had trouble persuading courts to apply antitrust remedies to health care and health insurance markets.[133]

The following sections discuss possible causes of market concentration. Determining which factors have been most important in promoting market concentration among health insurance markets may be difficult, but such analysis is critical to the assessment of the likely consequences of proposed reforms of the health insurance industry.

### *The Spread of Managed Care*

During the 1980s and 1990s, as noted above, the spread of managed care transformed the American health care system. Rising health care costs put pressure on insurers to find ways to control the growth of premiums by limiting utilization or by holding down medical costs. Many traditional insurers, according to some analysts, had difficulty implementing managed care techniques successfully. Not all insurers were able to balance the demands of managing care, maintaining consumer satisfaction, and responding to changing market conditions. This led some insurers to acquire or merge with existing health maintenance organizations or similar types of organizations as a way to gain the management capability to run managed care health plans.[134] While the spread of managed care might help explain increases in market concentration in the 1990s, it is less clear that it can explain changes in market structure once managed care strategies become more widespread and standardized.

### *Countervailing Power*

High levels of market concentration among health insurers may be a response to the market power of hospitals and other health care providers. Both hospitals and insurers may want to acquire "countervailing power" to enhance their bargaining strength.[135] In many geographic areas, market concentration among hospitals has steadily increased over the past few decades. Many hospitals banded together to create exclusive networks of providers, in part to increase in part bargaining power in negotiations with insurers.[136] Some hospitals viewed the hospital chain Columbia/HCA, which had expanded its networks rapidly in the early 1990s and had used aggressive business practices, both as a model and a potential competitive threat to independent hospitals.[137] Moreover, the introduction of Medicare's inpatient prospective payment system (IPPS) and the adoption of similar systems by private insurers in the early 1990s reduced average hospital lengths of stays and occupancy rates. Some hospitals viewed mergers as an easier way to eliminate excess capacity compared with other strategies. Some physicians also formed groups, which may have been, in part, motivated by the desire to enhance bargaining power in negotiations with payors.[138]

Increasing market concentration or strategic coordination among providers and insurers may create distortions that can lead to the misallocation of resources and suboptimal health access or availability. [139] While both insurers or providers may employ market strategies to build up countervailing power in response to increasing concentration on the opposite side of the market, many economists believe those measures weaken market competition and are likely to reduce consumer well-being and possibly reduce the availability of certain services.[140]

### *Economies of Scale*

Economies of scale play an important role in many industries. If larger firms can produce more cheaply than smaller rivals, then markets will be composed of a smaller number of large firms. In health insurance, economies of scale could be captured in claims processing, building compliance regimes, designing software systems, or negotiating provider networks. While larger employer groups are cheaper to administer than smaller ones, there is little relation between the size of major insurers and administrative costs, according to some industry analysts.[141] This suggests that the largest health insurers do not enjoy substantial scale economies unavailable to their smaller rivals and that economies of scale in administrative functions plays little role in explaining market concentration among health insurers. As noted above, some experts believe that a financially sound insurer would need a risk pool with about 25,000 policies covering about 50,000 people. Actuarial gains due to risk sharing across wider coverage pools may taper off above that point.

If indeed the health insurance industry lacks of economies of scale above a certain minimum point, then a public option might not achieve administrative cost efficiencies by simply being larger. It also suggests that efficiency losses would be small if incumbent firms were forced to contract the scale of their operations.

Some economists and financial analysts believe that in some industries that lack scale economies (above some minimal level), firms may seek to grow, not because they can become more efficient or more profitable, but because senior managers may obtain more benefits by leading a larger firm. According to this view, weak corporate governance, that prevents shareholders from focusing management attention on profits rather than perquisites, may motivate corporate growth.

### *Marketing and Brand Management*

The ability of firms to use marketing strategies to heighten customer loyalty can affect market structure and market concentration if the creation of strong brand identities hinders entry of potential rivals or changes the nature of competition with existing rivals.[142] For instance, the Blue Cross emblem has proved a potent marketing tool in the health insurance market. Marketing plays a larger role in the health insurance market and may complicate or retard the entry of new firms. Advertising and other marketing strategies can also provide potential consumers with information to help them choose among insurers. Where employees have had expanded choices among health plans, insurers have stepped up marketing efforts.

Health insurers spend considerable sums on marketing. According to one estimate, commercial health plans spent 4.6% of total premium revenues on marketing in 2007.[143] By contrast, marketing expenses for employers' self-insured plans administered by commercial insurers (administration services only [ASO] plans) were only 1.0% of total premium income in 2007. Marketing directed towards employers' human resources departments, who help select plans or design self-insured plans, may be more focused and therefore cheaper than marketing aimed at individuals.

### *Competitive Environment*

The nature of competition in the health insurance market may also affect market structure. Because most nonelderly Americans obtain health insurance coverage through their employers, insurers must compete for the business of both employers and employees.

Some aspects of health insurance promote competition. Many, but not all, employers allow workers to choose among different insurers. Those buying coverage on the individual market can use websites such as eHealthInsurance.com to compare plans. Consumers generally must decide which insurer to choose well in advance of the need to use health care. Many insurers provide detailed information about policies and procedures. On the other hand, even detailed plan brochures may omit important details, and comparing competing plans can be difficult even for sophisticated health care consumers.

Other aspects of health insurance can reduce the sharpness of competition. Employers are typically reluctant to switch insurers, which could require a major overhaul of human resources department procedures and a reorientation of employees.[144] Health insurance policies are often difficult to compare, and information on some important aspects of policies, such as promptness and fairness of claim handling, prompt and convenient access to plan representatives, and willingness to approve certain medical or surgical procedures, are often unavailable.

Some researchers have found underwriting cycles in some health insurance markets, suggesting that at times health insurers have engaged in aggressive price competition. Underwriting cycles are said to occur when insurers compete to gain market share by offering attractive premiums and then when investment or premium income threatens to fall short of claim costs, raise premiums. Some health insurance executives in 2004 said that better cost monitoring techniques and market consolidation would let health insurers link medical cost increases and premium growth more closely, making sharp price competition and large swings in premiums less likely in the future.[145]

## Health Insurance Company Profitability

Many have expressed concern about the rapid growth of health insurance premiums during the past half century. Rising premiums are linked to the growth of medical and other health care costs, which now make up about four-fifths of health insurance premium income. Many economists believe the extent of health insurance coverage has encouraged providers to increase the quantity of health care services, and over the longer term has led to higher prices for health care.[146] The portion of premiums not paid out as claims, often called the loading costs, includes administrative costs, taxes, and profits. Administrative costs include employee salaries, business overhead, marketing expenses, and other expenditures necessary to running an insurance firm. The rest of this section discusses trends in health insurance companies' profitability.

Evaluating the profitability of health insurers is complicated because insurers earn part of their profits from the difference between total premiums and total claims paid, and another part of their profits from the "float," that is, the lag between the payment of premiums and the payment of claims. Because claims lag premium payments, insurance companies can invest funds gathered from premiums until the claims are paid, thus allowing the insurer to collect investment income. This lag is generally shorter for health insurers than for many other lines of insurance. Some insurers suffered sharp declines in investment income in 2007 and 2008 due to lower interest rates on bonds and other fixed income securities as well as to steep declines in asset values in the wake of the economic recession. Profitability data for those years may therefore be atypical.[147]

Insurers typically participate in multiple segments of the health insurance market (large group, small group, individual, public insurance programs), but each segment differs in important ways. While most policies are issued through employer-provided plans, some insurers obtain a significant portion of their earnings from public programs such as Medicare Advantage, the Medicare Part D prescription drug program, and the State Children's Health Insurance Program (CHIP). Medicare Advantage (MA) may play a particularly important role in insurers' profitability. The Medicare Payment Advisory Commission (MedPAC) has calculated that MA plan costs are 18% higher than traditional fee-for-service (FFS) Medicare plan costs, in part because MA enrollees tend to be healthier than FFS enrollees.[148] Generous reimbursement policies, in turn, have helped encourage insurers to grow MA enrollments.

Some research has found that high market concentration in health insurance markets tends to accelerate increases in premiums on the consumer side, although one study found that HMO merger did not tend to higher premium growth rates.[149] Another study failed to find evidence that higher HMO market concentration reduced physician reimbursement rates, although a different study found an association between HMO concentration rates and lower hospital reimbursement rates.[150] Some economists believe that more empirical research is needed to explore links between health insurance market concentration and economic outcomes.

## Financial Results and Ratios

Insurance companies typically report financial data that include widely used measures of profitability such as net income, the medical loss ratio, return on revenues, and return on equity. Typically, analysts rely on several sources of financial data and various financial ratios to assess the profitability of a firm or industry.

Financial data for the health insurance industry can be sensitive to firms' accounting and financial reporting—accounting in the insurance industry can be complex because of the nature of the business. Insurance companies take in premiums from customers when a policy is issued and at some later time may pay claims on that policy. Insurers will make a profit if total premiums and investment income exceed total claims and operating expenses. In addition, because of the lag between the collection of a premium and the payment of a claim, insurers can invest funds in stocks, bonds, or direct investments that yield earnings.

Insurers typically keep three sets of books, so financial data reported for one purpose may differ from data reported for a different purpose. First, insurers use statutory accounting practices to compile reports to state regulators who monitor solvency of insurance companies or subsidiaries that write policies. Statutory accounting standards are issued by the National Association of Insurance Commissioners (NAIC). Second, insurers use generally accepted accounting principles (GAAP) to present financial data for investors in documents such as 10-Ks filed with the Securities and Exchange Commission (SEC). Third, insurers also keep a separate book for tax accounting, which is governed by state and federal tax rules. What insurers report as net income, a common measure of profitability, can depend on which accounting standards are used as well as accounting and actuarial judgments regarding investment cash flows and insurance reserves, although these are generally subject to state insurance regulation.[151] In particular, the link between data in state insurance filings for separate legal entities and financial results reported on a consolidated group basis by major insurers consisting of many subsidiaries is often unclear.

Financial indicators from three sources (Fortune magazine, the A.M. Best Company and the Sherlock Company) are discussed below. Because financial data presented below derive from different sources and may be calculated using different procedures, results may vary.

### *Comparing Profitability by Industry*

**Table 4** presents two indicators of profitability by major industrial sector. A third indicator, profits as a percentage of shareholder equity, is presented in **Table A-3**. For each industry, simple averages (means), weighted averages, and medians are presented.[152]

Profits as a percentage of revenues is widely used to compare performance of retail-oriented industries. This measure is sensitive to what funds pass through a firm as revenues. For example, for traditional commercial coverage, the insurer collects premiums (which are booked as revenues) and pays claims. When self-insured employers outsource health plan administration and claims processing to an insurer via an ASO plan, the insurer does not book premiums paid by workers as revenue, but instead collects administrative service fees. While the insurer may offer substantially the same services (apart from differences in risk-bearing) for both types of plans, profits as a percentage of revenues will generally be much lower for traditional commercial risk coverage than for ASO plans because those revenues include full premiums, not just administrative fees. For example, **Figure 2** shows how net margins for major health insurance companies vary depending on ASO plan enrollments as a share of total enrollments. In general, insurers with higher shares of ASO enrollments earn higher net margins.

Profits as a percentage of assets reflects an industry's profitability with its capital intensity. Profits as a percentage of equity indicate returns to stock investors. Return-on-equity ratios, unlike return-on-revenue, depends on how a firm raises its capital, and may change abruptly due to changes in corporate structures such as mergers and acquisitions. A firm that relies more on equity, rather than debt, may be less vulnerable to bankruptcy. Comparisons of profitability ratios across industries requires some caution, as each industry has a different cost structure and each faces a particular set of risks and opportunities. Industry profitability is also affect by temporary economic shocks and broader social trends. Individual firms, of course, vary from the industry averages, with some performing better on profit measures, and with others performing less well.

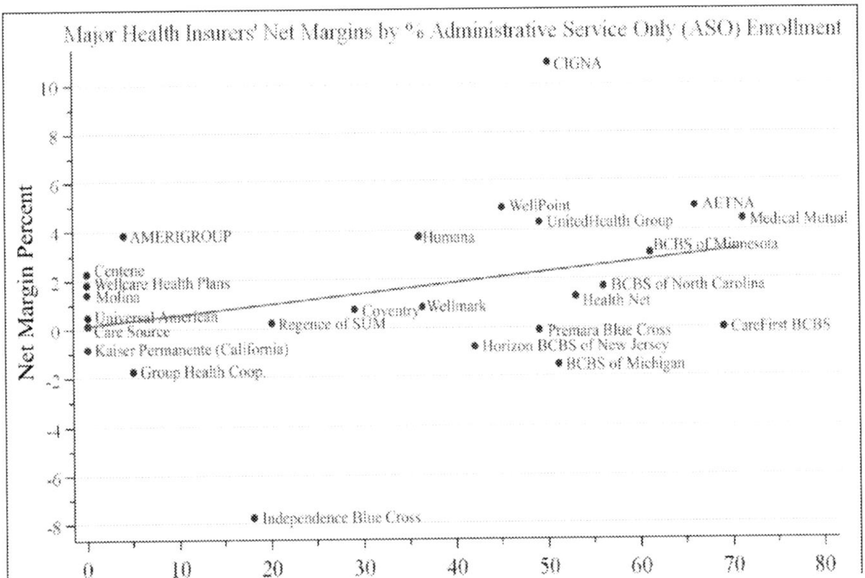


Source: Atlantic Information Service, *Directory of Health Plans: 2009* (Washington, D.C., 2009). Net margin is for second quarter of 2009. Graph by CRS.

Notes: CIGNA data may include non-health lines of insurance. ASO plans are generally self-insured plans. Data gathered from public sources.

Figure 2. Major Health Insurers' Net Margins by Percentage ASO Enrollments

Neither of the two health insurance sectors (Health Care: Insurance & Managed Care; and Insurance: Life, Health [stock]) are in the top 20 industries on either of the two profitability measures for 2009 presented in **Table 4**, nor among the top 20 industries in terms of profits as percentage of shareholder value (see **Table A-3**).

### *Profitability Measures Reported by the A.M. Best Company*

The A.M. Best Company provides ratings and analysis for the insurance industry, including GAAP financial indicators for major health insurers.[153] Which companies A.M. Best lists varies over time due to mergers, acquisitions, and the growth of smaller firms.

**Table 5** presents medical loss ratios for major health insurers over the period 2000-2008. Two other measures of profitability the health insurance industry, return on equity and return on revenues, are presented in **Table A-1** and **Table A-2**.

**Table 4. Two Profit Indicators for Fortune 1000 Firms By Industry, 2009**

| Industry Group | # Firms in Fortune 1000 | Profits As a Percentage of | | | | | | | |
|---|---|---|---|---|---|---|---|---|---|
| | | Revenues | | | | Assets | | | |
| | | Median | Average | Weighted Average | Rank | Median | Average | Weighted Average | Rank |
| Internet Services and Retailing | 7 | 20.9 | 23 | 22.3 | 1 | 13 | 13.4 | 14.2 | 1 |
| Savings Institutions | 2 | 20 | 20 | 19.4 | 2 | 0.9 | 0.9 | 0.9 | 60 |
| *Pharmaceuticals* | *21* | *17.3* | *17.7* | *24* | *3* | *8.2* | *9.9* | *10.2* | *5* |
| Tobacco | 6 | 15.2 | 15.4 | 19.9 | 4 | 8.1 | 13.8 | 12.2 | 6 |
| *Medical Products and Equipment* | *18* | *13.5* | *0.7* | *7.6* | *5* | *8.4* | *4.8* | *4.2* | *4* |
| Computer Software | 11 | 13.1 | -0.3 | 13.3 | 6 | 6.2 | -0.5 | 8.3 | 13 |
| Railroads | 4 | 12.9 | 12.9 | 12.9 | 7 | 4.4 | 4.2 | 4.3 | 26 |
| Network and Other Communications Equipment | 9 | 11.8 | 11.9 | 11.7 | 8 | 5.8 | 5 | 6.3 | 17 |
| Financial Data Services | 16 | 11.1 | 9 | 8.2 | 9 | 6.9 | 6 | 3.2 | 11 |
| Securities | 14 | 9.6 | 5 | 5.1 | 10 | 1.5 | 1.2 | 0.5 | 57 |
| Toys, Sporting Goods | 2 | 9.5 | 9.5 | 9.5 | 11 | 10.3 | 10.3 | 10.4 | 2 |
| Scientific, Photographic and Control Equipment | 10 | 9.1 | 6.7 | 6.1 | 12 | 4.7 | 3.9 | 3.4 | 22 |
| Household and Personal Products | 13 | 9 | 11.3 | 13.6 | 13 | 9.8 | 10.8 | 10.4 | 3 |
| Oil and Gas Equipment, Services | 14 | 8.3 | 7.4 | 6.9 | 14 | 5.4 | 4.6 | 4.8 | 18 |
| Food Consumer Products | 20 | 7.5 | 7.2 | 8.1 | 15 | 7 | 7.3 | 7.7 | 10 |
| Beverages | 8 | 7.3 | 9.7 | 11.5 | 16 | 5.3 | 6 | 8.4 | 21 |
| Waste Management | 2 | 7.2 | 7.2 | 7.4 | 17 | 3.6 | 3.6 | 3.7 | 30 |
| Utilities: Gas and Electric | 47 | 7.1 | 7.3 | 8.2 | 18 | 2.6 | 2.7 | 2.8 | 45 |
| Aerospace and Defense | 20 | 6.6 | 6.8 | 5.8 | 19 | 6 | 7.2 | 5.9 | 14 |
| Apparel | 13 | 6.4 | 4.2 | 5.4 | 20 | 6.9 | 4.9 | 7.1 | 12 |
| *Insurance: Life, Health (stock)* | *19* | *6.3* | *3.5* | *2.8* | *21* | *0.5* | *0.6* | *0.2* | *65* |
| Insurance: Property and Casualty (Mutual) | 5 | 6 | 4.1 | 1.8 | 22 | 1.3 | 1.3 | 0.6 | 59 |
| Diversified Outsourcing Services | 15 | 6 | 6.2 | 5.9 | 23 | 3.6 | 4.8 | 4.3 | 33 |
| Information Technology Services | 9 | 5.4 | 7.1 | 11.4 | 24 | 7.1 | 8.5 | 11.1 | 7 |
| Diversified Financials | 15 | 5.3 | -14.1 | -24.7 | 25 | 1.4 | 1.8 | -2.7 | 58 |
| Insurance: Property and Casualty (Stock) | 31 | 4.9 | 1 | 2.1 | 26 | 1.9 | 1 | 0.4 | 55 |
| Education | 4 | 4.8 | 6.7 | 7.1 | 27 | 3.8 | 6.9 | 6.1 | 28 |
| Electronics, Electrical Equip. | 14 | 4.7 | 2.4 | 3.8 | 28 | 4.4 | 2.4 | 3.9 | 25 |
| Packaging, Containers | 18 | 4.5 | 4.6 | 4.2 | 29 | 4.6 | 4.5 | 3.9 | 23 |
| Advertising, marketing | 2 | 4.4 | 4.4 | 5.2 | 30 | 2.7 | 2.7 | 3 | 39 |
| Telecommunications | 24 | 4.4 | 2 | 4.9 | 31 | 2.4 | 0 | 2.2 | 48 |

**Table 4. (Continued)**

| Industry Group | # Firms in Fortune 1000 | Profits As a Percentage of | | | | | | | |
|---|---|---|---|---|---|---|---|---|---|
| | | Revenues | | | | Assets | | | |
| | | Median | Average | Weighted Average | Rank | Median | Average | Weighted Average | Rank |
| Industrial Machinery | 23 | 4.3 | 2.5 | 3.7 | 32 | 3.3 | 2.8 | 3.2 | 34 |
| Food Services | 11 | 4 | 5.3 | 10 | 33 | 7 | 6.6 | 11 | 9 |
| Computer Peripherals | 5 | 3.8 | 3.6 | 5.7 | 34 | 4.1 | 3.2 | 4.1 | 27 |
| Energy | 21 | 3.6 | 5.3 | 7.7 | 35 | 2.7 | 3.5 | 3 | 42 |
| Chemicals | 37 | 3.6 | 4.7 | 5.4 | 36 | 4.6 | 4.1 | 4.2 | 24 |
| *Health Care: Pharmacy and Other Services* | *14* | *3.4* | *5* | *3.5* | *37* | *7* | *5.9* | *6.2* | *8* |
| Mining, Crude-Oil Production | 20 | 3.1 | 0.4 | 1.7 | 38 | 1.9 | 1.1 | 0.6 | 54 |
| Engineering, Construction | 14 | 3.1 | 3.2 | 3.1 | 39 | 5.3 | 5.8 | 5.9 | 20 |
| Pipelines | 14 | 3 | 3.5 | 3.2 | 40 | 2.4 | 2.1 | 1.8 | 49 |
| Computers, Office Equipment | 8 | 3 | 2.1 | 5.5 | 41 | 3.1 | 1.1 | 5.3 | 36 |
| *Health Care: Insurance and Managed Care* | *15* | *2.9* | *3.1* | *4.4* | *42* | *3.7* | *4.5* | *5.6* | *29* |
| Building Materials, Glass | 7 | 2.8 | 0 | -0.9 | 43 | 2.4 | 0.4 | -0.6 | 50 |
| Construction and Farm Machinery | 9 | 2.8 | 1.3 | 2.2 | 44 | 2.1 | 1.8 | 1.5 | 52 |
| Specialty Retailers | 64 | 2.7 | 2.3 | 2.7 | 45 | 6 | 4.4 | 5.2 | 16 |
| Home Equipment, Furnishings | 10 | 2.6 | 2.1 | 2 | 46 | 2.3 | 2.3 | 1.7 | 51 |
| Semiconductors and Other Electronic Components | 19 | 2.6 | 1.7 | 3.8 | 47 | 2.5 | 1 | 2.9 | 47 |
| Mail, Package, and Freight Delivery | 2 | 2.5 | 2.5 | 2.8 | 48 | 3.6 | 3.6 | 4 | 32 |
| *Health Care: Medical Facilities* | *16* | *2.5* | *2.2* | *2.7* | *49* | *2.7* | *2.1* | *2.7* | *40* |
| Commercial Banks | 29 | 2.4 | -8.6 | 4 | 50 | 0.1 | -0.5 | 0.3 | 67 |
| Trucking, Truck Leasing | 6 | 2.3 | 0.2 | -1.5 | 51 | 2.9 | 0.6 | -1.7 | 38 |
| Petroleum Refining | 15 | 2.2 | 1.5 | 4.2 | 52 | 3.1 | 1.3 | 4.9 | 37 |
| Food Production | 8 | 1.8 | 1 | 0.9 | 53 | 2.7 | 1.9 | 1.9 | 41 |
| Wholesalers: Diversified | 18 | 1.8 | 1.8 | 2.3 | 54 | 3.6 | 3.1 | 3.8 | 31 |
| Entertainment | 15 | 1.7 | -2.9 | 0.3 | 55 | 0.8 | -0.3 | 0.1 | 61 |
| General Merchandisers | 13 | 1.5 | 1.9 | 3.2 | 56 | 2 | 3.2 | 6.3 | 53 |
| Wholesalers: Food and Grocery | 7 | 1.5 | 1.3 | 1.9 | 57 | 5.4 | 5 | 7.1 | 19 |
| Forest and Paper Products | 7 | 1.5 | -5.4 | -2.8 | 58 | 2.6 | -2.1 | -2.1 | 44 |
| *Wholesalers: Health Care* | *7* | *1.3* | *2.6* | *1.1* | *59* | *6* | *6* | *4.3* | *15* |
| Transportation and Logistics | 4 | 1.1 | -0.7 | 1.8 | 60 | 3.3 | -9.2 | 4.4 | 35 |
| Airlines | 11 | 1 | -0.2 | -3 | 61 | 0.7 | -0.4 | -2.3 | 62 |
| Food and Drug Stores | 17 | 0.9 | -0.1 | 0.1 | 62 | 2.6 | -1.3 | 0.2 | 43 |
| Wholesalers: Electronics and Office Equipment | 10 | 0.8 | 0.3 | -0.3 | 63 | 2.5 | 1.1 | -0.9 | 46 |

**Table 4. (Continued)**

| Industry Group | # Firms in Fortune 1000 | Profits As a Percentage of | | | | | | | |
|---|---|---|---|---|---|---|---|---|---|
| | | Revenues | | | | Assets | | | |
| | | Median | Average | Weighted Average | Rank | Median | Average | Weighted Average | Rank |
| Real estate | 7 | 0.8 | -2.4 | -3.3 | 64 | 0.5 | -0.5 | -0.7 | 64 |
| Automotive Retailing, Services | 11 | 0.8 | 1 | 0.7 | 65 | 1.7 | 1.4 | 0.8 | 56 |
| Insurance: Life, Health (Mutual) | 11 | 0.3 | 0.3 | 0.4 | 66 | 0 | 0.1 | 0 | 68 |
| Publishing, Printing | 13 | 0.3 | -26.2 | -15.1 | 67 | 0.2 | -14 | -13 | 66 |
| Miscellaneous | 10 | 0 | 6.3 | 8.1 | 68 | 0.6 | 2.3 | 4.9 | 63 |
| Temporary Help | 4 | -0.2 | -0.4 | -0.3 | 69 | -0.7 | -1.6 | -0.9 | 71 |
| Motor Vehicles and Parts | 22 | -0.5 | -3.4 | -0.1 | 70 | -0.6 | -5.3 | -0.1 | 70 |
| Hotels, Casinos, Resorts | 11 | -1.3 | -2.9 | -2.5 | 71 | -0.6 | -1.2 | -1 | 69 |
| Metals | 10 | -2.2 | -6.8 | -6.3 | 72 | -2.4 | -10.1 | -4.8 | 73 |
| Transportation Equipment | 4 | -3.2 | -5.3 | -5.8 | 73 | -1.8 | -3 | -3.9 | 72 |
| Homebuilders | 8 | - 21.9 | -22.5 | -21.7 | 74 | -9.9 | -11.6 | -11.3 | 74 |

Source: *Fortune, May 3, 2010, and data provided by Fortune. Calculations by CRS.*

Notes: Health insurance and health care industries are emphasized for ease of comparison. For additional notes, see "The Largest U.S. Corporations," Fortune, vol. 161, no. 6 (May 3, 2010), pp. F-28-29

The medical loss ratio, defined as total health benefits paid divided by premium income, is a commonly used, albeit rough, indicator of profitability and administrative efficiency. The proportion of premium revenues not paid through benefits is used to cover administrative costs, taxes, interest payments, and profits. Investment income, which can be much more volatile than premium income due to occasional rapid price changes in asset markets, is excluded. To industry analysts, the medical loss ratio reflects how well premiums are keeping up with increases in medical costs. To consumers, the medical loss ratio shows what proportion of premiums, on average, are returned through benefits. State insurance regulators typically monitor health insurers' medical loss ratios to ensure adequate benefits are paid out and that premiums do not rise much more quickly than claims expenses. Some financial analysts perceive that lower medical loss ratios signal profit potential. Some have proposed stricter federal requirements on medical loss ratios (see below). Medical loss ratios typically do not include data from ASO plans used by self-insured plans, which make up the bulk of enrollments for larger firms (see **Table 3**).

**Table 5. Medical Loss Ratios for Major Publicly Traded Health Insurers, 2000-2008**

| | 2000 | 2001 | 2002 | 2003 | 2004 | 2005 | 2006 | 2007 | 2008 |
|---|---|---|---|---|---|---|---|---|---|
| Aetna Inc. | 92.1 | 89.8 | 89.8 | 76.6 | 78.3 | 77.4 | 79.9 | 80.4 | 81.5 |
| Amerigroup Corp. | 81.0 | 80.6 | 80.6 | 80.2 | 81.0 | 84.7 | 81.1 | 83.1 | 81.4 |
| Anthem Inc. | 84.7 | 84.5 | 84.5 | 82.4 | | | | | |
| Centene Corp. | 84.3 | 82.8 | 82.8 | 83.4 | 81.5 | 82.6 | 85.9 | 83.8 | 82.0 |
| Cigna HealthCare Inc. | 84.2 | 86.3 | 70.5 | 75.5 | 71.5 | 72.1 | 71.5 | 72.2 | 70.7 |
| Cobalt Corp. | 81.8 | 77.9 | 89.2 | 85.0 | | | | | |
| Coventry Health Care Inc. | 85.8 | 86.0 | 86.0 | 81.2 | 80.5 | 79.4 | 79.3 | 79.6 | 84.0 |
| Health Net Inc. | 82.8 | 84.4 | 84.4 | 82.6 | 89.3 | 86.5 | 85.0 | 86.6 | 88.4 |
| Humana Inc. | 84.5 | 83.3 | 83.3 | 83.5 | 84.1 | 83.2 | 84.0 | 83.0 | 84.5 |
| Molina Healthcare Inc. | | | | 83.4 | 84.4 | 86.9 | 84.6 | 84.5 | 84.8 |
| Mid Atlantic Medical Services Inc. | 86.1 | 85.3 | 86.4 | 85.0 | | | | | |
| Oxford Health Plans Inc. | 77.5 | 78.9 | 78.9 | 79.4 | | | | | |
| PacifiCare Health Systems Inc. | 87.5 | 89.7 | 89.7 | 86.8 | 88.5 | | | | |
| RightCHOICE Managed Care, Inc. | 81.7 | 80.3 | | | | | | | |
| Sierra Health Services Inc. | 95.4 | 91.0 | 84.8 | 79.2 | 79.5 | 79.1 | 79.9 | 84.2 | |
| Trigon Healthcare, Inc. | 83.6 | 84.0 | | | | | | | |
| Triple-S Manag-ement, Corp. | | | | | | | 87.6 | 87.0 | 88.9 |
| United Health Group | 85.4 | 85.3 | 85.3 | 81.4 | 80.6 | 80.0 | 81.2 | 80.6 | 82.0 |
| Universal American Corp. | | | | | | | | 80.4 | 83.3 |
| WellCare Health Plans Inc. | | | | 82.5 | 80.9 | 81.2 | 81.1 | 79.4 | 85.3 |
| WellChoice Inc. | | | 88.1 | 85.4 | 86.3 | | | | |
| WellPoint Health Networks Inc. | 80.8 | 81.5 | 81.5 | 81.0 | 82.5 | 80.9 | 82.0 | 83.2 | 84.4 |

Source: A.M. Best Company, Special Reports, various years. The medical loss ratio is defined as total health benefits divided by total premium revenue.

Notes: Anthem Inc. acquired WellPoint in late 2004 and operates under the WellPoint name. Cobalt Corp. was acquired by WellPoint in late 2003. Mid Atlantic Medical Services, Inc. (also known as MAMSI) was acquired by UnitedHealth Corp. in

February 2004. PacifiCare Health Systems Inc. was acquired by UnitedHealth on December 20, 2005. RightCHOICE Managed Care, Inc. was acquired by WellPoint on January 31, 2002. Sierra Health Services Inc. was acquired by UnitedHealth on February 25, 2008. Trigon Healthcare, Inc. merged with Anthem on July 31, 2002. Triple-S Management, Corp., the Blue Cross/Blue Shield affiliate for Puerto Rico, became a publicly traded company in 2006. As of December 28, 2005, WellChoice Inc. has operated as a subsidiary of WellPoint Inc. See source for additional notes.

Some contend that the medical loss ratio is a seriously flawed measure of administrative costs, profitability, and plan efficiency, and argue that customer satisfaction and cost-per-coveredperson-per-month data on specific health insurance market segments would be more informative.[154] Medical loss ratios can differ by market segment. For instance, administrative costs are typically higher, and medical loss ratios are therefore generally lower, for individual plans than for large group plans. Medical loss ratios are typically higher when health insurers shift insurance risks to consumers through cost-sharing or to providers through capitation arrangements. The allocation of overhead costs, which is inherently arbitrary to some degree, will typically depend on accounting judgments, which may vary from insurer to insurer, although computation of medical loss ratios is generally constrained by some state regulators and by generally accepted accounting principles.[155] While many insurance companies and some large employers use those data to track health plan performance, those data are typically considered proprietary. A more stringent limit on medical loss ratios might require careful attention to how those ratios are defined.[156]

In the latest data (2008), medical loss ratios among major insurers range from a low of 70.7% to almost 89%. Some major commercial insurers have had significant decreases in medical expense ratios in the past decade. For example, CIGNA HealthCare's medical loss ratio, 86.3% in 2001, fell to 70.7% in 2008, according to A.M. Best reports. In general, medical loss ratios are somewhat volatile and can change dramatically from one year to the next. Such swings may be explained by aggressive pricing intended to increase market share or by unexpectedly high medical costs.

Trends in medical loss ratios may also reflect changes in insurers' administrative costs. A major component of insurers' administrative costs is linked to processing of claims and running call centers, which are both closely linked to information technology. While many other businesses saw rapid productivity advances in the 1 990s due to better and cheaper information technology, some evidence suggests that productivity in the insurance industry grew less rapidly. While productivity in the finance industry (in value added terms) *grew* by 1.3% per year in the first half of the 1 990s and by 4.9% in the second half, according to one estimate, productivity in the insurance industry *fell* by 1.5% in the first half of the 1990s and fell by 0.06% in the second half of that decade.[157] In recent years, some insurers have claimed that better information technology management has helped constrain administrative costs.[158] Finally, as noted above, health insurers in some market segments have significant marketing expenses. Trends in marketing costs may therefore affect medical loss ratios.

***Profitability Measures Reported by the Sherlock Company***

The Sherlock Company tracks administrative expenses for health insurance companies by collecting financial and operating data from a large number of health insurance firms. These data are checked and compiled in a consistent manner. Sherlock Company estimates are widely used in the industry. The Sherlock data are not drawn by random sample; therefore, if firms not cooperating with the Sherlock Company's data collection were more profitable than average, the profitability measures would be skewed downwards.

The tables below present Sherlock Company data for 2007 and 2008. Profit margins for 2007 and 2008 in the health insurance industry may reflect substantial job losses, which reduce the number of employees covered by employer plans. Losses due to asset price declines following the turmoil in financial markets in late 2007 and 2008 have also adversely affected some insurers' profits. Thus, profitability measures for 2007 and 2008 might be atypical for the insurance industry.

Profit margins in the health insurance industry for 2007 appear to be lower than profit margins reported for other parts of the health sector, such as the pharmaceutical industry, reflecting different investment, risk, and opportunities in each industry. **Table 6** presents data for 2007 on profit margins for standard commercial plans and administrative service only (ASO) plans used by firms that self insure. [159] Within each category, unweighted averages (means), medians, and weighted averages are presented. [160] These profit margin estimates exclude investment income as well as interest expenses and many taxes. Results for 2007 presented in **Table 6** suggest that standard commercial plans were more profitable than ASO plans. When the weighted average margins are higher than the unweighted mean, it suggests that larger firms in 2007 tended to be more profitable than smaller firms.

**Table 6. Profit Margins of Health Plans**
**Operating Profits as a Percentage of Premium Equivalents, 2007**

| | Commercial Insured | | | Commercial ASO | | | Commercial Total | | |
|---|---|---|---|---|---|---|---|---|---|
| | **Mean** | **Weighted** | **Median** | **Mean** | **Weighted** | **Median** | **Mean** | **Weighted** | **Median** |
| Blue Cross | 0.63% | 0.10% | 1.95% | -0.30% | 0.27% | -0.11% | 0.39% | 0.22% | 0.59% |
| Independent/ Provider-Sponsored | 1.87% | 1.93% | 1.26% | -1.09% | -1.24% | -0.18% | 1.56% | 1.16% | 1.19% |
| Total | 0.63% | 0.37% | 1.95% | -0.30% | 0.17% | -0.11% | 0.39% | 0.32% | 0.59% |

Source: Sherlock Company, Sherlock Expense Evaluation Reports data.

Notes: Mean is an unweighted average. Weighted averages are weighted by enrollments. Income taxes, certain state taxes, investment income and interest expense are excluded from these calculations. Premium equivalents for administrative service only (ASO) plans are fees plus health benefits. Operating Profits include pharmacy and mental health expenses and exclude miscellaneous business taxes. Premium equivalents exclude miscellaneous business taxes. Provider-sponsored plans are owned by non-profit health systems. Independent plans are regionally based and often are closely associated with a provider network.

**Table 6** includes an adjustment that helps make profit margins on standard and ASO plans more comparable. Insurers that run ASO plans charge firms fees, but the firms pay claims themselves (aside from any reinsurance provisions) out of funds collected from employees. [161] For example, out of every $100 of employee health insurance funds, a hypothetical firm might pay $90 in benefits and pay an insurance firm $10 to administer the program. In standard plans, firms pass on premiums from employees to insurers, who then pay claims. Thus, for an ASO plan the insurance firm would receive $10, but would get $100 in premium income in a standard plan. Therefore, calculating ASO profit margins by using premium equivalents in the denominator puts profit margins on ASO and standard plans on a more comparable basis.

**Table 7** presents profit data for all Blue Cross/Blue Shield plans in 2008 taken from publicly reported data, such as filings with the Securities and Exchange Commission (SEC). Unlike the profit data in **Table 6** these data include investment income and may include income from other lines of insurance. The adjustment for ASO plans used for profit margins presented in **Table 6** is not included in margins reported in **Table 7**.

**Table 7. Profit Margins of Blue Cross/Blue Shield Plans, 2008 Computed Using Publicly Reported Data**

| | Mean | Weighted | Median |
|---|---|---|---|
| Operating Margins | 1.02% | 2.84% | 1.18% |
| Pretax Margin | 1.65% | 2.55% | 1.67% |
| Margin After Taxes | 1.52% | 1.64% | 1.24% |
| Federal Income Tax Rate | 23.45% | 35.41% | 13.71% |

Source: Sherlock Company analysis of public data (e.g., SEC, NAIC).
Notes: Includes data for all 39 Blue Cross/Blue Shield plans. See notes for **Table 6**.

**Table 8** shows profit margins for the six largest national commercial insurers in 2008 (Aetna, CIGNA, Coventry, Health Net, Humana and UnitedHealth), whose plans covered 73 million members. Profit margins in **Table 8** were computed in the same way as in **Table 7**. These data suggest that large commercial insurers enjoyed higher profit margins in 2008 than Blue Cross/Blue Shield plans. To the extent that the 2007 data reported in **Table 6** is similar to 2008 profit data, the profit margins reported in **Table 7** and **Table 8** suggest that investment income is a significant source of insurer's profits.

Many insurers are active in many different segments of the health insurance market. **Table 9** shows profit margins for the individual market, the small group insurance market, and the ASO market. These markets, according to these data, were less profitable in 2008 than standard commercial plans. Health insurers on average had negative profit margins in the small group and commercial ASO markets, but had positive margins in the individual market. That the weighted mean margin for the individual market is less than the unweighted mean suggests that smaller insurers in 2007 tended to have higher profit margins in that market segment.

**Table 8. Profit Margins of National Commercial Insurers, 2008 Computed Using Publicly Reported Data**

| | Mean | Weighted | Median |
|---|---|---|---|
| Operating Margins | 6.0 1% | 5.96% | 5.32% |
| Pretax Margin | 5.40% | 5.90% | 5.13% |
| Margin After Taxes | 3.62% | 3.81% | 3.35% |
| Federal Income Tax Rate | 35.6 1% | 35.35% | 34.75% |

Source: Sherlock Company analysis of public data (e.g., SEC, NAIC).
Notes: See text and notes for **Table 6**.

**Table 9. Profit Margins By Line of Health Insurance, 2008**

| | **Individual** | |
|---|---|---|
| Mean | Weighted | Median |
| 2.17% | 1.04% | 6.41% |
| | **Small Group** | |
| Mean | Weighted | Median |
| -5.96% | -8.47% | -6.28% |
| | **Commercial ASO** | |
| Mean | Weighted | Median |
| -0.30% | 0.27% | -0.11% |

Source: Sherlock Company, Sherlock Expense Evaluation Reports and publicly reported data.
Notes: Profit margins for Commercial ASO using data for Blue Cross/Blue Shield Commercial ASO plans (**Table 6**). Profit margins for the small group and individual markets were estimated using data from 10 plans serving policyholders in 13 states. See text and notes for **Table 6**.

# Options for Congress

In the wake of health care reform measures enacted in March 2010, congressional concern over health insurance policy is likely to persist, even if health reform takes a less central role in legislative deliberations. Congress could take several further actions to affect the behavior and structure of health insurance markets. Important policy details remain to be resolved through federal rule-making, agency actions, and possibly through further legislation. The remainder of this section discusses some possible policy responses to perceived problems in the health insurance market.

## More Aggressive Antitrust Enforcement

More aggressive antitrust enforcement is one potential response to perceived problems resulting from high levels of market concentration among health insurers. Federal agencies with antitrust enforcement responsibilities have been active in health care markets, opposing many hospital mergers and putting restrictions on some health insurance mergers. The U.S. Department of Justice and the Federal Trade Commission issued a major report on competition, antitrust policy, and the health care sector in 2004, which urged policies to enhance competition in the health care and health insurance markets.[162] State governments, which generally have primary responsibility for insurance regulation, also have antitrust enforcement capabilities.[163]

Strong antitrust action is preferable to allowing both health insurers and providers to build up countervailing power, according to some economists who argue that a more fully competitive market would better protect consumers.[164] Such antitrust remedies may be most effective in promoting economic efficiency if applied to both the health insurance market and key health care provider markets.

On the other hand, the federal government in the past has had trouble using antitrust remedies to increase the competitiveness in the health sector. The federal government lost many antitrust cases intended to promote competition among hospitals.[165] While federal antitrust authorities have forced alterations of some health insurance mergers, federal antitrust policies do not appear to have had a determining influence on the structure of health insurance markets.[166] One former FTC official contends that modifying the McCarran-Fergusson Act (P.L. 79-15) and removing other impediments could strengthen federal antitrust policy in the health care market. [167] Congress could amend antitrust laws to facilitate stronger pro-competition policies among health insurers.

Other measures could also inject greater competition into health insurance markets. Some analysts contend that simplifying regulatory policies encourages new entrants. Standardization of claims processes and payment mechanisms could also lower barriers to entry. Other policies might allow insurers in related lines of business, such as life and disability insurance, to provide more competition in ASO markets for firms that self-insure.

## Stronger Regulatory Measures

Congress could adopt more stringent regulatory measures designed to improve performance in private health insurance markets. This may require a realignment of regulatory responsibilities with state governments, which now play the leading role in insurance regulation. Congress has taken some steps in the past to regulate health insurance. For example, the Health Insurance Portability and Accountability Act of 1996 (HIPAA; P.L. 104-191) imposed several federal requirements on health insurance plans. [168] Although HIPAA provided uniform federal standards on certain aspects of insurance plans, some contend that HIPAA had only limited effects on health insurance markets. Legislative changes to the Employee Retirement Income Security Act (ERISA), which provides a federal exemption to many state health insurance requirements, could also have important consequences in the health insurance market. Many large corporations, which typically operate in many states, oppose changes in ERISA.

### *Regulation of Medical Underwriting*

The Protection and Affordable Care Act (H.R. 3590; P.L. 111-148) bars some medical underwriting practices, which may change how health insurance companies compete.[169] The practice of medical underwriting, which consists of offering better prices and conditions to the healthy, rearranges the cost burden of health care but has little or no effect on overall costs. Although an individual insurer earns higher profits by attracting a healthier risk pool via medical underwriting, total costs to society are not reduced. Because underwriting consumes real resources, a system with extensive medical underwriting may have higher administrative costs, which provide little social benefit.

Individual firms, however, could face major financial risks by unilaterally dropping medical underwriting practices. The health insurers' trade association, America's Health Insurance Plans (AHIP), had said it would accept limitations of pre-existing condition exclusions, but only if individuals are required to purchase coverage, so that not just the sick enroll.[170]

Regulations barring medical underwriting practices, such as limiting coverage of those with preexisting conditions, could change the nature of competition in health insurance markets. If those regulations motivated health insurers to compete on the basis of how well they served consumers rather than on the ability to shift risks to others, economic efficiency could be enhanced. Even with limits on medical underwriting, however, health insurers may affect the composition of their risk pools through marketing, customer service practices, and by other means. The implementation of individual mandate provisions that encourage purchase of health insurance may have important interactions with management and marketing decisions of health insurers.

### *Minimum Loss Ratio Requirements*

Some critics of the health insurance industry contend that medical loss ratios (defined as total claims divided by premium income) are too low, which in their view has helped push health insurance premiums up. Health insurance industry analysts argue that high medical loss ratios could undermine insurers' ability to raise capital and could lead to cuts in cost of care coordination activities, chronic disease management activities and quality assurance programs. A few states have minimum medical loss ratio requirements for some segments of the health insurance market.[171]

The Protection and Affordable Care Act (H.R. 3590; P.L. 111-148, Sec. 1331(b)(3)) requires that plans offered through state health insurance exchanges (which are to be operational at the beginning of 2014) have a medical loss ratio of at least 85%. The act also will require large group health insurance plans to have a medical loss ratio of at least 85%. Small-group and individual plans will have to satisfy an 80% threshold.

That requirement may require the Secretary of the Department of Health and Human Services to specify how medical loss ratio will be calculated, and how that requirement will interact with state-level insurance regulation. A request for comments on defining medical loss ratios was issued in April 2010.[172]

## Individual and Employer Health Insurance Mandates

Individual or employer mandates could affect the health insurance market in important ways. An individual mandate would require individuals to offer proof of health insurance either to avoid financial penalties or to qualify for certain tax benefits. An individual health insurance mandate in some ways would resemble the individual mandate most states impose on automobile drivers that require either minimum insurance coverage levels, or proof of financial responsibility. The aim of these mandates is to widen the insurance risk pool as broadly as possible and to discourage individuals from forgoing insurance and then transferring the costs of an accident or illness onto others. Of course, enforcing a health insurance mandate would likely require different administrative mechanisms than an automobile insurance mandate.

Critics note that an individual mandate could compel purchase of an insurance policy that in the individual's view would cost more than its expected benefits. In particular, if premiums were not adjusted for age and other relevant risk factors, an individual mandate could be seen as helping transfer economic resources from younger and healthier people to older and sicker people. In Massachusetts, the individual health insurance mandate was tied to the availability of "affordable" policies, which required a state panel to judge what "affordable" meant.[173]

An employer mandate would require certain firms to offer qualifying health insurance to their employees or pay some amount into a government health fund or alternatively, face the loss of some tax benefits. Some argue that health costs of uncovered employees are to some degree borne by those with private insurance coverage because providers shift some costs of uncompensated care onto others. Some argue that imposing a employer mandate would level the playing field among larger firms, who are more likely to offer health insurance benefits, and smaller firms, which are most likely not to offer those benefits. On the other hand, an employer mandate could force some firms to lower wages and other benefits. Some employees may value those forgone wages and benefits more than new health benefits.

Employer mandates would affect the health insurance market more broadly as well. The number and proportion of American workers receiving employer-provided health insurance has been declining over time. Imposing an employer mandate would probably slow or even reverse that trend.

Employer-provided health care has important advantages and disadvantages. As noted above, employer-provided health insurance coverage can be administratively efficient and helps mitigate adverse selection problems that could lead to splintering of risk pools. On the other hand, tying health benefits to employment can reduce job mobility and hinder efficient matching of workers to positions that make the best use of their skills. Making the individual health insurance market more attractive (see discussion of Wyden-Bennett plan below) or providing health coverage on the basis of citizenship, as do many other advanced industrial countries, could enhance job mobility.

## Health Insurance Exchanges

Some proposals that Congress considered contained measures partially intended to heighten competition in the market for health care.[174] For example, H.R. 3200 proposed creation of a "Health Insurance Exchange" that would provide an alternative to employer-based health coverage for groups that have had difficulty obtaining affordable health insurance. The Health Insurance Exchange proposed in H.R. 3200 includes a "public option" insurance plan intended to spur greater competition among health insurers. Critics of H.R. 3200 expressed concern that a federally financed public option would enjoy special advantages unavailable to private health insurers and that creation of a public option might be a first step towards a much broader federal role in health care finance.

The Affordable Health Choices Act (S. 1679), approved by the Senate Health, Education, Labor, and Pensions (HELP) Committee on July 15, 2009, proposes new federal private health insurance standards and the creation of an "Affordable Health Benefit Gateway" in each state, along with a public option plan called the "Community Health Insurance Plan." On September 16, 2009, the Chairman of the Senate Finance Committee, Senator Baucus, released a chairman's mark of the America's Healthy Futures Act of 2009, which also included new federal health insurance standards and health insurance exchanges, but does not include a public option plan.[175] On November 19, Senator Reid proposed a measure that melded provisions of the HELP and Finance Committee bills, which allowed states to include a public option in health insurance exchanges.[176] The version of H.R. 3590 that passed the Senate on December 24, 2009, however, omitted the public option.[177]

### *Lessons from the Massachusetts Connector*

The proposed Health Insurance Exchange in some ways resembles the Massachusetts Connector created in 2006 and implemented at the end of 2007. Both the proposed federal Health Insurance Exchange and the Massachusetts

Connector act as an intermediary between insurance companies and eligible enrollees, playing a similar role to employers who act as health insurance intermediaries for most Americans.[178] Massachusetts mandates that individuals have health insurance (as long as "affordable" insurance options are available) or face financial penalties. All but the smallest firms (fewer than 10 employees) that offer no (qualifying) health insurance benefits must pay an annual penalty of $295 per full-time employee. The program has roughly halved the number of uninsured people in the state.[179]

#### *What Role Would Exchanges Play: Traffic Cops vs. Gatekeepers*

The role played by a Health Insurance Exchange could have important effects. The exchange could act as a "traffic cop" that imposed minimal requirements on plans, in order to allow a large number of insurers to offer coverage to eligible individuals. Alternatively, the exchange could act as a "gatekeeper," as most large employers do, and preselect a limited number of alternatives. In Medicare Part D, which offers prescription drug coverage, the Center for Medicare and Medicaid Services (CMS) acts more like a traffic cop, allowing a wide range of insurers to enter that market. This policy allows Medicare beneficiaries to choose among a wide array of plans. Prices for actuarially equivalent plans, however, are widely dispersed, which suggests that market competition has been ineffective in weeding out plans that offer less value for the money.

Alternatively, an exchange could also play a more active "gatekeeper" role. Many employers have played a very active role in designing health insurance offerings.[180] The exchange could either select a limited number of plans judged to be more attractive or impose stricter requirements on plans. Some economists have found that consumers have difficulty choosing among plans when alternatives are numerous and when differences among plans are difficult to compare. [181] Congress arguably acted as a gatekeeper by requiring standardization of Medigap policies in order to encourage more effective competition among insurers.[182]

## The Public Option

Creation of a public option within the proposed Health Insurance Exchanges would have arguably been one way to expand health insurance coverage and control the growth of health insurance costs. The public option proposals responded to concerns about high levels of market concentration and the exercise of market power in health care markets, as well as to concerns about some industry practices in the individual and small-group market segments. Proponents of the public option argued that it would help limit costs in two ways.[183] First, a public option plan could institute administrative efficiencies. Second, some argued that a public plan could negotiate better discounts with providers.

Government intervention in the market motivated by concerns about market concentration and the exercise of market power could have unintended consequences if the determinants of market structure are not well understood. The bargaining power of a public option could enhance economic efficiency by counteracting monopoly power exerted by providers, thus lowering prices and increasing output.[184] But if providers are operating efficiently, then increased bargaining power by insurers could lead to economic inefficiency in the health care market. Evidence suggests, however, that many providers are not operating efficiently.[185]

Without further regulation, however, a public plan would have likely attracted high-cost individuals—those who, because of health or age, can only buy insurance for very high premiums, or who are medically uninsurable because of pre-existing conditions. This adverse selection would have threatened the viability and stability of a public option. As an example, many states have high-risk health insurance pools (HRPs) to cover these high-cost individuals. But state HRPs typically charge premiums higher than premiums charged by private plans offered to healthier individuals and all operate at a loss.[186] To avoid or mitigate adverse selection problems, most public option proposals mandated health insurance coverage by all, require community rating, and prohibit denial of insurance based on health or pre-existing conditions by private insurance plans.

## Cooperatives

Some proposed creation of health insurance cooperatives as an alternative to a public plan. 187 Cooperative health insurance policies would be available to eligible individuals through health insurance exchanges created by health insurance reform legislation. Proponents argued that cooperative-run plans would increase competition in the health insurance market without requiring more direct federal involvement.[188] Others contended that cooperatives would be unable to improve performance of the health insurance industry.[189]

Some medical cooperatives were created in the 1930s, such as the Group Health Association in Washington, DC, and the Group Health Cooperative of Puget Sound. The AMA and local medical societies, however, vigorously opposed medical cooperatives and succeeded in driving many of them out of business.[190] The Farm Security Administration (FSA) created several programs to provide medical care to low-income rural households, which included cooperatives that at their peak reached 600,000 people.[191] Some historians argue the success of these cooperatives was limited by the lack of clear direction from FSA administrators and opposition from traditional farm groups.[192] These programs were discontinued starting in 1946. The United Mine Workers' Welfare and Retirement Fund, created in the 1940s, might provide another model of a health cooperative.[193]

The early history of Blue Cross may be instructive. The Blue Cross idea, incorporated through a stream of new organizations, spread rapidly across the country during the 1930s and 1940s, demonstrating that a suitable design with support from existing organizations could transform the American health finance system. Blue Cross was able to piggyback on local hospitals and the AHA, and Blue Shield initially piggybacked on local medical societies. Links between hospitals and Blue Cross had profound effects on the governance and structure of Blue Cross. Though the modern health care sector is very different than when Blue Cross began, the strategy of linking new structures, such as cooperatives, to existing organizations could accelerate implementation. Those organizations would likely have a strong imprint on how proposed health insurance cooperatives were run.

Blue Cross, in its earliest days, was originally strongly community oriented. This, in part, reflected the ideals of the "voluntary hospital" movement. Yet while charity and altruism have played important roles in the hospital industry, business-like behavior has also been prominent.[194] By 1986, Congress concluded that Blue Cross organizations did not act much differently than commercial insurers.[195] Competitive pressures on cooperatives may also be strong enough to motivate them to act much like other insurers.

## Other Options

Some have proposed more fundamental reforms of the health care sector. Senators Wyden and Bennett have introduced a medical voucher proposal, the Healthy Americans Act, which was introduced in the 110th Congress as S. 334 and in the 111th Congress as S. 391.[196] The WydenBennett plan would mandate that individuals carry private health insurance and would create state-run pools to restructure the individual health insurance market. The federal government would support the plan by providing subsidies to certain individuals.

The Empowering Patients First Act (H.R. 3400), introduced by Representative Tom Price on July 30, 2009, would provide additional tax incentives to individuals and employers to maintain or expand health insurance coverage; modify federal regulations governing insurance pools for individual purchasers; would take steps to ease purchase of individual insurance policies across state lines; would modify remedies for alleged medical malpractice; and would ban certain applications of comparative effectiveness research data in health care.

Others have proposed more limited reforms that would reintroduce cash indemnity payments under certain circumstances. For example, one proposal would allow patients in end-of-life care to choose between standard care or a package of palliative care and a cash payment that could be used for other purposes. [197] The option of indemnity benefits could make providers more conscious of the costs and benefits of the care they deliver.

## CONCLUDING REMARKS

Evidence suggests that health insurance markets in many local areas are highly concentrated. Many large firms have reacted to market conditions by self-insuring, which may provide some competitive pressure on insurers, although this is unlikely to improve market conditions for other consumers. The exercise of market power by firms in concentrated markets generally leads to higher prices and reduced output—high premiums and limited access to health insurance—combined with high profits. Many other characteristics of the health insurance markets, however, also contribute to rising costs and limited access to affordable health insurance.

Some evidence suggests that insurance companies' profits are not large, especially during the current economic recession; although some of those estimates exclude investment income. Even if health insurers were highly profitable, it is unclear how much reducing insurance industry profits would do to reduce total health care costs or even reduce administrative costs. Nor is it clear that more vigorous enforcement of antitrust laws and regulations would succeed in courts or would significantly reduce health insurance premiums or expanded health insurance coverage.

Health insurance is intertwined with the whole health care system. Health costs appear to have increased over time in large part because of complex interactions among health insurance, health care providers, employers, pharmaceutical manufacturers, tax policy, and the medical technology industry. Reducing the growth trajectory of health care costs may require policies that affect these interactions. Policies focused on health insurance sector reform may yield some results, but are unlikely to solve larger cost growth and problems of limited access to health care if other parts of the health are left unchanged.

## APPENDIX. ADDITIONAL INDICATORS OF HEALTH INSURERS' PROFITABILITY

This appendix presents two indicators of health insurer profitability for the period 2000-2008, and profits as a percentage of shareholder equity for Fortune 1000 firms by industry in 2008.

**Table A-1** presents return-on-equity figures for major publicly traded health insurers over the period 2000-2008. Return on equity measures a company's overall after-tax profitability from underwriting and investment activity, and is defined as the sum of after-tax net income and unrealized capital gains divided by equity. Return on equity provides a useful comparison to profits in other lines of business, but can be volatile, especially when accounting changes require adjustments of equity levels. Firms obtain capital through equity (typically through the sale of shares that entitle shareholders to dividend payments and certain voting rights) and debt (typically through loans or bonds that require fixed or specified interest payments). Firms can increase return on equity by increasing their debt-to-capital ratio, but at an increased risk of bankruptcy in the event of adverse business conditions that make interest payments to debt holders hard to sustain.

**Table A-2** presents return-on-revenue figures for major publicly traded health insurers over the period 2000-2008. Return-on-revenue ratios are roughly analogous to return-on-sales figures in other industries. Return-on-revenue figures, unlike return-on-equity, measures profitability independently of how a firm raises its capital.[198]

## Table A-1. Return on Equity for Major Publicly Traded Insurers, 2000-2008

| | 2000 | 2001 | 2002 | 2003 | | | | 2004 | 2005 | 2006 | 2007 | 2008 |
|---|---|---|---|---|---|---|---|---|---|---|---|---|
| Aetna Inc. | -0.4 | -5.9 | -6.1 | -41.3 | | 3.0[a] | 15.1 | 13.4 | 15.4 | 18.6 | 18.2 | 16.9 |
| Amerigroup Corp. | 520.0 | 19.7 | 19.7 | | 20.1 | | 14.5 | 15.1 | 8.4 | 14.0 | 12.8 | -6.0 |
| Anthem Inc. | 11.8 | 16.6 | 16.6 | | 10.2 | | | | | | | |
| Centene Corp. | -100.0 | 20.3 | 20.3 | | 25.5 | | 15.0 | 16.5 | 15.9 | -13.4 | 17.7 | 16.7 |
| Cigna HealthCare Inc. | 14.2 | 15.4 | 14.4 | | 15.0 | | 9.8 | 27.6 | 30.3 | 26.7 | 23.5 | 8.1 |
| Cobalt Corp. | -23.7 | -10.6 | -10.6 | | 24.5 | | | | | | | |
| Coventry Health Care Inc. | 10.2 | 12.2 | 12.2 | | 22.6 | | 27.0 | 27.8 | 19.6 | 19.0 | 19.0 | 11.1 |
| Health Net Inc. | 15.5 | 7.4 | 7.4 | 17.5 | | 18.2[a] | 18.1 | 3.4 | 14.5 | 18.5 | 10.3 | 5.4 |
| Humana Inc. | 6.6 | 7.8 | 7.8 | | 8.9 | | 12.5 | 13.4 | 11.8 | 16.0 | 20.7 | 14.5 |
| Molina Healthcare Inc. | | | | | | | 19.5 | 16.9 | 7.7 | 10.9 | 11.9 | 12.2 |
| Mid Atlantic Medical Services Inc. | 17.7 | 20.6 | 20.6 | | 28.0 | | | | | | | |
| Oxford Health Plans Inc. | 41.8 | 69.8 | 69.8 | | 44.7 | | | | | | | |
| PacifiCare Health Systems Inc. | 8.0 | 0.9 | 0.9 | -57.1 | | 10.5a | 13.1 | 13.8 | | | | |
| RightCHOICE Managed Care, Inc. | 11.9 | 16.2 | | | | | | | | | | |
| Sierra Health Services Inc. | -222.2 | 3.1 | 4.2 | | 23.1 | | 41.1 | 60.9 | 42.3 | 64.5 | 29.1 | |
| Trigon Healthcare, Inc. | 11.0 | 11.4 | | | | | | | | | | |

**Table A-1. (Continued)**

| | 2000 | 2001 | 2002 | 2003 | | | | 2004 | 2005 | 2006 | 2007 | 2008 |
|---|---|---|---|---|---|---|---|---|---|---|---|---|
| Triple-S Management, Corp. | | | | | | | | | | 16.0 | 12.1 | 5.1 |
| UnitedHealth Group | 19.1 | 23.5 | 23.5 | | 30.5 | | 35.6 | 24.1 | 17.3 | 20.0 | 23.2 | 14.3 |
| Universal American Corp. | | | | | | | | | | | 6.2 | 7.2 |
| WellCare Health Plans Inc. | | | | | | | 24.0 | 15.9 | 14.1 | 24.8 | 26.8 | -4.6 |
| WellChoice Inc. | | | 15.8 | | 30.6 | | 14.0 | 14.7 | | | | |
| WellPoint Health Networks Inc. | 20.9 | 19.5 | 19.5 | | 17.7 | | 12.9 | 4.9 | 9.9 | 12.6 | 14.6 | 11.6 |

Source: A.M. Best Company, Special Reports, various years.

Notes: Return on equity is the sum of after-tax net income and unrealized capital gains, to the mean of prior and current year-end policyholder surplus, expressed as a percentage. This ratio measures a company's overall after-tax profitability from underwriting and investment activity. Leftmost columns for year ending Dec. 3 1, 2003 were taken from A.M. Best Company, Special Report surveying 2003 GAAP results; right column taken from report surveying 2004 GAAP results. See notes for Table 6.

a. Calculated before the cumulative effect of change in accounting principle. Return on revenue, return on equity and return on capital for Aetna Inc., Health Net Inc., and Pacificare Health Systems Inc. were calculated using net income before the cumulative effect of accounting principle changes. "Change in accounting principle" is a technical accounting term that refers to changes due to the adoption of a generally accepted accounting principle different from the one used previously for reporting purposes.

## Table A-2. Return on Revenue for Major Publicly Traded Health Insurers, 2000-2008

| | 2000 | 2001 | 2002[a] | | 2003 | 2004 | 2005 | 2006 | 2007 | 2008 |
|---|---|---|---|---|---|---|---|---|---|---|
| Aetna Inc. | -0.17 | -2.61 | -16.10 | *1.31* | 4.60 | 6.10 | 7.00 | 6.80 | 6.60 | 4.50 |
| Amerigroup Corp. | 3.94 | 4.04 | 4.13 | *4.16* | 4.10 | 4.70 | 2.30 | 3.80 | 3.00 | -1.10 |
| Anthem Inc. | 2.59 | 3.28 | 4.13 | *4.60* | | | | | | |
| Centene Corp. | 4.04 | 3.94 | 5.52 | *5.64* | 4.30 | 4.40 | 3.70 | -2.20 | 2.60 | 2.50 |
| Cigna HealthCare | 5.26 | 4.96 | 3.67 | *4.04* | 3.30 | 7.90 | 9.70 | 7.00 | 6.30 | 1.50 |
| Cobalt Corp. | -6.28 | -1.57 | 4.71 | *5.39* | | | | | | |
| Coventry Health Care Inc. | 2.31 | 2.63 | 4.04 | *4.17* | 5.50 | 6.30 | 7.50 | 7.10 | 6.20 | 3.20 |
| Health Net Inc. | 1.81 | 0.98 | 2.62 | *2.77* | 2.50 | 0.40 | 1.90 | 2.50 | 1.40 | 0.60 |
| Humana Inc. | 0.85 | 1.15 | 1.27 | *1.31* | 1.90 | 2.10 | 2.10 | 2.30 | 3.30 | 2.20 |
| Molina Healthcare | | | | | 5.40 | 4.80 | 1.70 | 2.30 | 2.30 | 2.00 |
| Mid Atlantic Medical Services | 2.70 | 3.21 | 4.17 | *4.28* | | | | | | |
| Oxford Health Plans | 4.67 | 7.31 | 4.47 | *4.58* | | | | | | |
| PacifiCare Health Systems Inc. | 1.39 | 0.16 | -6.79 | *1.28* | 2.20 | 2.50 | | | | |
| RightCHOICE Managed Care, | 3.33 | 5.43 | | | | | | | | |
| Sierra Health Services Inc. | -17.26 | 0.53 | 3.95 | *4.20* | 6.10 | 7.80 | 8.70 | 8.10 | 4.90 | |
| Trigon Healthcare | 4.29 | 3.90 | | | | | | | | |
| Triple-S Management, Corp. | | | | | | | | 3.50 | 3.80 | 1.40 |
| UnitedHealth Group | 3.34 | 3.89 | 5.40 | *6.17* | 6.30 | 7.00 | 6.60 | 5.80 | 6.20 | 3.70 |
| Universal American Corp. | | | | | | | | | 2.80 | 2.00 |
| WellCare Health Plans | | | | | 2.30 | 3.50 | 2.80 | | 4.00 | -0.60 |
| WellChoice Inc. | | 2.84 | 7.40 | *8.17* | 3.70 | 4.20 | | | | |
| WellPoint Health Networks Inc. | 3.72 | 3.34 | 4.05 | *4.34* | 4.60 | 4.60 | 5.50 | 5.40 | 5.50 | 4.10 |

Source: A.M. Best Company, Special Reports, various years.

Notes: See notes for Table 6. Return-on-revenue is sum of after-tax net income and unrealized capital gains divided by premium income.

a. Second column for 2002 (in italics) calculated before the cumulative effect of change in accounting principle. Insurers financial data separates investment income and premium income (sometimes called underwriting income). Because investment income fluctuates with trends in asset markets, analysts often focus on premium income, which is more stable. Premium income is affected by employment growth and pricing decisions.

**Table A-3. Profits As a Percentage of Shareholder Equity By Industry for Fortune 1000 Firms, 2009**

| Industry | Fortune 1000 Firms in Industry | Profits As a % of Shareholder Equity | | | |
|---|---|---|---|---|---|
| | | Mean | Weighted Mean Median | | Rank |
| Tobacco | 5 | 21.5 | 61.3 | 74.3 | 6 |
| Computer Software | 10 | 21.4 | 20.0 | 29.4 | 8 |
| *Pharmaceuticals* | *21* | *15.3* | *15.2* | *21.1* | *27* |
| Railroads | 5 | 17.0 | 15.7 | 16.7 | 20 |
| Financial Data Services | 15 | 15.7 | -744.3 | 2.0 | 24 |
| Network and Other Communications Equip. | 8 | 13.1 | -1.2 | 13.9 | 36 |
| Oil and Gas Equip., Services | 19 | 18.3 | 12.4 | 15.8 | 14 |
| Scientific, Photographic and Control Equip. | 8 | 13.9 | 10.4 | 10.2 | 32 |
| Mining, Crude-oil production | 22 | 11.5 | 0.9 | 3.9 | 38 |
| Education | 2 | 31.7 | 31.7 | 30.1 | 1 |
| *Medical Products and Equip.* | *18* | *14.3* | *13.0* | *9.8* | *30* |
| Computer Peripherals | 5 | 18.2 | 17.3 | 14.2 | 15 |
| Securities | 14 | 10.0 | 0.3 | -24.2 | 45 |
| Internet Services and Retailing | 8 | 15.5 | -1.1 | 10.1 | 26 |
| Household and Personal Products | 12 | 30.9 | 29.1 | 21.8 | 2 |
| Utilities: Gas and Electric | 46 | 11.0 | 10.8 | 12.0 | 41 |
| Toys, Sporting Goods | 2 | 20.0 | 20.0 | 19.6 | 10 |
| Industrial Machinery | 26 | 18.2 | 21.6 | 16.6 | 16 |
| Transportation Equip. | 4 | 23.3 | 6.1 | 5.6 | 5 |
| Aerospace and Defense | 20 | 19.5 | 11.4 | 27.0 | 12 |
| Food Consumer Products | 20 | 19.8 | 30.3 | 23.3 | 11 |
| Advertising, marketing | 2 | 20.2 | 20.2 | 21.6 | 9 |
| Telecommunications | 21 | 4.2 | -4.4 | 9.2 | 57 |
| Construction and Farm Machinery | 11 | 23.4 | 12.3 | 30.2 | 4 |
| Electronics, Electrical Equip. | 17 | 13.9 | 13.0 | 18.2 | 31 |
| Waste Management | 2 | 9.7 | 9.7 | 8.8 | 46 |
| Metals | 12 | 18.6 | 5.4 | 13.0 | 13 |
| Mail, Package and Freight Delivery | 2 | 26.0 | 26.0 | 19.4 | 3 |
| Information Technology Services | 10 | 13.8 | 24.3 | 53.5 | 33 |

**Table A-3. (Continued)**

| Industry | Fortune 1000 Firms in Industry | Profits As a % of Shareholder Equity | | | |
|---|---|---|---|---|---|
| | | Mean | Weighted Mean | Median | Rank |
| Computers, Office Equip. | 7 | 21.4 | -8.3 | 22.2 | 7 |
| Chemicals | 40 | 17.1 | 13.9 | 15.3 | 19 |
| Commercial Banks | 28 | 2.8 | -3.6 | -1.2 | 60 |
| Food Services | 10 | 17.6 | -70.2 | 27.0 | 17 |
| Transportation and Logistics | 6 | 15.5 | 15.2 | 19.1 | 25 |
| Apparel | 11 | 9.2 | -17.0 | 9.1 | 48 |
| Packaging, Containers | 18 | 13.2 | 17.0 | -5.5 | 35 |
| Trucking, Truck Leasing | 7 | 9.1 | -12.3 | -6.3 | 50 |
| Wholesalers: Diversified | 17 | 17.3 | 1.0 | 14.4 | 18 |
| Real estate | 9 | 7.7 | -64.8 | -5.4 | 52 |
| Beverages | 8 | 13.5 | 1778.4 | 4.7 | 34 |
| Specialty Retailers | 60 | 10.2 | -18.6 | 8.8 | 44 |
| Engineering, Construction | 12 | 12.9 | 12.8 | 13.6 | 37 |
| Diversified Outsourcing Services | 15 | 14.9 | -13.1 | 16.2 | 29 |
| *Health Care: Pharmacy and Other Services* | *9* | *16.1* | *10.7* | *19.5* | *23* |
| *Health Care: Medical Facilities* | *17* | *7.3* | *-9.1* | *175.6* | *53* |
| *Health Care: Insurance and Managed Care* | *14* | *11.4* | *9.4* | *12.4* | *39* |
| Insurance: Property and Casualty (mutual) | 4 | 1.4 | 1.5 | -0.4 | 61 |
| Miscellaneous | 8 | 9.1 | 335.7 | 8.6 | 49 |
| Building materials, Glass | 7 | -0.1 | -12.9 | -8.3 | 63 |
| Home Equip., Furnishings | 11 | 6.3 | 52.0 | -0.4 | 55 |
| Petroleum Refining | 15 | 16.5 | 7.9 | 18.8 | 21 |
| Food and Drug Stores | 16 | 10.9 | 11.8 | 10.7 | 42 |
| Energy | 20 | 15.0 | 10.1 | 7.7 | 28 |
| Pipelines | 15 | 11.2 | -27.9 | -3.0 | 40 |
| *Wholesalers: Health Care* | *7* | *16.2* | *15.4* | *15.4* | *22* |
| Wholesalers: Food and Grocery | 7 | 10.8 | 16.0 | 26.2 | 43 |
| General Merchandisers | 13 | 3.8 | -12.8 | 11.0 | 58 |
| Food Production | 8 | 3.0 | -40.0 | 4.2 | 59 |

**Table A-3. (Continued)**

| Industry | Fortune 1000 Firms in Industry | Profits As a % of Shareholder Equity | | | |
|---|---|---|---|---|---|
| | | Mean | Weighted Mean | Median | Rank |
| Wholesalers: Electronics and Office Equip. | 9 | 7.2 | -15.4 | -4.7 | 54 |
| Semiconductors and Other Elec. Components | 26 | 8.0 | 139.9 | -8.5 | 51 |
| Entertainment | 14 | 9.7 | 25.9 | -18.4 | 47 |
| Temporary Help | 6 | -1.9 | -5.9 | 1.8 | 66 |
| Motor vehicles and Parts | 29 | 0.9 | -24.5 | 49.8 | 62 |
| Diversified Financials | 11 | 4.8 | 52.4 | -100.6 | 56 |
| Insurance: Property and Casualty (stock) | 29 | -1.7 | -12.1 | -27.4 | 65 |
| Publishing, Printing | 14 | -2.1 | -278.0 | -542.4 | 67 |
| *Insurance: Life, Health (mutual)* | *10* | *-5.1* | *-4.1* | *-7.2* | *69* |
| *Insurance: Life, Health (stock)* | *16* | *-5.2* | *-7.4* | *2.0* | *70* |
| Forest and Paper Products | 9 | -24.4 | 106.7 | -33.8 | 72 |
| Airlines | 10 | -1.2 | -97.8 | -556.9 | 64 |
| Hotels, Casinos, Resorts | 9 | -3.7 | 36.7 | -39.5 | 68 |
| Automotive Retailing, Services | 10 | -69.3 | -202.8 | -62.5 | 73 |
| Homebuilders | 10 | -73.8 | -107.1 | -66.0 | 74 |
| Savings Institutions | 2 | -16.5 | -16.5 | -18.1 | 71 |

Source: Fortune, May 4, 2009 and other Fortune data, and CRS calculations.

Notes: Health insurance and health care industries are emphasized for ease of comparison. For additional notes, see "The Largest U.S. Corporations," Fortune, vol. 1 59, no. 9 (May 4, 2009), pp. F-28-29. Firms with negative shareholder equity (66 firms in total) were excluded from calculations of profits as a percentage of shareholder equity.

**Table A-3** presents profits as a percentage of shareholder equity for Fortune 1000 firms by industry in 2008, which complements other profitability measures presented in **Table 4**. Shareholder equity can change dramatically when a firm's capital structure changes, and can be affected by the timing of major writedowns on a firm's financial statements.

As in **Table 4**, which presented profits as a percentage of revenues and as a percentage of assets, neither of the two health insurance sectors listed (Health Care: Insurance & Managed Care; and Insurance: Life, Health [stock]) are in the top 20 industries in terms of profits as a percentage of shareholder value for 2008.

## End Notes

[1] CRS Report R41124, *Medicare: Changes Made by the Reconciliation Act of 2010 to the Patient Protection and Affordable Care Act* (P.L. 111-148), coordinated by Patricia A. Davis; CRS Report R41128, *Health-Related Revenue Provisions: Changes Made by H.R. 4872, the Health Care and Education Reconciliation Act of 2010* , by Janemarie Mulvey.

[2] CRS Report R40968, *Limiting McCarran-Ferguson Act's Antitrust Exemption for the "Business of Insurance": Impact on Health Insurers and Issuers of Medical Malpractice Insurance*, by Janice E. Rubin and Baird Webel.

[3] U.S. Census Bureau, "Health Insurance Coverage: 2008," September 10, 2009, available at http://www.census.gov/hhes/www/hlthins/hlthin08/hlth08asc.html. See also CRS Report 96-891, *Health Insurance Coverage: Characteristics of the Insured and Uninsured in 2008*, by Chris L. Peterson.

[4] Todd Gilmer and Richard Kronick, "It's The Premiums, Stupid: Projections of the Uninsured Through 2013," Health Affairs, Web Exclusive, April 5, 2005, available at http://content.healthaffairs.org/cgi/content/full/hlthaff.w5.143/DC1.

[5] For example, see American Medical Association, *Competition in Health Insurance: A Comprehensive Study of U.S. Markets* (Chicago: AMA, 2008), p. 1; and David Balto, "Why A Public Health Insurance Option Is Essential," blog posting, *Health Affairs*, September 17, 2009.

[6] One leading insurance rating agency recently described the commercial health sector as "very competitive." A.M. Best Company, *Multiple Issues Adversely Impact Health Care Results for 2008*, May 4, 2009, p. 2.

[7] Congressional Budget Office, *The Budgetary Treatment of Proposals to Change the Nations Health Insurance System*, Economic and Budget Issue Brief, May 27, 2009.

[8] Laura A. Scofea, "The Development and Growth of Employer-Provided Health Insurance," *Monthly Labor Review*, vol. 117, no. 3 (March 1994), pp. 3-10.

[9] For a discussion of insurance before the Great Depression, see David T. Beito, "'This Enormous Army:' The Mutual-Aid Tradition of American Fraternal Societies Before the 20th Century," in David T. Beito, Peter Gordon, and Alexander Tabarrok, eds., *The Voluntary City* (Ann Arbor, MI: Michigan University Press, 2002).

[10] Crystal Eastman, *Work-Accidents and the Law* (New York: Survey Associates, 1910), available at http://books.google= ACfU3U1rXY2JDamyzoybhpuDxNPKQ-Lr-Q&source=gbs_v2_summary_r&cad=0; David Rosner and Gerald Markowitz, "The Struggle over Employee Benefits: The Role of Labor in Influencing Modern Health Policy," *Milbank Quarterly*, vol. 81, no. 1 (2003), pp. 45-73.

[11] Robert D. Eilers, *Regulation of Blue Cross and Blue Shield Plans* (Homewood, IL: R.D. Irwin, 1963), pp. 10-11.

[12] Robert Cunningham III and Robert M. Cunningham Jr., *The Blues: A History of the Blue Cross and Blue Shield System* (Dekalb, IL: Northern Illinois University Press, 1997).

[13] American Hospital Association, "Essentials of an Acceptable Plan for Group Hospitalization," 1933.

[14] Paul Starr, *The Social Transformation of American Medicine* (New York: Basic Books, 1983), pp. 296-297; Eilers, p. 12.

[15] Starr, p. 298.

[16] Rosemary Stevens, *In Sickness and In Wealth: American Hospitals in the 20$^{th}$ Century* (New York: Basic Books, 1989), p. 156.

[17] Starr, p. 297.

[18] Anthony J. Badger, *The New Deal: The Depression Years, 1933-1940* (New York: Hill and Wang, 1989), p. 75.

[19] Carl Shapiro, Deputy Assistant Attorney General for Economics, Antitrust Division, U.S. Department of Justice, "Competition Policy In Distressed Industries," Speech delivered at ABA Antitrust Symposium: Competition as Public Policy, May 13, 2009, available at http://www.usdoj.gov/atr/public/speeches/245857.htm; Michael M. Weinstein, Recovery and Redistribution under the NIRA (Amsterdam: North-Holland, 1980); and Harold L. Cole and Lee E. Ohanian, "New Deal Policies and the Persistence of the Great Depression: A General Equilibrium Analysis," *Journal of Political Economy*, vol. 112, no. 4 (August 2004), pp. 779-816. De Long and Summers contend that certain wage and price rigidities may help with macroeconomic stability in some situations, but admit that anticompetitive policies in the early 1930s "may have had contractionary macroeconomic effects." J. Bradford De Long and Lawrence H. Summers, "Is Increased Price Flexibility Stabilizing?" *American Economic Review*, vol. 76, no. 5 (December 1986), pp. 1031-1044.

[20] Starr, pp. 306-309.

[21] Testimony of C. Rufus Rorem, Executive Director, Hospital Service Plan Commission, in U.S. Congress, Senate Committee on Education, 79th Cong., 2nd sess., 1946, available at http://www.sigmondpapers.org/shapers_pdf/shapers_appendix_k.pdf.

[22] Wage and price controls and the War Labor Board was authorized by the October 2, 1942, entitled "An Act to Amend the Emergency Price Control Act of 1942, to Aid in Preventing Inflation, and for Other Purposes," (P.L. 77-729, 56 Stat. 765) enacted October 2, 1942. President Franklin Roosevelt's Executive Order issued the following day "exclud[ed] insurance and pension benefits in a reasonable amount as determined by the Director" from wages and salaries covered by the act (Title VI).

[23] Two key cases were Inland Steel Co. v. NLRB, 170 F.2d 247 (7th Cir. 1948), cert, denied 336 US 960 (1949) over retirement and pension issues, and W.W. Cross & Co. v. NLRB, 174 F.2d. 875 (1st Cir. 1949) regarding insurance benefits.

[24] For a brief review of the history of the exclusion see CRS Report RL34767, *The Tax Exclusion for Employer-Provided Health Insurance: Policy Issues Regarding the Repeal Debate*, by Janemarie Mulvey.

[25] IRS Special Ruling, Letter to Mr. Russell L. Davenport, October 26, 1943, quoted in 3 CCH 1943 Fed. Tax Rep. ¶6587 (1943); IRS Ruling Letter dated August 26, 1943, P-H 1943-44 Fed. Tax Serv. ¶ 66,294, cited in "Employer Health or Accident Plans: Taxfree Protection and Proceeds," *University of Chicago Law Review*, Vol. 21, No. 2 (Winter, 1954), pp. 277-286.

[26] Melissa Thomasson, "The Importance of Group Coverage: How Tax Policy Shaped U.S. Health Insurance," *American Economic Review*, vol. 93, no. 4 (September 2003), pp. 1373-1384.

[27] Eilers, pp. 12-13.

[28] Starr, pp. 327-328.

[29] Robert Cunningham III and Robert M. Cunningham Jr., *The Blues: A History of the Blue Cross and Blue Shield System* (Dekalb, IL: Northern Illinois University Press, 1997).

[30] Robin A. Cohen et al., "Health Insurance Coverage Trends, 1959–2007: Estimates from the National Health Interview Survey, National Health Statistics Report," No. 17, July 1, 2009, available at http://www.cdc.gov/nchs/data/nhsr/nhsr017.pdf.

[31] Federal Employees Health Benefits Act of 1959 (P.L. 86-382).

[32] Sallyanne Payton and Rhoda M. Powsner, "Regulation Through the Looking Glass: Hospitals, Blue Cross, and Certificate-of-Need," Michigan Law Review, vol. 79 (December 1980), pp. 203-277.

[33] Social Security Amendments of 1950 (P.L. 81-831), 1956 (P.L. 84-8 80), 1960 (P.L. 86-778). See Wilbur J. Cohen, "Reflections on the Enactment of Medicare and Medicaid," Health Care Financing Review, Annual Supplement 1985, pp. 3-11. Certain other groups, including

low-income children deprived of parental support and their caretaker relatives, the elderly, the blind, and individuals with disabilities, also became eligible for Medicare benefits. In later years, Medicare benefits have been extended to other groups, such as those requiring end-stage renal dialysis.

[34] Judith D. Moore and David G. Smith, "Legislating Medicaid: Considering Medicaid and its Origins," *Health Care Financing Review*, vol. 27, no. 2 (winter 2005), pp. 45-52, available at http://www.cms.hhs.gov/ HealthCareFinancingReview/downloads/05-06Winpg45.pdf.

[35] U.S. Congress, House Committee on Energy and Commerce, Subcommittee on Health and the Environment, *Medicaid Source Book: Background Data and Analysis* (A 1993 Update), committee print, 103rd Cong., 1st sess., January 1993, CP 103-A, p. 29.

[36] Moore and Smith, p. 47.

[37] Enacted as the Social Security Amendments of 1965 (P.L. 89-97).

[38] See CRS Report R40425, Medicare Primer, coordinated by Hinda Chaikind.

[39] For more information about Medicaid eligibility, see CRS Report R40490, *Medicaid Checklist: Considerations in Adding a Mandatory Eligibility Group*, by Chris L. Peterson, Elicia J. Herz, and Julie Stone.

[40] Starr, pp. 303-305.

[41] Stevens, p. 155.

[42] Cooperatives created by the Farm Security Administration are discussed in the Options for Congress section below.

[43] See CRS Report 91-261, *Health Maintenance Organizations and Employer Group Health Plans*, by Mark Merlis (out of print, available from the author of this chapter).

[44] Jon Gabel, et al., "The Commercial Health Insurance Industry In Transition," *Health Affairs*, vol. 6, no. 3 (fall 1987), pp. 46-60.

[45] M. Susan Marquis, Jeannette A. Rogowski, and José J. Escarce, "The Managed Care Backlash: Did Consumers Vote with Their Feet?" *Inquiry*, vol. 41, no. 4 (2004), pp. 376-390.

[46] As managed care spread in the 1990s, staff-model HMOs became much less common. Karen L. Trespacz, "Staff- Model HMOs: Don't Blink or You'll Miss Them," *Managed Care*, July 1999, available at http://www.managedcaremag.com/archives/9907/9907.staffmodel.html.

[47] U.S. General Accounting Office, *Health Insurance: Comparing Blue Cross and Blue Shield Plans With Commercial Insurers*, HRD-86-1 10, July 11, 1986 , available at http://archive.gao.gov/d4t4/130462.pdf.

[48] James J. McGovern, "Federal Tax Exemption of Prepaid Health Care Plans." *The Tax Adviser*, vol. 7 (February 1976), pp. 76-81.

[49] U.S. Congress, Joint Committee on Taxation. "Tax Exempt Organizations Engaged in Insurance Activities." In General Explanation of the Tax Reform Act of 1986. Joint Committee Print, 100th Cong., 1st sess. Washington, DC: Government Printing Office, May 4, 1987, pp. 583-592.

[50] The small-group market is typically defined as covering firms with fifty or fewer employees.

[51] U.S. General Accounting Office, *Blue Cross and Blue Shield: Experiences of Weak Plans Underscore the Role of Effective State Oversight*, April 1994, GAO/HEHS-94-71, available at http://archive.gao.gov/t2pbat3/151562.pdf. A Senate staff report issued in 1992 concluded that the West Virginia Blue Cross and Blue Shield Plan failed in part because of mismanagement by senior officials, diversion of resources to non-insurance activities, conflicts of interest among the plan's board, creation of unsuccessful affiliates and subsidiaries, as well as increased health care costs. See Staff Statement, Part VII, in U.S. Congress, Senate Committee on Governmental Affairs, Permanent Subcommittee on Investigations, *Efforts to Combat Fraud and Abuse in the Insurance Industry*, 1 02nd Cong., 2nd sess., July 2, 29 and 30, 1992; and Robert Pear, "Money Shortage Puts Blue Cross on Shaky Ground," *New York Times*, July 20, 1992, p. A1.

[52] Robert Cunningham III and Robert M. Cunningham Jr., *The Blues: A History of the Blue Cross and Blue Shield System* (DeKalb, IL: Northern Illinois University Press, 1997); Christopher J. Conover, "Impact of For-Profit Conversion of Blue Cross Plans: Empirical Evidence,"

paper presented at the Conversion Summit, Princeton University, December 5, 2008. Regulators have blocked several other proposals to convert Blue Cross organizations to for-profit status.

[53] For a more complete description of market conditions in health insurance and health care, see Federal Trade Commission and U.S. Department of Justice, *Improving Health Care: A Dose of Competition*, July 2004, available at http://www.usdoj.gov/atr/public/health_care/204694.pdf. Also, see notes to **Table 5**.

[54] For details, see Steven B. Larsen, Commissioner of the Maryland Insurance Administration, *Report Regarding the Proposed Conversion of CareFirst Inc. to For-Profit Status and Acquisition by WellPoint Health Networks*, Inc., March 5, 2003, available at http://www.mdinsurance.state.md.us/sa/documents/FinalMIAReport-CareFirst3-5-03.pdf.

[55] Enrollments in **Table 1** total 181 million, which includes enrollments in some public insurance plans such as Medical Advantage and certain Medicaid plans. Some individuals may obtain health coverage from more than one source.

[56] Archer MSAs were introduced in the Health Insurance Portability and Accountability Act of 1996 (P.L. 104-19 1). HSAs were authorized by the Medicare Prescription Drug, Improvement, and Modernization Act of 2003 (MMA, P.L. 108-173). For details, see CRS Report RL3 3257, *Health Savings Accounts: Overview of Rules for 2010*, by Janemarie Mulvey.

[57] America's Health Insurance Plans, "January 2009 Census Shows 8 Million People Covered By HSA/HighDeductible Health Plans," May 2009, available at http://www.ahipresearch.org/pdfs/2009hsacensus.pdf.

[58] A analysis of 2002 Medical Expenditure Panel Survey data found that "[h]alf of the population spends little or nothing on health care, while 5 percent of the population spends almost half of the total amount." For details, see Mark W. Stanton, "The High Concentration of U.S. Health Care Expenditures," U.S. Department of Health and Human Services, Agency for Healthcare Research, *Research in Action*, Issue 19, June 2006, available at http://www.ahrq.gov/ research/ria19/expendria.pdf.

[59] In some cases the insurer and the provider are a single entity as in the case of staff-model HMOs.

[60] Gary Claxton, Jon Gabel, and Bianca DiJulio, et al., "Health Benefits in 2007: Premium Increases Fall to an Eight- Year Low, While Offer Rates and Enrollment Remain Stable," *Health Affairs*, vol. 26, no. 5 (September/October 2007), pp. 1407-1416.

[61] This is the familiar condition of supply equaling demand in a market with no third-party effects. In the absence of third-party effects, the demand curve reflects social benefits and the supply curve reflects social costs of production.

[62] Robin W. Boadway and David E. Wildasin, *Public Sector Economics*, Second Edition (New York: Little, Brown, 1984), pp. 1-4.

[63] For an explanation, see Peter Zweifel and Friedrich Breyer, *Health Economics* (New York; Oxford University Press, 1997), p. 238.

[64] Randall D. Cebul, "Organizational Fragmentation and Care Quality in the U.S. Healthcare System," *Journal of Economic Perspectives*, vol. 22, no. 4 (fall 2008), pp. 93-113.

[65] CRS Report RL34101, *Does Price Transparency Improve Market Efficiency? Implications of Empirical Evidence in Other Markets for the Health Sector*, by D. Andrew Austin and Jane G. Gravelle.

[66] For a discussion of complementary agents (intermediaries), see Zweifel and Breyer, pp. 239-257.

[67] Insurance plans typically have out-of-pocket limits and global payment caps, and coinsurance requirements differ for care obtained through in-network and out-of-network providers. This example ignores investment income made possible by the lag between premiums and claims payments.

[68] More explicitly, premiums (R) thus equal $R=(1+L).(1-C).p_m.m^*$, where L is the load factor, C is the average cost- sharing rate (percentage of covered expenses paid out of pocket by the

individual), $p_m$ is the average price of medical care, and m* is the average quantity of medical care of the insured. The costs of medical care and insurance in this stylized example are split as follows:

- Consumer pays out of pocket C.$p_m$ .m* in addition to the premiums
- Insurer retains L.(1-C). $p_m$ .m* (amount remaining after paying claims)
- Provider receives $p_m$ .m*.

[69] See, for example, Katherine Baicker and Amitabh Chandra, "The Labor Market Effects of Rising Health Insurance Premiums," *Journal of Labor Economics*, vol. 24, no. 3 (2006), pp. 609-634; and Dana Goldman, Neeraj Sood, and Arleen Leibowitz, "Wage and Benefit Changes in Response to Rising Health Insurance Costs," *Forum for Health Economics and Policy*, vol. 8, article 3 (2005).

[70] On the other hand, health insurers may have much more sophisticated information about average health risks for specific categories of people.

[71] For a literature review see David M. Cutler and Richard J. Zeckhauser, "The Anatomy of Health Insurance," in *Handbook of Health Economics*, ed. A.J. Culyer and J.P. Newhouse, vol. 1A (Amsterdam: Elsevier, 2000), pp. 563- 643.

[72] See, for example, Katherine Baicker and Amitabh Chandra, "The Labor Market Effects of Rising Health Insurance Premiums," *Journal of Labor Economics*, vol. 24, no. 3 (2006), pp. 609-634; and Dana Goldman, Neeraj Sood, and Arleen Leibowitz, "Wage and Benefit Changes in Response to Rising Health Insurance Costs, " *Forum for Health Economics and Policy*, vol. 8, article 3 (2005).

[73] See, for example, David M. Cutler and Sarah J. Reber, "Paying for Health Insurance: The Trade-off Between Competition and Adverse Selection," *Quarterly Journal of Economics*, vol. 113, no. 2 (May 1998), pp. 433-466. The authors analyze the case of Harvard University's relatively generous Blue Cross/Blue Shield PPO, which was one of several plans offered in Harvard's health insurance program. Faced with a deficit in the employee benefits budget in the mid-1990s, Harvard implemented pricing reforms that raised the employee's costs of the PPO.

[74] See, for example, Thomas Buchmueller and John DiNardo, "Did Community Rating Induce an Adverse Selection Death Spiral? Evidence from New York, Pennsylvania, and Connecticut," *American Economic Review*, vol. 92, no. 1 (March 2002), pp. 280-294.

[75] Arson is perhaps the clearest example of moral hazard. Few owners are tempted to ignite an uninsured building.

[76] The price paid by the insured individual depends on cost-sharing through coinsurance, deductibles, and copayments.

[77] The RAND Health Insurance Experiment examined this issue in the 1970s with a randomized trial. See Willard G. Manning et al., "Health Insurance and the Demand for Medical Care: Evidence from a Randomized Experiment," *American Economic Review*, vol. 77, no. 3 (June 1987), pp. 25 1-277; Emmett B. Keeler, "Effects of Cost Sharing on Use of Medical Services and Health," *Journal of Medical Practice Management*, vol. 8 (summer 1992), pp. 3 17-321; and RAND, *The Health Insurance Experiment*, RAND Corporation, Research Highlights, Santa Monica, CA, 2006, available at http://www.rand.org.

[78] CRS Report RL34101, *Does Price Transparency Improve Market Efficiency? Implications of Empirical Evidence in Other Markets for the Health Sector*, by D. Andrew Austin and Jane G. Gravelle.

[79] For details, see Thomas G. McGuire, "Physician Agency," in *Handbook of Health Economics* (Amsterdam: Elsevier, 2000), vol. 1, pt. 1, pp. 461-536.

[80] Gerald B. Hickson, William A. Altemeier, and James M. Perrin, "Physician Reimbursement by Salary or Fee-forService: Effect on Physician Practice Behavior in a Randomized Prospective Study," *Pediatrics*, vol. 80, no. 3 (September 1987), pp. 344-350.

[81] Defining and measuring "defensive medicine" is hard because many procedures that may lower physicians' risk of malpractice litigation also provide at least some diagnostic or therapeutic benefit to the patient.

[82] See Charles E. Phelps, *Health Economics, Fourth Edition* (New York: Addison-Wesley, 2009), p. 334 for a summary of the early literature estimating the price sensitivity of health insurance demand.

[83] See Linda J. Blumberg, Len M. Nichols, and Jessica S. Banthin, "Worker Decisions to Purchase Health Insurance," *International Journal of Health Care Finance and Economics*, vol. 1 (2001), pp. 305-325; Michael Chernew, Kevin Frick, and Catherine G. McLaughlin, "The Demand for Health Insurance Coverage by Low-Income Workers: Can Reduced Premiums Achieve Full Coverage?" *Health Services Research*, vol. 32, no. 4 (October 1997), pp. 453-470; and Jonathan Gruber and Ebonya Washington, "Subsidies to Employee Health Insurance Premiums and the Health Insurance Market," *Journal of Health Economics*, vol. 24, no. 2 (March 2005), pp. 253-276.

[84] Jonathan Gruber, "Covering the Uninsured in the United States," *Journal of Economic Literature*, vol. 46, no. 3 (September 2008), p. 590.

[85] M. Susan Marquis and Stephen H. Long, "Worker Demand for Health Insurance in the Non-Group Market," *Journal of Health Economics*, vol. 14, no. 1 (January 1995), pp. 47-63.

[86] Francis W. Ahking, Carmelo Giaccotto, and Rexford E. Santerre, "The Aggregate Demand for Private Health Insurance Coverage in the United States," *Journal of Risk and Insurance*, vol. 76, no. 1 (March 2009), pp. 133-157.

[87] Providing subsidies for workers that are not offered health benefits might motivate some employers to drop health coverage benefits. For details, see Jonathan Gruber, "Incremental Universalism for the United States: The States Move First?" *Journal of Economic Perspectives*, vol. 22, no. 4 (fall 2008), pp. 65–66. Maine's Dirigo Health Plan provides some subsidies for low-income workers. See Commonwealth Fund, "Expanding Health Coverage: Maine's Dirigo Health Reform Act," Innovations Note, May 2005, available at http://www.commonwealthfund.org/Content/Innovations/State-Profiles/2004/Aug/Expanding-Health-Coverage—Maines-Dirigo-Health-Reform-Act.aspx.

[88] For 2008, the estimate is $226.2 billion of which $132.7 billion is forgone income tax and $93.5 billion is forgone payroll tax. See U.S. Congress, Joint Committee on Taxation, *Background Materials for Senate Committee on Finance Roundtable on Health Care Financing*, May 8, 2009, JCX-27-09.

[89] The two deductions for health insurance of the self-employed and health savings accounts are above-the-line deductions. Furthermore, individuals can exclude from taxable income the contributions their employer makes to their health savings account.

[90] See Thomas E. Getzen, *Health Economics: Fundamentals and Flow of Funds*, Second Edition (New York: John Wiley & Sons, 2004), pp. 72-73 for a discussion.

[91] The law of large numbers is a mathematical theorem stating that the average of a randomly drawn sample of observations will converge to the true value of the underlying probability distribution as the sample size increases under certain conditions. See Charles M. Grinstead and J. Laurie Snell, *Introduction to Probability* (Providence, RI: American Mathematical Society, 2003).

[92] American Academy of Actuaries, private communication, August 26, 2009.

[93] David M. Cutler and Richard J. Zeckhauser, "The Anatomy of Health Insurance," *in Handbook of Health Economics*, ed. A.J. Culyer and J.P. Newhouse, vol. 1A (Amsterdam: Elsevier, 2000), pp. 563-643.

[94] See Charles E. Phelps, *Health Economics, Fourth Edition* (New York: Addison-Wesley, 2009), pp. 350-3 52; and CRS Report RL32237, *Health Insurance: A Primer*, by Bernadette Fernandez.

[95] The Federal Employees Health Benefits program, which provides health benefits to most federal workers, has a national Blue Cross option. Beneficiaries in that plan receive benefits from the Blue Cross affiliate where they live.

[96] Thomas C. Buchmueller and Alan C. Monheit, Employer-Sponsored Health Insurance and the Promise of Health Insurance Reform, National Bureau of Economic Research, Working Paper 14839, Cambridge, MA, April 2009.

[97] Kaiser Family Foundation and Health Research and Educational Trust, *Employer Health Benefits: 2009 Annual Survey, Kaiser Family Foundation and Health Research and Educational Trust*, 2009, Exhibit 4.1, available at http://ehbs.kff.org/pdf/2009/7936.pdf.

[98] Barbara Steinberg Schone and Philip F. Cooper, "Assessing the Impact of Health Plan Choice," *Health Affairs*, vol. 20, no. 1 (January/February 2001), pp. 267-275.

[99] Kaiser Family Foundation and Health Research and Educational Trust, *Employer Health Benefits: 2009 Annual Survey*, Kaiser Family Foundation and Health Research and Educational Trust, 2009, Exhibit 6.4. Inflation adjustment made using U.S. Bureau of Economic Analysis GDP price index.

[100] See, for example, M. Susan Marquis and Stephen H. Long, "To Offer or Not to Offer: The Role of Price in Employers' *Health Insurance Decisions*," Health Services Research, vol. 36, no. 5 (October 2001), pp. 935-958.

[101] For a discussion of state differences see Mila Kofman and Karen Pollitz, *Health Insurance Regulation by States and the Federal Government: A Review of Current Approaches and Proposals for Change,* Health Policy Institute, Georgetown University, Washington, DC, April 2006.

[102] See CRS Report RL32237, *Health Insurance: A Primer*, by Bernadette Fernandez.

[103] See CRS Report RL33759, *Health Care and Markets*, by D. Andrew Austin for details.

[104] For details, see CRS Report R40 142, *Health Insurance Continuation Coverage Under COBRA,* by Janet Kinzer and Meredith Peterson.

[105] Vip Patel and Mark V. Pauly, "Guaranteed Renewability And the Problem of Risk Variation in Individual Health Insurance Markets," *Health Affairs Web Exclusive*, August 28, 2002, available at http://content.healthaffairs.org/cgi/ content/abstract/hlthaff.w2.280.

[106] For details, see CRS Report RL3 1634, *The Health Insurance Portability and Accountability Act (HIPAA) of 1996: Overview and Guidance on Frequently Asked Questions*, by Hinda Chaikind et al.

[107] A single seller in a market is a monopolist and a small group of firms in a market are called oligopolists.

[108] A single buyer in a market is a monopsonist and a small group of firms in a market are called oligopsonists.

[109] Horizontal mergers are those among firms that compete in the same product market.

[110] U.S. Department of Justice, *Merger Guidelines, 47 Federal Register 28493*, June 30, 1982; U.S. Department of Justice and the Federal Trade Commission, *Horizontal Merger Guidelines*, April 8, 1997, available at http://www.usdoj.gov/atr/public/guidelines

[111] According to the guidelines, HHI increases of 100 or more in moderately concentrated markets or 50 or more in highly concentrated markets raise significant competitive concerns, although other factors play a role.

[112] For instance, many economists would argue that Google acquired its dominance of internet search engines by developing superior technologies and better marketing strategies rather than through anticompetitive measures.

[113] For an economic analysis of the merger guidelines, see Janusz A. Ordover and Robert D. Willig, "The 1982 Department of Justice Merger Guidelines: An Economic Assessment," *California Law Review*, vol. 71, no. 2 (March 1983), pp. 53 5-574.

[114] This view was rejected by the judge. F.T.C. v. Coca Cola Co., 641 F Supp. 1128.

[115] David A. Hyman and William E. Kovacic, "Monopoly, Monopsony, And Market Definition: An Antitrust Perspective on Market Concentration Among Health Insurers," *Health Affairs*, vol. 23, no. 6 (2004), pp. 25-28.

[116] The AMA publishes an annual report that lists a two-firm concentration ratio (CR-2) and the HHI for health insurers by metropolitan statistical areas (MSAs) across the country. The 2008 AMA report lists market concentration data for 42 states and 314 MSAs (out of 362 MSAs in the United States). Other states and MSAs were excluded due to data limitations. American Medical Association, *Competition in Health Insurance: A Comprehensive Study*

*of U.S. Markets 2007 Update* (AMA: Chicago, 2007), available at http://www.ama-assn.org/ama1/pub/upload/mm/368/compstudy_52006.pdf.

[117] U.S. Government Accountability Office, "Private Health Insurance: Number and Market Share of Carriers in the Small Group Health Insurance Market in 2004," letter to Senator Olympia J. Snowe, GAO-06-155R, October 13, 2005.

[118] If a firm self-insures through an ERISA plan administered by an insurance company, or if an insurance company bears some risk, then those enrollments are probably included in the AMA market share data. Data for employees covered in employer self-insured plans administered by health insurers were checked to avoid double-counting. For additional information on ERISA, see CRS Report RS22643, *Regulation of Health Benefits Under ERISA: An Outline*, by Jennifer Staman. Enrollments in some employer self-insure plans that are self-administered or administered by a servicer that is not a health insurer may be excluded from the AMA data. Combining administrative data on coverage, on which the AMA report is based, with survey data on, such as MEPS data presented in Table 4, is probably too imprecise to impute the extent of health insurance coverage offered by self-insured plans not run by a health insurer.

[119] James Reschovsky, J. Lee.Hargraves, Albert F. Smith, "Consumer Beliefs and Health Plan Performance: It's Not Whether You Are in an HMO but Whether You Think You Are," *Journal of Health Politics, Policy and Law*, vol. 27, no. 3 (June 2002).

[120] A.M. Best Company, *Earnings Decline, Expenses Are Up, But BCBS Results Remain Favorable*, July 28, 2008, p. 3.

[121] For an overview of research examining links between market concentration and health insurance profitability, see Government Accountability Office, *Private Health Insurance: Research on Competition in the Insurance Industry*, GAO-09-864R, letter to Senator Herb Kohl, July 31, 2009, available at http://www.gao.gov/new.items/d09864r.pdf.

[122] For a systematic overview of research on differences between profit and non-profit health care organizations, see Allyson M. Pollock et al., "A Literature Review on the Structure and Performance of Not-For-Profit Health Care Organisations," Report for the National Coordinating Centre for NHS Service Delivery and Organisation R&D (NCCSDO), February 2007, chapter 3, available at http://www.sdo.nihr.ac.uk/files/project. The authors contend that much of the research on this issue is flawed.

[123] Jack Needleman, "The Role of Nonprofits in Health Care," *Journal of Health Politics, Policy and Law*, vol. 26 (2001), pp. 1113-1130.

[124] Leonard Weiss, ed., *Concentration and Price* (Cambridge, MA: MIT Press, 1990).

[125] Leemore Dafny, "Are Health Insurance Markets Competitive?" forthcoming *American Economic Review*, available at http://www.kellogg.northwestern.edu/faculty/dafny/personal/Documents/Working%20Papers/Dafny5_09.pdf.

[126] Leemore Dafny, Mark Duggan, Subramaniam Ramanarayanan, "Paying A Premium On Your Premium? Consolidation In The U.S. Health Insurance Industry," National Bureau of Economic Research (NBER) Working Paper 15434, October 2009, available at http://www.nber.org/papers/w15434.

[127] American Medical Association, *Competition in Health Insurance: A Comprehensive Study of U.S. Markets 2007 Update* (AMA: Chicago, 2007).

[128] Laurie J. Bates and Rexford E. Santerre, "Do Health Insurers Possess Monopsony Power in the Hospital Services Industry?" *International Journal of Health Care Finance and Economics*, vol. 8 (March 2008), pp. 1-11.

[129] Testimony of Len M. Nichols, Ph.D., Director, Health Policy Program, New America Foundation, in U.S. Congress, Senate Committee On Commerce, Science, and Transportation, "Competition In The Healthcare Marketplace," hearings, 111th Cong., 1st sess., July 16, 2009, available at http://www.newamerica.net/files /NICHOLS_ Commerce . pdf.

[130] This view, known as the structure-conduct-performance approach, is presented in Frederic M. Scherer, and David Ross, *Industrial Market Structure and Economic Performance, Third Edition* (Boston: Houghton-Mifflin, 1990).

[131] John Sutton, *Sunk Costs and Market Structure* (Cambridge, MA: MIT Press, 1991).

[132] Networks of health care providers are not obviously similar to networks in transportation or communications. A hospital not within a network of other hospitals generates much the same benefits as a hospital within a network. By contrast, a road or telephone not connected to a network of other roads or telephones generates few, if any, benefits.

[133] Martin Gaynor, "Why Don't Courts Treat Hospitals Like Tanks for Liquefied Gases? Some Reflections on Health Care Antitrust Enforcement," *Journal of Health Politics, Policy, and Law*, vol. 31, no. 3 (June 2006), pp. 497-510.

[134] Paul B. Ginsburg, "Competition In Health Care: Its Evolution Over The Past Decade," *Health Affairs*, vol. 24, no. 6 (2005), pp. 15 12-1522.

[135] J. Kenneth Galbraith introduced the term "countervailing power" to describe the use of one large organization to check the power of another. As noted above, consumers use the bargaining power of large retailers to counteract the power of large suppliers. J. Kenneth Galbraith, *American Capitalism: The Concept of Countervailing Power* (Boston: Houghton Mifflin, 1952).

[136] Boston Globe, "A Healthcare System Badly Out of Balance: Call It the 'Partners Effect,'" November 16, 2008, available at *http://www.boston.com/news/ local/articles/ 2008/11/16/ a_healthcare_system_badly_out_of_balance/.*

[137] Robert Kuttner, "Columbia/HCA and the Resurgence of the For-Profit Hospital Business," *New England Journal of Medicine*, vol. 335, no. 5 (Aug 1, 1996) , p. 362 and no. 6 (August 8, 1996), p. 446-453. Columbia/HCA was subject to several major fraud lawsuits and investigations. For details, see U.S. Department of Justice, Largest Health Care Fraud Case In U.S. History Settled: HCA Investigation Nets Record Total of $1.7 Billion," Press release #03 -386, June 26, 2003, available at *http://www.justice.gov/ opa/pr/2003/ June/03 _civ_ 386.htm.*

[138] U. S. Department of Justice and Federal Trade Commission, Improving Health Care: A Dose of Competition, July 2004, p. 14. The report concluded that "countervailing power should not be considered an effective response to disparities in bargaining power between payors and providers. (p. 27)

[139] Martin Gaynor, "Why Don't Courts Treat Hospitals Like Tanks for Liquefied Gases? Some Reflections on Health Care Antitrust Enforcement," *Journal of Health Politics, Policy and Law*, 2006, vol. 31, no. 3, pp. 497-510.

[140] See Kuttner (1996); and Joyce Gelb and Colleen J. Shogan, "Community Activism in the USA: Catholic Hospital Mergers and Reproductive Access," Social Movement Studies, vol. 4 no. 3 (December 2005), pp. 209-229.

[141] Douglas B. Sherlock and Christopher de Garay, "Administrative Expenses of Health Plans, and for the Small Groups and Individual Markets," presentation to CRS staff, April 2009.

[142] John Sutton, *Sunk Costs and Market Structure* (Cambridge, MA: MIT Press, 1991).

[143] Sherlock and de Garay, 2009.

[144] Randall Cebul et al., "Employer-Based Insurance Markets and Investments in Health," Case Western Reserve University Working Paper, July 2007, available at http://wsomfaculty.case.edu/rebitzer/EmployerBased%20Insurance%20Markets%20and%20Investments%20in%20Health_02.pdf.

[145] Joy M. Grossman and Paul B. Ginsburg, "As The Health Insurance Underwriting Cycle Turns: What Next?" *Health Affairs*, vol. 23, no. 6 (2004), pp. 91-102.

[146] Amy Finkelstein, "The Aggregate Effects of Health Insurance: Evidence from the Introduction of Medicare," *Quarterly Journal of Economics*, vol. 122, no. 1 (2007).

[147] A.M. Best Company, Inc., *Earnings Decline, Expenses are Up, But BCBS Results Remain Favorable*, Special Report, July 28, 2008; *Multiple Issues Adversely Impact Health Care Results for 2008*, Special Report, May 4, 2009. According to the latter report, net income

for the managed care industry fell by 36.5% year over year, as underwriting income fell 22.5% and investment income fell by almost 60%.

[148] Medicare Payment Advisory Commission, *A Data Book: Healthcare Spending and the Medicare Program*, June 2009, Table 10-7; U.S. Government Accountability Office, *Medicare Advantage: Increased Spending Relative to Medicare Fee-for-Service May Not Always Reduce Beneficiary Out-of-Pocket Costs*, February 2008, GAO-08-359.

[149] For a literature review of research on the effects of market concentration in the health insurance market, see U.S. Government Accountability Office, *Private Health Insurance: Research on Competition in the Insurance Industry, letter to Sen.* Herb Kohl, July 31, 2009, GAO-09-864, available at http://www.gao.gov/new.items/d09864r.pdf.

[150] Ibid., pp. 3-4.

[151] Douglas Sherlock, President of the Sherlock Company, letter to Ms. Janet Kinzer, CRS, dated June 25, 2009.

[152] Half of the firms have profits below the median and half have profits above. Weighted means are computed using industry totals for firms within the Fortune 1000.

[153] Most of these reports provide GAAP data for the previous two years. Thus, for many companies two sets of financial results are reported for the same year, which might not agree due to accounting revisions or other factors.

[154] James C. Robinson, "Use and Abuse of the Medical Loss Ratio to Measure *Health Plan Performance*," Health Affairs, vol. 16, no. 4 (1997), pp. 176-187, available at http://content.healthaffairs.orglcgi/reprintl16/4/176.pdf.

[155] The Securities and Exchange Commission has sued Wellcare Health Plans alleging that it manipulated medical loss ratio data in order to avoid refunding the State of Florida certain Medicaid costs. For details, see U.S. SEC v. Wellcare Health Plans, U.S. District Court, Middle District of Florida, Civil Action 8:09.CV.00910-T-33EAS, available at http://www.sec.gov/litigation

[156] American Academy of Actuaries, *Critical Issues in Health Reform: Minimum Loss Ratios*, July 2009, available at http://www.actuary.org/pdf/health/loss_july09.pdf.

[157] Susanto Basu et al., "The Case of the Missing Productivity Growth: Or, Does Information Technology Explain Why Productivity Accelerated in the United States but not the United Kingdom?" Federal Reserve Bank of Chicago Working Paper 2003-08, June 2003.

[158] Atlantic Information Services, Inc., *Health Plan Facts, Trends and Data: 2008-2009* (Washington, DC: Atlantic Information Services, 2009), p. 25.

[159] Douglas Sherlock, President of the Sherlock Company, letter to Ms. Janet Kinzer, CRS, dated June 25, 2009.

[160] Half of reporting firms have profits below the median and half have profits above. Weighted means are weighted by enrollments. These match means weighted by revenues to the extent that revenue per enrollee is the same for insurers.

[161] These payments might be routed through the insurer running the ASO plan, but are not typically booked as revenues by the insurer.

[162] U. S. Department of Justice and Federal Trade Commission, Improving Health Care: A Dose of Competition, July 2004. The report recommended that (1) experiments to find ways to motivate providers to reduce costs and improve quality should continue; (2) states should remove barriers to entry for providers such as certificate of need (CON) programs; (3) governments should reconsider health care subsidies, especially indirect subsidies that may create distortions; (4) governments should not let physicians bargain collectively; (5) states should consider costs and benefits of pharmacy benefit manager regulation; and (6) governments should reconsider the use of health care mandates (i.e., requirements that insurance plans cover certain types of benefits).

[163] The McCarran-Fergusson Act (P.L. 79-15) delineates state and federal responsibilities for insurance regulation and exempts insurers from certain antitrust actions. The act, however, allows federal regulation of the "business of insurance," including antitrust actions. The act also leaves some regulatory and antitrust options to the discretion of states. For a detailed

discussion, see CRS Report RL33683, Courts Narrow McCarran-Ferguson Antitrust Exemption for "Business of Insurance": *Viability of "State Action" Doctrine as an Alternative*, by Janice E. Rubin; and CRS Report R40968, *Limiting McCarran-Ferguson Act's Antitrust Exemption for the "Business of Insurance": Impact on Health Insurers and Issuers of Medical Malpractice Insurance*, by Janice E. Rubin and Baird Webel.

164 Martin Gaynor, "Why Don't Courts Treat Hospitals Like Tanks for Liquefied Gases? Some Reflections on Health Care Antitrust Enforcement," *Journal of Health Politics, Policy, and Law*, vol. 31, no. 3 (June 2006), pp. 497-510.

165 Ibid.

166 Some contend that the George W. Bush Administration undertook very little federal antitrust enforcement. The DOJ in the past decade required minor adjustments to three health insurance mergers, out of a total of nearly 400 such mergers during that period. For case citations, see Leemore Dafny, "Are Health Insurance Markets Competitive?" forthcoming *American Economic Review*, available at *http://www.kellogg.northwestern.edu/faculty/dafny/personal/* Documents/Working%20Papers/Dafny5_09.pdf; also see David Balto, "Why a Public Health Insurance Option is Essential," blog posting, *Health Affairs*, September 17, 2009.

167 Testimony of David Balto, Senior Fellow, Center for American Progress, in U.S. Congress, House Committee on the Judiciary, Subcommittee on Courts and Competition Policy, "Health Insurance Industry Antitrust Enforcement Act of 2009 (H.R. 3596)," hearings, 111th Cong., 1st sess., October 8, 2009, available at http://judiciary pdf/Balto091008.pdf.

168 For more information, see CRS Report RL3 1634, *The Health Insurance Portability and Accountability Act (HIPAA) of 1996: Overview and Guidance on Frequently Asked Questions*, by Hinda Chaikind et al.

169 The act directs the HHS Secretary to work with states to create high-risk insurance pools that do not impose preexisting condition limitations, and a more general prohibition on preexisting condition limitations in group insurance plans takes effect for plans years after the beginning of 2014.

170 AHIP, "Health Plans Propose Guaranteed Coverage for Pre-Existing Conditions and Individual Coverage Mandate," November 19, 2008, available at *http://www. ahip.org/content/pressrelease.aspx?docid=25068.*

171 For details, see Families USA, *Medical Loss Ratios: Evidence from the States*, June 2008, available at http://www.familiesusa.org/assets

172 Internal Revenue Service, Department of the Treasury; Employee Benefits Security Administration, Department of Labor; Office of the Secretary, Department of Health and Human Services, "Medical Loss Ratios; Request for Comments Regarding Section 2718 of the Public Health Service Act," *75 Federal Register 71*, April 14, 2010.

173 See Jonathan Gruber, "Incremental Universalism for the United States: The States Move First?" *Journal of Economic Perspectives*, vol. 22, no. 4 (fall 2008), pp. 51–59.

174 For a summary of H.R. 3200's provisions and information on current legislative status, see CRS Report R40724, *Private Health Insurance Provisions of H.R. 3200*, by Hinda Chaikind et al.

175 A revised mark of the bill was released on September 22, 2009.

176 S.Amndt. 2786 to H.R. 3590, November 19, 2009.

177 See *New York Times* website, "Public Health Insurance Option," Times Topics website, updated March 25, 2010, available at http://www.nytimes.com/info/public-health-insurance-option/.

178 For a description of recent Massachusetts experience with health insurance reform, see Jonathan Gruber, "Incremental Universalism for the United States: The States Move First?" *Journal of Economic Perspectives*, vol. 22, no. 4 (fall 2008), pp. 51–68; John Holahan and Linda Blumberg, "Massachusetts Health Reform: Solving the Long-Run Cost Problem," Robert Wood Johnson/Urban Institute issue brief, January 2009, available at http://www.urban.org/ UploadedPDF/41 1 820_mass_health_reform.pdf.

[179] Ibid.

[180] Henry Aaron, "A Funny Thing Happened on the Way to Managed Health Competition," *Journal of Health Politics, Policy and Law*, vol. 27, no. 1 (2002), pp. 31-36.

[181] Richard G. Frank and Richard J. Zeckhauser, "Health Insurance Exchanges—Making the Markets Work," *New England Journal of Medicine website*, July 22, 2009, available at http://content.nejm.org/cgi/reprint/NEJMp0906246.pdf.

[182] CRS Report RL33300, *Standardized Choices: Medigap Lessons for Medicare Part D*, by Jim Hahn.

[183] See, for example, Jacob S. Hacker, The Case for Public Plan Choice in National Health Reform, Institute for America's Future and Center on Health, Economic and Family Security, Berkeley, CA, December 2008, *http://www.law.berkeley.edu/chefs.htm;* and Jacob S. Hacker, *Healthy Competition: How to Structure Public Health Insurance Plan Choice to Ensure Risk-Sharing, Cost Control, and Quality Improvement*, Institute for America's Future and the Berkeley Center on Health, Economic and Family Security, Policy Brief, Berkeley, CA, April 2009.

[184] Economic efficiency would be enhanced only to the extent that providers did not shift costs to other insurers with less bargaining power.

[185] See, for example, Medicare Payment Advisory Commission, *Report to the Congress: Medicare Payment Policy*, Washington, DC, March 2008, available at *http://www.medpac.gov/documents/mar08_entirereport.pdf.*

[186] U. S. Government Accountability Office, *State High-Risk Health Insurance Pools*, GAO-09-730R, July 22, 2009, http://www.gao.gov.

[187] Ezra Klein, "Has Kent Conrad Solved the Public Plan Problem? An Interview," *Washington Post*, blog, posted June 11, 2009, available at http://voices.washingtonpost.com/ezra-klein/2009/06/has_kent_conrad_solved_the_pub.html.

[188] The proposed health insurance cooperatives would not resemble health insurance purchasing cooperatives (HIPC), which several states have set up to improve access to coverage.

[189] Jacob S. Hacker, "Un-Cooperative: The Trouble with Conrad's Compromise," The New Republic, The Treatment Blog, posted June 14, 2009, available at http://blogs

[190] Starr, pp. 302-306, 320-327.

[191] Michael R. Grey, New Deal Medicine: *The Rural Health Programs of the Farm Security Administration* (Baltimore: Johns Hopkins University Press, 1999). The Bankhead-Jones Farm Tenancy Act of July 1937 (P.L. 75-210) authorized the Farm Security Administration, and the Farmers' Home Administration Act of 1946 (P.L. 79-731) liquidated it.

[192] Anthony J. Badger, The New Deal: The Depression Years, 1933-1940 (New York: Hill and Wang, 1989), p. 185; Kevin R. Kosar, "A Nearly Forgotten Classic Study in Public Administration: Edward C. Banfield's Government Project," *Public Administration Review*, vol. 69, no. 5 (Sept/Oct, 2009), pp. 993-997.

[193] Ivana Krajcinovic, *From Company Doctors to Managed Care: The United Mine Workers' Noble Experiment*. Cornell Studies in Industrial and Labor Relations, no. 31 (Ithaca: Cornell University Press, 1997).

[194] See Rosemary Stevens, *In Sickness and In Wealth: American Hospitals in the 20th Century* (New York: Basic Books, 1989).

[195] U.S. Congress, Joint Committee on Taxation, "Tax Exempt Organizations Engaged in Insurance Activities." In General Explanation of the Tax Reform Act of 1986, Joint Committee Print, 100th Cong., 1st sess. (Washington, DC: Government Printing Office, May 4, 1987), pp. 5 83-592.

[196] For more detailed analyses of the Wyden-Bennett proposals, see Congressional Budget Office, letter to Senators Ron Wyden and Robert Bennett, May 1, 2008, available at http://cbo.gov/ftpdocs/91xx/doc9184/05-01-HealthCareLetter.pdf; and Edwin Park, "An Examination of the Wyden-Bennett Health Reform Plan: Key Issues in a New Approach to Universal Coverage," Center on Budget and Policy Priorities working paper, September 24, 2008, available at http://www.cbpp.org/cms/?fa=view&id=674.

[197] Margaret M. Byrne and Peter Thompson, "Death and Dignity: Terminal Illness and the Market for Non-Treatment," *Journal of Public Economics*, vol. 76, no. 2 (May 2000), pp. 263-294.

[198] Return-on-revenue figures for health insurers, however, may depend on how fees for administrative service only (ASO) contracts are included. See discussion of premium equivalents at p. 44.

In: Health Insurance Industry Market... ISBN: 978-1-61761-289-3
Editors: Brent C. Jenner 

*Chapter 2*

# HEALTH INSURANCE: A PRIMER

***Bernadette Fernandez***

## SUMMARY

People buy insurance to protect themselves against the possibility of financial loss in the future. Such losses may be due to a motor vehicle collision, natural disaster, or other circumstance. For patients, financial losses may result from the use of health care services. Health insurance then provides protection against the possibility of financial loss due to high health care expenses. Also, people do not know ahead of time exactly what their health care expenses will be, so paying for health insurance on a regular basis helps smooth out their out-of-pocket spending.

While health coverage continues to be mostly a private enterprise in this country, government plays an increasingly significant role. Especially during the latter half of the 20$^{th}$ century, the government both initiated and responded to dynamics in medicine, the economy, and the workplace through legislation and public policies. For example, the Internal Revenue System clarified that employer contributions to employee health benefits are exempt from taxation, which encouraged the growth of employment-based health coverage. Given the frequent introduction of legislation aimed at modifying or building on the current health insurance system, understanding the potential impact of such proposals requires a working knowledge of how health insurance is designed, provided, purchased, and regulated. This chapter provides background information about these topics.

Individuals and families without health coverage are more likely than those with coverage to forgo needed health care, which often leads to worse health outcomes and the need for expensive medical treatment. Since uninsured persons are more likely to be poor than insured persons, the uninsured are less able to afford the health care they need. Uninsurance can lead to health care access problems for communities, such as increased problems obtaining specialty care. Taxpayers and the nation as a whole are affected through increased taxes and health care prices to cover the uncompensated care expenses of uninsured persons.

Americans obtain health insurance in different settings and through a variety of methods. People may get health coverage through the private sector, or from a publicly funded program. Consumers may purchase health insurance on their own, as part of an employee group, or through a trade or professional association. However, approximately 46 million Americans did not have health coverage for the entire year of 2007.

Health insurance benefits are delivered and financed under different systems. The factors that distinguish one delivery system from another are many, including how health care is financed, how much access to providers and services is controlled, and how much authority the enrollee has to design her/his health plan. To illustrate, managed care is characterized by predetermined restrictions on accessing services and providers, whereas individual decision-making regarding use of health benefits is a hallmark of consumer driven health care, such as health savings accounts. As economic conditions change, a specific delivery system may gain or lose the interest of affected parties. This chapter will be updated periodically.

## INTRODUCTION

As health insurance coverage has evolved from an uncommon benefit to a routine one, government's role in subsidizing and regulating that coverage also has changed. While most insured Americans obtain health coverage through the private sector, public entities play an increasingly significant role.

Government's involvement in health coverage expanded dramatically in the latter half of the $20^{th}$ century:

- A long-standing rule issued by the Internal Revenue Service (IRS) stated that an employer's contributions to employment-based health insurance could not be included in an employee's gross income for tax purposes (Internal Revenue Code, Section 106). This ruling helped spur the growth of employer-sponsored health benefits. The IRS also stated separately that employers could deduct such contributions as part of business expenses.
- Advances in medicine led to escalating consumer demand for newer, better treatments. At the same time, the cost of some treatments increased, which was especially problematic for certain groups of consumers who lacked health coverage. This led to government efforts to assist health care consumers in paying for medical services through social insurance programs.[1]
- More and more employees began to work for more than one employer over their lifetimes. Government was called on to address a problem many workers faced: keeping health coverage as workers moved from job to job.

Given the frequent introduction of legislation aimed at modifying or building on the current health insurance system, understanding the potential impact of such proposals requires a working knowledge of how health insurance is designed, provided, purchased, and regulated. This chapter provides background information about these topics.

## WHAT IS HEALTH INSURANCE?

### Definitions and Principles

People buy insurance to protect themselves against the possibility of financial loss in the future. Such losses may be due to a motor vehicle collision, natural disaster, or other circumstance. For patients, financial losses may result from the use of health care services. Health insurance then provides protection against the possibility of financial loss due to high health care expenses. Also, people do not know ahead of time exactly what their health care expenses will be, so paying for health insurance on a regular basis helps smooth out their out-of-pocket spending.

The concept underlying insurance is “risk” (i.e., the likelihood and magnitude of financial loss). In any type of insurance arrangement, all parties seek to minimize their own risk. In health insurance, consumers and insurers approach the management of insurance risk differently. From the consumer’s point of view, a person (or family) buys health insurance for protection against financial losses resulting from the future use of medical care. From the insurer’s point of view, it employs a variety of methods to minimize the risk it takes on when providing health coverage to consumers, to assure that it operates a profitable business. One method is to cover only those expenses arising from a pre-defined set of services (generally called “covered” services). Another method for limiting risk is to encourage healthier people to obtain health coverage, presumably because healthier people would not need as many medical services as sicker people, leading to fewer claims that the insurer would have to cover.

While the methods employed by an insurer differ from those of a consumer, each has the same goal: to minimize risk in an uncertain future. It is this uncertainty of the future and risk of financial loss which form the context for insurance, and the strategies to make financial loss more predictable and manageable which drive insurance arrangements.

### *Uneven Distribution of Health Care Expenses*

In health care, a minority of consumers are responsible for a majority of expenses. According to a longitudinal study conducted by the federal Agency for Healthcare Research and Quality, 5% of the population accounted for about half of all health expenditures in 2003, and 10% of the population accounted for nearly two-thirds of expenditures in the same year.[2] Given the unevenness of health care spending and the improbability of identifying all of the highest spenders before they use medical services, insurers employ various strategies in order to minimize the risk they bear.

### *Risk Pool and Rate Setting*

A function of insurance is to spread risk across a group of people. This is achieved in health insurance when people contribute to a common pool (“risk pool”) an amount at least equal to the *expected* cost resulting from use of covered services by the group as a whole. In this way, the *actual* costs of health services used by a few people are spread over the entire group. This is the reason why insuring larger groups is considered less risky—the more individuals participating in a risk pool, the less likely that the serious medical experiences of one or a few persons will result in catastrophic financial loss for the entire pool.

An insurer calculates and charges a rate (i.e., a "premium") in order to finance the health coverage it provides. The premium reflects several factors, including the expected cost of claims for health care use in a year, administrative expenses associated with running the plan, and a profit margin. If the insurer accurately estimates future costs and sets appropriate premium levels, then that risk pool has reached equilibrium where premiums paid by healthy persons in the risk pool help subsidize the higher-than-average costs of less-healthy persons in the pool.

### *Risk Pool Composition and Adverse Selection*

As noted above, one of the ways insurers attempt to make future costs more predictable is by spreading the risk of a few high-cost individuals across many people. But the number of people in a risk pool is not the only significant factor. Equally as important, if not more so, is the composition of the group.

A consumer's decision to obtain health coverage is based on a variety of factors, such as individual health status, estimated need for future medical care, and disposable income. Consumers with different health conditions, as well as varying degrees of comfort towards risk- taking, will differ on whether they consider health insurance necessary. This is a circumstance that insurers will consider when estimating their expenses to cover future health care use. With this in mind, insurers generally will vary the premiums they charge and the health services they cover (subject to state and federal rules) in order to attract various segments of the population. This flexibility in rate setting and benefit determination is particularly important in a competitive insurance market where insurers try to provide the most attractive rates to increase their market share.

However, some risk pools do attract a disproportionate share of unhealthy individuals. In part, this is because individuals generally know more about their own health conditions than anyone else, including an insurer. Therefore, health care consumers have an advantage over insurers in terms of knowing the kind and amount of health services they will use, at least in the short- to mid-term. This "information asymmetry" between what consumers know compared to what insurers know gives consumers an advantage when looking for health coverage that will meet their future demand for health care. For example, if a consumer plans on obtaining orthodontic care in the near future, that consumer will look for a health plan with generous dental benefits.

Information asymmetry is another source of uncertainty that insurers take into account when developing and pricing insurance products.

When a disproportionate share of unhealthy people make up a risk pool, a phenomenon known as "adverse selection," the cost for each person in the pool rises. The higher costs may encourage the departure of healthier members from the group, and discourage the entrance of other healthy people, since healthier people may be able to find cheaper coverage elsewhere or decide that coverage is too costly and become uninsured. In either situation, it leaves an even less healthy group of people in the risk pool, which again causes the cost to rise for the remaining participants. If there is no change in this dynamic, the group may experience a "death spiral" as it suffers substantial adverse selection leading to an increasingly expensive risk pool and possibly dissolution of the pool altogether. Therefore, despite the consumer's information advantage, it does not guarantee access to affordable and adequate health coverage.

***Group Market, Nongroup Market, and Medical Underwriting***

Health insurance can be provided to groups of people that are drawn together by an employer or other organization, such as a trade union. Such groups are generally formed for some purpose other than obtaining insurance, like employment. When insurance is provided to a group, it is referred to as "group coverage" or "group insurance." In the group market, the entity that purchases health insurance on behalf of a group is referred to as the plan "sponsor."

Consumers who are not associated with a group can obtain health coverage by purchasing it directly from an insurer in the individual (or nongroup) insurance market. Insurance carriers in the nongroup market conduct an analysis of each applicant's insurability. An applicant usually must provide the insurer with an extensive medical history and, while uncommon, may be asked to provide blood samples or other physical specimens. The information is used by carriers to assess the potential medical claims for each person by comparing characteristics of the applicant to the loss experience of others with similar characteristics. Once such an evaluation has been conducted, the carrier decides whether or not to provide health coverage and determines the terms for coverage. This evaluation and determination process is referred to as "medical underwriting."

Medical underwriting is standard practice in the individual insurance market, though a carrier's ability to reject applicants or vary the terms of coverage are restricted to some degree by federal and state requirements. In the group health insurance market, insurers forgo underwriting in the traditional sense (i.e., reviewing *each* person's demographics and medical history). Instead, an insurer looks at the characteristics of the collective group, such as its claims history, group demographics, and geographic location. The insurer then charges a premium based on the analysis of the group's characteristics. There are exceptions to this for very small groups. For example, when a firm with only a handful of employees applies for health coverage, the insurer may choose to review the health conditions of each person in order to establish a premium for the entire group. Or, the insurer may charge a larger premium due to the larger risk attributed to smaller groups, if permitted under law.[3]

### *Fully-Insured vs. Self-Insured Plans*

A common distinction made between types of health insurance products is whether they are fully- insured or self-insured. A fully-insured health plan is one in which the plan sponsor purchases health coverage from a state-licensed insurance carrier. The insurer assumes the risk of providing health benefits to the sponsor's enrolled members. In contrast, organizations who self insure (or self fund) do *not* purchase health coverage from state-licensed insurers. Self-insured plans refer to health coverage that is provided directly by the organization seeking coverage for its members (e.g., a firm providing health benefits to its employees). Such organizations set aside funds and pay for health benefits directly. Under self insurance, the organization directly takes on the risk for covering medical expenses, and such benefit plans are not subject to state insurance regulations. Firms that self fund typically contract with third-party administrators (TPAs) to handle administrative duties such as member services, premium collection, and utilization review. TPAs do not underwrite insurance risk.

### *Self-only vs. Family Coverage*

Another common distinction made in health insurance is the tiers of coverage provided under a policy; that is, whether the policy covers one person, a family, or other groupings. Under self- only coverage, the holder of the insurance policy is the only person insured. (Self-only coverage is also called individual coverage. Individual coverage in this sense should not be confused with health coverage from the individual insurance market—see discussion above.) Family coverage applies to the policyholder, her/his spouse, and children.[4] Other tiers of coverage include self plus one (two adults), and self plus children. Policies providing different tiers of coverage may differ from each other in terms of the services they cover and the cost-sharing they impose.

***Administrative Expenses***

Costs for administrative functions encompass a wide range of operational activities. Administrative expenses include costs associated with contracting with providers, sales and marketing, enrollment and billing, customer service, utilization review, case management, and other functions. Because of economies of scale, administrative expenses in the group market are a smaller portion of overall costs, compared to those in the nongroup market.[5]

## Tax Preference

Unlike most industrialized countries, the United States does not guarantee health coverage to all of its citizens. Instead, it relies on a patchwork approach that combines private and public means for providing health insurance and health care. One of the key pieces of this approach encouraged the growth of employment-based health coverage via the tax code.

Section 106 of the Internal Revenue Code states that employer contributions to employment- based health insurance are not included in workers' gross incomes for tax purposes. This tax preference encourages workers to sign up for ("take-up") health coverage within the work setting. A separate ruling by the Internal Revenue Service clarified that such employer contributions are business expenses and, therefore, deductible from employers' taxable income. Both parties benefit: employers use health insurance coverage as a means to recruit and retain workers, while workers typically get access to more services at better rates (see discussion below). However, workers generally receive reduced wages to compensate for richer benefits.

The tax exclusion of health benefits is one of the primary reasons why health insurance coverage is provided mainly through the workplace in the United States. Approximately two out of three nonelderly (under 65) Americans have employer-sponsored insurance. Moreover, of nonelderly persons with private health coverage, approximately nine out of 10 obtain it through the workplace.[6]

## Health Insurance Regulation

Health insurance regulation addresses a wide variety of issues: the benefits that must be offered, the individuals to whom the insurance is made available, and the responsibilities insurers have to plan enrollees, to name a few. One of the most contentious issues regarding health insurance regulation is whether it is the responsibility of individual states or the federal government. This distinction is important because federal and state laws governing health plans differ on issues such as patient compensation in courts, consumer access to care, and mandated coverage for certain benefits.

### *Responsibility of the States*

The regulation of insurance traditionally has been a state responsibility, as clarified by the 1945 McCarran-Ferguson Act. However, overlapping federal requirements complicate the matter with respect to health insurance. Individual states have established standards and regulations overseeing the "business of insurance," including requirements related to the finances, management, and business practices of an insurer. For example, all states have laws that require state-licensed insurance carriers to offer coverage for specified health care services (known as "mandated benefits"). Because fully-insured plans are subject to state-established requirements, those plans must offer those mandated benefits. On the other hand, self-insured plans are not subject to state insurance regulations so they are exempt from such requirements.

### *Key Federal Statutes*

Regardless of whether health plans are fully-insured or self-funded, they all are subject to a number of federal laws. Two of these federal laws, the Employee Retirement Income Security Act of 1974 (ERISA, P.L. 93-406) and the Health Insurance Portability and Accountability Act of 1996 (HIPAA, P.L. 104-191), have significant impact on how health insurance is provided.

ERISA outlines minimum federal standards for private-sector employer-sponsored benefits. (Public employee benefits and plans sponsored by churches are exempt from ERISA). Passed in response to abuses in the private pension system, the act was developed with a focus on pensions but the law applies to a long list of "welfare benefits" including health insurance. ERISA requires that funds be handled prudently and in the best interest of beneficiaries, participants be informed of their rights, and there be adequate disclosure of a plan's financial activities. It preempts state laws that "relate to" employee benefit plans. (In other words, the federal law overrides state laws affecting private-sector employee benefits). This portion of ERISA was designed to ensure that plans would be subject to the same benefit laws across all states, partly in consideration of firms that operate in multiple states. However, state laws still apply for issues which involve the "business of insurance." The delineation of issues attributable to the phrases "relate to" and "business of insurance" is not clear, and have led to longstanding debates and active litigation over the scope of ERISA preemption.[7]

The core motivation behind the Health Insurance Portability and Accountability Act of 1996 (HIPAA) is to address the concern that insured persons have about losing their coverage if they switch jobs or change health plans ("portability" of health coverage). The act's health insurance provisions established federal requirements on private and public employer-sponsored health plans and insurers. It ensures the availability and renewability of coverage for certain employees and other persons under specified circumstances. HIPAA limits the amount of time that coverage for pre-existing medical conditions can be excluded, and prohibits discrimination on the basis of health status-related factors. The act also includes tax provisions designed to encourage the expansion of health coverage through several mechanisms, such as authorizing tax-advantaged medical savings accounts and a graduated increase of the portion of premiums self-employed persons may deduct from their federal income tax calculations. Another set of HIPAA provisions addresses the electronic transmission of health information and the privacy of personally identifiable medical information (administrative simplification and privacy provisions, respectively).[8]

## Health Insurance Premiums

The most current, publicly-available data on employer health benefits found that the average annual premium for self-only coverage was around $4,700 in 2008. The average premium for a family of four was about $12,700.[9] Together, these premiums represent a 5% increase in the cost for employer-sponsored health benefits compared to the previous year's average premiums. While this signals a reprieve from double-digit increases in recent years,[10] the premium growth rate nonetheless outpaces the growth in prices for goods and services.[11]

## WHY IS HEALTH INSURANCE CONSIDERED IMPORTANT?

While health insurance coverage is not necessary to obtain health care, it is a useful mechanism for accessing services in an environment of increasingly expensive health care. As health care costs continue to rise, more people need greater assistance with covering medical expenses. Health insurance provides some measure of protection for consumers, especially those who have limited means or greater-than-average need for medical care.

Health insurance is considered important also because of the well-documented, far-reaching consequences of uninsurance. For instance, uninsured persons are more likely to forgo needed health care than people with health coverage. This includes forgoing services for preventable or chronic conditions which often leads to worse health outcomes.[12] Uninsured persons also are less likely to have a "usual source of care," that is, a person or place identified as the source to which the patient *usually* goes for health services or medical advice (not including emergency rooms). Having a usual source is important because people who establish ongoing relationships with health care providers or facilities are more likely to access preventive health services and have regular visits with a physician, compared with individuals without a usual source.[13] Therefore, to the extent that health insurance coverage facilitates access to basic medical services, people without coverage face substantial barriers in the pursuit of the health care they need. For 2003-04, almost 10% of nonelderly adults with private health insurance identified no usual source of care, compared with around 49% of uninsured, nonelderly adults who reported no usual source.[14]

The negative consequences of uninsurance extends beyond the persons directly involved. For example, the Institute of Medicine found that the insurance status of parents affects the amount of health care their children receive.[15] Another study has found negative spillover effects of uninsurance to the community at large. For instance, *insured* adults in communities where uninsurance is high are less likely to have a usual source of care compared to insured adults in low-uninsurance communities. And "a higher proportion of insured adults also reported having more problems getting a referral to see a needed specialist in high-uninsurance communities than in low-uninsurance communities."[16] In addition, many uninsured persons forgo preventive health care and end up developing more serious conditions requiring complex, expensive medical services. Since health coverage is positively related to income, uninsured persons are less likely to be able to afford this level of care. In cases where patients are unable to cover the costs associated with receiving health services, the facilities that provided those services must take it as a financial loss (i.e., uncompensated care). These losses can be staggering. For example, one study estimated that uninsured individuals received approximately $56 billion worth of uncompensated care in 2008.[17]

Ultimately, though, the costs for caring for the uninsured are "passed down to all taxpayers and consumers of health care in the form of higher taxes and higher prices for services and insurance."[18] Taxpayers are affected because the federal government makes payments to hospitals, which take into account the share of poor people treated. The assumption is that facilities that treat a larger proportion of poor people have a greater problem with uninsurance and uncompensated care. The federal government also provides grants to many health centers and other facilities that serve poor communities. In addition, states and localities fund local health programs, public hospitals, and clinics—facilities that generally serve an uninsured or medically underserved population. Health care consumers are affected by uninsurance because in order for physician practices and hospitals to survive financially they have to make-up the losses they sustain. Hospitals and physicians may raise rates for certain services or discontinue unprofitable programs in order to recoup those losses, thereby affecting consumers' pocketbooks and access to services. Uninsurance, then, has negative health and financial consequences for uninsured persons, their families, communities, and the nation as a whole.

## WHERE DO PEOPLE GET HEALTH INSURANCE?

Americans obtain health insurance through a variety of methods and from different sources. People may get it through the private sector, or from a publicly-funded social insurance program. Consumers may purchase health coverage on their own, as part of an employee group, or through a trade or professional association. A small minority of employees get health insurance at no upfront cost because their employer pays the total premium. However, approximately 46 million Americans did not have health insurance coverage for 2007; that is, around 15% of the total population were uninsured.[19]

## Employer-Sponsored Insurance

Most Americans obtain health coverage through the workplace. In 2007, approximately 177 million persons had employment-based health insurance, which accounts for nearly 60% of the total population.

Under employer-sponsored insurance, risk pools may be comprised of active workers, dependents, and retirees. Insurers use a number of strategies to increase the likelihood that each risk pool includes a good proportion of healthy individuals, thus avoiding adverse selection. For instance, insurers may restrict employees' opportunities to take-up health coverage or switch health plans by designating a specific time frame each year for such activities ("open enrollment period"). This strategy decreases the likelihood that people will "game" the system by taking up coverage only when they plan on using health services (e.g., for pregnancy and childbirth), and dropping coverage when they no longer plan to access care. Insurers also may require the employer to enroll a certain proportion of the firm's eligible population. Assuming that the eligible population consists of a good percentage of healthy people, requiring a certain proportion of all eligibles to enroll leads to an enrollee population which contains at least some healthy people. Employers also use strategies to encourage insurance take-up by healthy people. For example, employers pay, on average, the majority of health insurance premiums. This practice makes health coverage a more attractive benefit, even to those workers who do not plan to use medical services on a regular basis. By encouraging healthy workers to take-up health insurance, the employer subsidy helps to avoid adverse selection and contributes to the stability and diversity of the risk pool.

### *Advantages*

ESI plans retain enrollees better than the individual health insurance market. As previously mentioned, health benefits provided at the workplace are exempt from income and employment taxes, encouraging the growth and continuity of employer-sponsored health insurance. Large risk pools with a good proportion of healthy enrollees tend to be more stable than small pools or those with a higher proportion of unhealthy enrollees. Given the strategies discussed above to discourage adverse selection, insurers assume that ESI pools—particularly large, diverse ones— are relatively stable. Generally, this translates into less volatile costs and better premiums overall in the group market compared to the nongroup market. Also, large ESI groups can use their size to negotiate for better benefits and lower cost-sharing, in contrast to individual applicants in the nongroup market. Plan sponsors negotiate and interact with insurers on behalf of all of their insured members, unlike in the individual market where each consumer must deal with the insurance carrier directly in order to apply for and purchase coverage. In addition, there are economies of scale for enrollees in the group market compared to the nongroup market for administrative functions such as sales, billing, and customer service. For these reasons, workers and their families benefit from receiving coverage through the workplace. For plan sponsors, the main advantage is to use health benefits for recruitment and retention of workers. This is particularly appealing in a growing economy—such as during most of the 1990s—when there may be high demand for workers.

***Disadvantages***

While there are many advantages to obtaining ESI coverage, there are challenges as well. From the vantage point of the enrollee, one of the biggest disadvantages is the general lack of portability. Because ESI coverage is tied to the job and not the person, any change in employment (such as going from full-time to part-time status, or changing jobs) may alter the health care providers or services to which the worker has access, or disrupt health coverage altogether. Also, in firms that offer health coverage, there is a trade off made between wages and benefits. For workers who do not take up health insurance from those firms, they end up accepting lower wages for a set of benefits they do not use. From the perspective of the sponsor, an underlying challenge is the lack of enrollee awareness of the true costs of health care. Because the sponsor usually contributes to the cost of the premium, enrollees do not bear the full cost of obtaining health coverage. Also, enrollees generally do not have to cover the entire cost of the services they use, since sponsors negotiate for lower rates and better cost-sharing arrangements from insurers. Consumers enrolled in managed care plans particularly are shielded from health care's true costs. Some observers contend that this lack of cost awareness gives little incentive to consumers to utilize medical services prudently, which leads to greater use of services and more health care spending. In addition, sponsors' efforts to constrain their health spending—by increasing the employee share of the premium or cost-sharing—are made even more difficult to justify or implement. Finally, from the perspective of the federal budget, the tax exclusion of employer- sponsored health insurance represents a lost source for Treasury funds. (The Joint Committee on Taxation estimated the FY2009 tax exclusion for employer-paid health insurance, health care, and long-term care insurance premiums to be around $127 billion.)[20]

### *Large vs. Small Groups*

The group health insurance market often is thought of as consisting of large and small groups. The underlying reason for this distinction is rooted in the inverse relationship between insurance risk and group size (i.e., the risk associated with a group grows as the size of the group shrinks). This concept affects employers' offers of health benefits. For instance, a very large employer often is able to offer multiple health plan options to its members (e.g., the Federal Employee Health Benefit Program (FEHBP)). A large business can leverage its size to get a more comprehensive set of benefits. In contrast, small employers are less able to provide health coverage at all because of the greater risk associated with small groups. Even when small employers do offer coverage, the benefits are often limited. Small employers also are much less likely to self-fund health coverage, since there is a smaller pool for spreading risk and protecting against catastrophic loss. Furthermore, such firms generally do not have the necessary administrative capacity to negotiate with multiple provider groups and handle all the day-to-day operational functions. It is conditions such as these which prompt legislators to develop proposals for expanding small group participation in health insurance; for example, by establishing association health plans, and opening up FEHBP to small businesses.

Association health plans are just one example among the spectrum of entities which bring groups of people together for the purpose of buying health insurance. These entities include trade and professional associations that offer health coverage to their members ("association-sponsored plans"), and small firms that band together to purchase coverage as a group ("health insurance purchasing cooperatives"). The premise behind group purchasing arrangements is to decrease the administrative burden on and increase the negotiating capacity of participants who cannot afford to offer or purchase coverage on their own. Around one-third of small firms buy health coverage through some type of purchasing pool.[21]

## Public Programs

While most Americans with health insurance obtain it through the private-sector, tens of millions of people get health coverage through public programs. Below are descriptions of selected federal and state programs which provide payments on behalf of many persons who, due to low incomes or high health care expenses, could not afford health care otherwise.

### *Medicare*

The Medicare program was established in 1965, and is a federal program for persons age 65 and older and certain persons with disabilities. Medicare consists of four parts: Part A, Hospital Insurance; Part B, Supplementary Medical Insurance; Part C, Medicare Advantage (replaced the Medicare+Choice program with the passage of the Medicare, Prescription Drug, and Modernization Act of 2003 (MMA, P.L. 108-173); and Part D, the prescription drug benefit also added by MMA. The Medicare program provides coverage for a wide range of medical services, such as care provided in hospitals and skilled nursing facilities, hospice care, home health care, physician services, physical and occupational therapy, outpatient prescription drug benefits, and other services. By 2008, the program provided coverage to approximately 45 million beneficiaries. Medicare has been so successful in covering the elderly that the problem of uninsurance usually is described in terms of the under-65 population.[22]

### *Medicaid and the Children's Health Insurance Program (CHIP)*

Medicaid is the main health insurance program for low-income Americans. It is a means-tested program, and applicants must meet financial and other criteria in order to be eligible for services. Everyone who meets the eligibility criteria is entitled to Medicaid benefits available in their state of residence. Medicaid provides coverage for health care and long-term-care services to certain adults (generally parents and pregnant women), children, the elderly, and persons with disabilities. It is jointly funded by federal and state governments, and is administered by the states within federally-set guidelines. State Medicaid programs provide a comprehensive set of services, reflecting its diverse enrollee population. These programs must provide a set of federally- specified benefits, such as hospital services (both inpatient and outpatient), physician services, nursing home care for ages 21 and over, home health care for those entitled to services from nursing facilities, and certain services for children. States may also cover additional optional services. Some states have used waiver authority under Medicaid to extend coverage to uninsured persons who do not meet the program's categorical and/or financial tests.[23]

The Children's Health Insurance Program was established in 1997 to allow states to cover uninsured low-income children who are ineligible for Medicaid. In designing their programs, states can choose among three options: expand Medicaid, create a new "separate state" insurance program, or devise a combination of both approaches. States that choose to expand Medicaid to

CHIP eligibles must provide the full range of mandatory Medicaid benefits, as well as all optional services specified in their state Medicaid plans. States that establish CHIP programs that are separate from Medicaid choose one of three benefit options. All 50 states, the District of Columbia, and five territories have established some type of CHIP program. CHIP 's eligibility rules target uninsured children under 19 years of age whose families' incomes are above Medicaid eligibility levels. States may raise the upper income level for low-income children up to 200% of the federal poverty level, or higher under certain circumstances.[24]

## Individual Health Insurance

The individual insurance ("nongroup") market is often referred to as a "residual" market. The reason is because this market provides coverage to persons who cannot obtain health insurance through the workplace and do not qualify for public programs such as Medicare, Medicaid, or CHIP. Consequently, the enrollee population for this private health insurance market is small.

The residual nature of the nongroup market is evident in the demographic make-up of those who purchase coverage from it. The market is over-represented by the near elderly (55-64 years old); a group that has relatively weak attachments to the workplace. The individual market disproportionately consists of part-time workers, part-year workers, and the self-employed, groups unlikely to have access to ESI coverage.[25] Also, some people use the nongroup market as a temporary source of coverage, such as those in-between jobs or early retirees who are not yet eligible for Medicare.

Applicants to the individual insurance market must go through robust underwriting. Insurance carriers in most states conduct an exhaustive analysis of each applicant's insurability. An applicant provides her/his medical history, and may undergo a physical exam though this is uncommon. This medical information is used by carriers to assess the insurance risk for each person. From this assessment, insurers decide whether to offer coverage to the applicant, and under what terms. Federal and state requirements restrict somewhat insurers' ability to reject applications or design coverage based on health factors and other characteristics. Nonetheless, some applicants are rejected from the nongroup market altogether, and others who are approved may receive limited benefits or are charged premiums that are higher than those in the group market for similar coverage.[26] Rigorous medical underwriting results in an enrollee population that is fairly healthy (three out of four enrollees report that their health is excellent or very good[27]), thereby excluding persons with moderate to severe health problems from the private nongroup insurance market.

### State High Risk Pools

A majority of states have established high risk health insurance pools. These programs target individuals who cannot obtain or afford health insurance in the private market, primarily because of pre-existing health conditions. If such individuals are not eligible for public programs (e.g., their incomes may exceed the financial eligibility requirements), they have very few options for obtaining coverage. In general, high risk pools tend to be small and enroll a small percentage of the uninsured. As of the first half of 2006, 34 states had high risk pools with participation of nearly 193,000 enrollees.[28] While health benefits vary across states and plans, they generally reflect coverage that is available in the private insurance market, with required cost-sharing for enrollees. The majority of high risk pools cap premiums between 125% to 200% of market rates, and pools often are subsidized through assessments imposed on insurance companies, general revenue, or other funding mechanisms.[29]

## The Uninsured

Despite the multiple private and public sources of health insurance, millions of Americans are without health coverage. In 2007, nearly 46 million people were without health insurance coverage. For the vast majority of the uninsured, they lack coverage because they cannot *access* coverage (e.g., their employer does not offer health insurance as an employment benefit) or they cannot *afford* it.

Uninsurance is characterized as a problem of the under-65 population, given near-universal coverage of seniors through Medicare. One of the most striking characteristics of persons who lack coverage is that a significant proportion are in low-income families. For instance, among all uninsured persons under age 65, more than half were in poor or near poor families in 2007.[30]

A defining characteristic of the nonelderly uninsured population is that most have ties to the paid labor force. In 2007, 81% of uninsured persons under age 65 were employed individuals or their dependents. Even more surprising is that 55% of the nonelderly uninsured were workers with full-time, full-year status, or the dependents of such workers. While such findings may be counter-intuitive, there are multiple reasons why employed persons and their families may lack health coverage. For example, a worker may be offered health insurance by his/her employer, but declines it because he/she thinks it is too expensive. An employee may work for a small firm which is less likely than a large firm to offer health insurance as a benefit. A low-wage employee, even working full time, is less likely to be offered health insurance at work, and less likely to be able to afford it than higher-wage workers in the same firm. Finally, a healthy worker may be willing to take on the risk of being uninsured and choose not to purchase insurance at all. So despite the dominance of employer-sponsored health insurance, the dynamics of work, insurance risk, and financial resources intersect to impede the coverage of all workers and their families.

The problem of the uninsured is an ongoing concern to many policymakers and legislators. One persistent topic of debate is the overall number of uninsured individuals and the direction of the uninsurance rate. These issues have generated some controversy over dueling analyses which show slightly different (and sometimes moderately different) findings.[31] But despite the forceful discussions regarding trends in uninsurance, the year-to-year changes in the uninsurance rate actually are small. For example, from 1987 to 2007, the change in the uninsurance rate from year to year has been less than 1%.[32] Nonetheless, tens of millions of Americans were without coverage during that time period. Such circumstances beg the questions: why does pervasive uninsurance persist (even during the robust economy of the mid-1990s), and what are the implications for legislation and public policies to expand health coverage?

## HOW ARE PRIVATE HEALTH BENEFITS DELIVERED?

Given the complexity of the health care system overall, it is no surprise that health benefits are delivered and financed through different arrangements. Those arrangements vary due to numerous factors such as: how health care is financed, how much access to providers and services are controlled, and how much authority the enrollee has to design her/his health plan. While delivery systems may share certain characteristics, general distinctions can be made based on payment, access, and other critical variables.

## Indemnity (Traditional) Insurance

Under indemnity insurance, the insured person decides when and from whom to seek health services. If the services the enrollee receives are covered under his/her insurance, the enrollee or the enrollee's provider files a claim with the insurer. Thus, insurers make payments *retrospectively* (i.e., after the health services have been rendered), up to the maximum amounts specified for each covered service. In this model of health care delivery, the financing of health services and the obtaining of those services are kept separate.

This bifurcated arrangement was unquestioned for a time. But as medical costs began to rise, sometimes faster than other sectors of the national economy, many observers criticized this delivery model as contributing to increasing expenditures. Because providers were compensated on a fee-for-service basis, some argued that providers were not given incentives to provide efficient health care. In fact, some critics accused health care practitioners and institutions of providing an over-abundance of health care in order to generate greater revenue. By the early 1970s, legislators, analysts, and others expressed considerable interest in alternative models, such as managed care models, with cost control as a key feature.

## Managed Care

While managed care means different things to different people, several key characteristics set it apart from traditional (indemnity) insurance. One of the main differences is that the service delivery and financing functions are integrated under managed care. Managed care organizations (MCOs) employ various techniques to control costs and manage health service use *prospectively*. Among those techniques are restricting enrollee access to certain providers ("in-network" providers); requiring primary-care-physician approval for access to specialty care ("gatekeeping"); coordinating care for persons with certain conditions ("disease management" or "case management"); and requiring prior authorization for routine hospital inpatient care ("pre- certification"). MCOs may offer different types of health plans that vary in the degree to which cost and medical decision-making is controlled. As a consequence, enrollee cost-sharing also varies. Generally, the more tightly managed a plan is, the less the premium charged. Other distinguishing features of the managed care approach include an emphasis on preventive health care and implementation of quality assurance processes.

Managed care was touted as the antidote to rapidly rising health care costs. Starting with the passage of federal legislation in the 1970s which supported the growth of managed care (specifically in the form of health maintenance organizations (HMOs)), the number of MCOs grew quickly. Increased market competition among these organizations led to decreases in premiums, in order to gain market share. With high medical inflation in the 1980s and early 1990s, enrollees flocked to these less-costly managed care plans. By the mid-1990s, more insured workers were enrolled in HMOs than any other health plan type, and health insurance premiums had stabilized.

But in the latter half of the 1990s, a "backlash" of sorts against managed care grew.[33] Some enrollees had grown weary of provider and service restrictions. Many MCOs that had increased market share through artificially-low premiums began to raise them in order to increase revenue.[34] Consumers and others accused the managed care industry of caring more about controlling costs than providing health care. Some providers resented the role managed care played in medical decision-making. Many enrollees began to leave HMOs. The industry responded by developing insurance products that were less-tightly managed, but more costly. Some traditional HMOs widened their provider networks and eliminated the gatekeeping function, while employers began to offer plan types that were less tightly managed, such as preferred provider organizations (PPOs). In fact, by the end of the 1990s, more people with work- based health coverage were enrolled in PPOs than in HMOs.[35]

As the influence of managed care waned and health care costs began to rise at an increasing paceduring the late 1990s, the impact on consumers began to be felt. For example, in the employment setting, employers absorbed the extra costs at first in order to recruit and retain workers during the booming economy of the mid to late 1990s.[36] But as the economy soured, employers began to pass these expenses along to enrollees in the form of greater cost-sharing.[37]

## Consumer-Driven Health Care

By the end of the 1990s, large increases in health costs again became commonplace. With the belief by some observers that the age of managed care was over, they began to search for alternatives. Consumer-driven (or consumer-directed) health care have been offered as one such option.

Consumer-driven health care refers to a broad spectrum of approaches that give incentives to consumers to control their use of health services and/or ration their own health benefits. In the workplace, at one extreme employers may choose to provide an array of insurance products from which workers can choose, while at the other end an employer could increase wages but not offer any health coverage allowing workers to decide how to spend that extra money to meet their health care needs. Within those two endpoints, the consumer-directed approach varies in the degree to which consumers are responsible for health care decision-making.[38]

For example, one example that is at the heart of discussions about consumer-driven care is the health savings account (HSA). An HSA, in and of itself, is not a health insurance plan. Instead, it is an investment account in which contributions earn interest tax free. Consumers, their employers, or both may make contributions to HSAs. Consumers withdraw funds on a tax-free basis to cover medical expenses not covered by health insurance. Unused contributions roll over to the next year. HSAs are paired with high-deductible health plans. If the HSA funds are exhausted and the deductible level has not been reached, the consumer is responsible for covering that gap. Once the consumer's spending reaches the deductible level, then coverage from the health plan takes effect. HSAs received a legislative boost when they were authorized in November 2003 by the Medicare Prescription Drug, Improvement, and Modernization Act of 2003 (P.L. 108-173).[39]

While consumer-driven health care can take on many forms, the premise common to all of the approaches is that by making enrollees more responsible for their own health care, it creates incentives for people to use services prudently. The expectation is that greater cost-consciousness on the part of consumers will result in lower overall health costs. In essence, the service and cost control functions administered by MCOs and providers under managed care shifts to enrollees under the consumer-driven health care scenario.

Proponents of consumer-directed health care assert the merit in having people take increased responsibility for their own health care use and expenses. They predict that this approach will lead to better-informed consumers, more appropriate use of health services, and lower overall spending on health care. Opponents express concern that this approach does not recognize the possible range of health conditions in an enrolled population. They argue that these plans benefit the young and healthy who use relatively few services, and, therefore, would not need to expend a great deal of time and energy making these health care decisions. However, these plans impose a greater burden on individuals with moderate to severe health conditions because of their greater¬than-average use of medical services.

## End Notes

[1] Publicly funded health programs generally either provide funding for direct medical services or assist consumers in paying for health care. The latter are included in a broad category of programs based on "social insurance" principles. Social insurance refers to publicly funded insurance programs that are statutorily mandated for certain groups of people, such as low-income individuals.

[2] S. Zuvekas and J. Cohen, "Prescription Drugs and the Changing Concentration of Health Care Expenditures," Health Affairs, Vol. 26, No. 1, Jan./Feb. 2007.

[3] G. Claxton, "How Private Insurance Works: A Primer," Kaiser Family Foundation (KFF) website, April 2002, at http://www.kff.org/insurance/upload/How-Private-Insurance-Works-A-Primer-Report.pdf.

[4] Policies vary on the requirements children must meet (e.g., age, martial status, etc.) in order to become eligible for or stay on a family policy.

[5] Given that insurers monitor administrative costs as part of managing their businesses, such information is considered proprietary. Therefore, there are no reliable national estimates of the portion of insurers' expenses attributable to administrative functions.

[6] Paul Fronstin, "Sources of Health Insurance and Characteristics of the Uninsured: Analysis of the March 2008 Current Population Survey," Issue Brief No. 321, September 2008, at http://www.ebri.org/pdf/briefspdf/EBRI_IB_09a2008.pdf.

[7] For more information about ERISA regulation of health benefits, see CRS Report RS22643, *Regulation of Health Benefits Under ERISA: An Outline*, by Jennifer Staman.

[8] For more information about HIPAA, see CRS Report RL31634, *The Health Insurance Portability and Accountability Act (HIPAA) of 1996: Overview and Guidance on Frequently Asked Questions*, by Hinda Chaikind et al.

[9] These averages include both the employer and employee shares of the total premium. The Kaiser Family Foundation and Health Research and Educational Trust, *Employer Health Benefits 2008 Annual Survey*, http://ehbs.kff.org/.

[10] Other sources of premium data show a comparable trend in declining growth rates for health insurance costs. For example, see Mercer press release online, "Mercer survey finds $1,000 health plan deductible was the norm in 2008," November 19, 2008, at http://www.mercer.com/summary.htm?idContent=1328445.

[11] The annual inflation rate for 2008 was 3.8%. Bureau of Labor Statistics, "Table 1A. Consumer Price Index for All Urban Consumers (CPI-U)," at *http://www.bls.gov/cpi/cpid08av.pdf.*

[12] Kaiser Commission on Medicaid and the Uninsured, "The Uninsured and Their Access to Health Care," November 2005 at http://www.kff.org/uninsured

[13] J.E. DeVoe, et al., "Receipt of Preventive Care Among Adults: Insurance Status and Usual Source of Care," *American Journal of Public Health*, May 2003.

[14] National Center for Health Statistics, *Health, United States, 2006*, Table 77, at http://www.cdc.gov/nchs/data/hus/ hus06.pdf#executivesummary.

[15] Institute of Medicine, Committee on the Consequences of Uninsurance, *Coverage Matters: Insurance and Health Care*, 2001.

[16] M. Pauly and J. Pagan, "Spillovers and Vulnerability: The Case of Community Uninsurance," Health Affairs, Vol. 26, No. 5, p. 1309.

[17] J. Hadley et al., "Covering the Uninsured in 2008: Current Costs, Sources of Payment, and Incremental Costs," Health Affairs, Web Exclusives, August, 25, 2008.

[18] Institute of Medicine, Committee on the Consequences of Uninsurance, *A Shared Destiny*, 2003, p 122.

[19] U.S. Census Bureau, *Income, Poverty, and Health Insurance Coverage in the United States: 2007*, August 2008, p. 19 at http://www.census.gov/prod/2008pubs/p60-235.pdf.

[20] For additional information on the tax treatment of health benefits, see CRS Report RL33505, *Tax Benefits for Health Insurance and Expenses: Overview of Current Law and Legislation*, by Bob Lyke and Julie M. Whittaker.

[21] For additional information, see CRS Report RL31963, *Association Sponsored Health Plans: Legislation in the 109th Congress*, by Jean Hearne.

[22] For additional information about Medicare, see CRS Report RL33712, *Medicare: A Primer*, by Jennifer O'Sullivan.

[23] For additional information about Medicaid, see CRS Report RL33202, *Medicaid: A Primer*, by Elicia J. Herz.

[24] For additional information about SCHIP, see CRS Report RL30473, *State Children's Health Insurance Program (SCHIP): A Brief Overview*, by Elicia J. Herz, Chris L. Peterson, and Evelyne P. Baumrucker.

[25] D. J. Chollet, "Consumers, Insurers, and Market Behavior," *Journal of Health Politics, Policy and Law*, February 2000.

[26] M. V. Pauly and A.M. Percy, "Cost and Performance: A Comparison of the Individual and Group Health Insurance Markets," *Journal of Health Politics, Policy and Law*, February 2000.

[27] General Accounting Office, "Private Health Insurance: Millions Relying on Individual Market Face Cost and Coverage Trade-Offs," November 1996.

[28] States with high risk pools: AL, AK, AR, CA, CO, CT, FL, ID, IL, IN, IA, KS, KY, LA, MD, MN, MS, MO, MT, NE, NH, NM, ND, OK, OR, SC, SD, TN, TX, UT, WA, WI, WV, WY.

[29] For additional information about state high risk pools, see CRS Report RL31745, *Health Insurance: State High Risk Pools*, by Bernadette Fernandez.

[30] The poverty level for a family of four was an annual income of $21,027 (weighted average) in 2007; see http://www.census.gov/hhes/www/poverty/threshld/thresh07.html.

[31] For a discussion of the various sources of data on health insurance coverage, see CRS Report RL31275, *Health Insurance: Federal Data Sources for Analyses of the Uninsured*, by Chris Peterson and Christine Devere.

[32] Data available at http://www.census.gov/hhes/www/hlthins/historic/index.html.

[33] Richard Kronick, "Waiting for Godot: Wishes and Worries in Managed Care," *Journal of Health Politics, Policy and Law*, vol. 24, no. 5 (October 1999), pp. 1099-1106.

[34] Jon Gabel, et al., "Job-Based Health Insurance in 2001: Inflation Hits Double Digits, Managed Care Retreats," *Health Affairs*, vol. 20, no. 5 (September/October 2001), pp. 180-186.

[35] American Association of Health Plans, "Health Plans and Employer-Sponsored Plans," October 1999. Available at http://www.ahip.org/content/default.aspx?bc=41|331|366.

[36] Jon B. Christianson and Sally Trude, "Managing Costs, Managing Benefits: Employer Decisions in Local Health Care Markets," *Health Services Research*, pt. II, vol. 38, no. 1, (February 2003), pp. 357-373.

[37] Jon Gabel, et al., "Job-Based Health Benefits in 2002: Some Important Trends," *Health Affairs*, vol. 21, no. 5 (September/October 2002), pp. 143-151.

[38] P. Fronstin, ed., Employee Benefit Research Institute, *Consumer-Driven Health Benefits: A Continuing Evolution?* 2002.

[39] For more information about HSAs, see CRS Report RS22877, *Health Savings Accounts and High-Deductible Health Plans: A Data Primer*, by Carol Rapaport.

In: Health Insurance Industry Market...
Editors: Brent C. Jenner
ISBN: 978-1-61761-289-3


*Chapter 3*

# PRIVATE HEALTH INSURANCE: RESEARCH ON COMPETITION IN THE INSURANCE INDUSTRY

***United States Government Accountability Office***

July 31, 2009
The Honorable Herb Kohl
Chairman
Subcommittee on Antitrust, Competition Policy and Consumer Rights
Committee on the Judiciary
United States Senate

Subject: *Private Health Insurance: Research on Competition in the Insurance Industry*

Dear Mr. Chairman:

Health care providers and members of Congress have raised concerns that consolidation in the private health insurance industry may be resulting in less competitive markets and contributing to rising health insurance rates paid by consumers and employers. However, measuring the extent of changes in market competition over time or the effects of changes is challenging. In particular, reliable, longitudinal data to measure concentration, that is, the number of competitors and their relative market share, are only available on health maintenance organizations (HMO) but not on preferred provider organizations (PPO) or other insurance products that may comprise the market.[1] Further, data on health insurers are not available at all geographic levels. Despite these challenges, researchers have used the data available to study competition in health insurance markets, typically using one of two measures of competition: (1) HMO market concentration or (2) the number of HMOs in a market.[2] Researchers acknowledge that market concentration and the number of competitors are not perfect measures of competition in private health insurance markets and that there are limits to the conclusions to be drawn from studies that rely on the available data.[3] You asked us to review research completed on competition in the private health insurance industry. This chapter summarizes the findings of peer-reviewed research on concentration in private health insurance markets and the relationship between the level of competition and other variables, such as premium prices and provider reimbursement rates.

To identify research that examined the concentration of private health insurance markets and the relationship between the level of competition and other variables, we conducted a structured literature review, which resulted in 41 peer-reviewed articles we determined to be relevant to our objective. To conduct this review, we searched 17 reference databases, such as EconLit and Social SciSearch,[4] for scholarly articles published between January 1990 and March 2009 using a combination of search terms, such as "health insurance" and "competition."[5] We made a judgment as to whether the article was directly relevant if it included empirical analyses examining either of the following: (1) the extent of market concentration or consolidation in the private health insurance industry or (2) the relationship between the level of competition and other variables. We excluded articles published prior to 1999 that relied solely on pre-1990 data. We included articles with varying scopes. For example, one article focused on a sample of HMOs in a limited geographic area while others considered data on HMOs and PPOs nationwide. Of the 41 articles, 35 relied solely on HMO data while the remaining 6 also examined data on other health insurance products. Our review focused on studies meeting our specific criteria, though there has been other research completed that relates to competition in health insurance markets.[6] To confirm that our search captured all of the relevant peer-reviewed literature that met our criteria, we checked the bibliographies of the relevant articles to identify other potentially relevant studies. See the enclosure for a list of the 41 articles we identified through our literature review. We did not assess the methodologies of the studies identified in our review. Further, in summarizing the findings of the literature, we grouped the studies according to the topics covered and did not make judgments as to why studies may have reached different conclusions. We conducted our work from May 2009 through July 2009 in accordance with all sections of GAO's Quality Assurance Framework that are relevant to our objectives. The framework requires that we plan and perform the engagement to obtain sufficient and appropriate evidence to meet our stated objectives and to discuss any limitations in our work. We believe that the information and data obtained, and the analysis conducted, provide a reasonable basis for any findings and conclusions in this product. Because we did not evaluate the policies or operations of any federal agency to develop the information presented in this chapter, we did not seek comments from any agency.

In summary, our review found articles that measured the extent of concentration in private health insurance markets or focused on the relationship between competition in these markets and other variables, though the findings of these studies should be interpreted with caution. Several articles identified through our review examined the extent of concentration in private health insurance markets, though this research had limitations including, for example, relying on state-level data when the more appropriate geographic focus may be at a more local level. One study found that the HMO industry became more consolidated nationally from 1994 to 1997. According to the study, several national consolidations occurred during this period and contributed to the market share of the top five national firms growing from 43.2 percent in 1994 to 49.9 percent in 1997.[7,8] The study found that the effects of these national consolidations on concentration varied significantly, with some local markets experiencing no change and others facing increases significant enough to raise antitrust concerns.[9] While no other studies measured the extent of changes in the concentration of markets over time, several studies measured the concentration of local health insurance markets (defined as a state, metropolitan statistical area (MSA), or county depending on the study) at a point in time. For example, one study measured commercial health insurance concentration at the state level. The study reviewed data on HMO and PPO products for insured and self-insured employer funding arrangements across 48 states and the District of Columbia.[10] The study found that market concentration at the state level in 2003 was relatively high by federal standards[11] and that the top three firms typically dominated each market. The study noted that data were available at the state level only, even though some states include multiple geographic markets and some geographic markets cross state lines, and that the study results should be interpreted with caution.

In addition to measuring concentration, research we reviewed generally focused on examining the relationship between the level of competition in private health insurance markets (or "competition") and several variables—premium rates, rates paid to health care providers, utilization of medical services, quality of care, efficiency, and insurer profits. The results of this research should also be interpreted with caution because of data limitations and varying methodologies. For example, this research focused predominately on HMOs—and often did not include data on PPOs or other insurance products. Further, the research studies we reviewed defined geographic markets differently and controlled for different market characteristics.

## Competition and Premium Rates

Research on the relationship between competition and premium rates generally focused on the association between the level of HMO competition and premium rates or on the effects of HMO mergers on premium rates. The studies generally found that more competitive markets were associated with lower premium rates, but that mergers have not led to sustained premium increases, though they may if the merger does not result in efficiencies. For example:

- One study that reviewed data on all HMOs operating from 1988 to 2001 found that an increase in the number of competing HMOs increased the bargaining power of employers looking to contract with HMOs and led to lower premiums, especially for for-profit HMOs.[12]
- Another study examined a sample of 40 HMO mergers that occurred between 1988 and 1994 and found that the mergers did not result in increased pricing.[13]

## Competition and Reimbursement Rates

Studies that examined how competition in private health insurance markets was associated with provider payments focused on reimbursement rates to physicians and hospitals. The findings from these studies varied. For example:

- One study, which focused on markets in California, found that market concentration did not appear to be associated with physician rates including, for example, rates for evaluation and management, radiology, and pathology services.[14]
- Another study that examined data on all HMOs operating in the United States from 1985 through 1997 found that greater HMO market concentration was associated with a reduction in hospital rates.[15]

## Competition and Utilization of Medical Services

Research examining the relationship between competition in private health insurance markets and utilization of medical services focused on inpatient hospital services and outpatient care. Together, the findings of these studies generally suggested that greater competition may be associated with decreased utilization of inpatient services, but the association with outpatient utilization was unclear. For example:

- One study that examined HMO and PPO data from selected metropolitan statistical areas from 2001 to 2004 found that greater HMO concentration was associated with an increased use of inpatient services.[16] The study also found that higher PPO concentration was associated with more outpatient visits.
- Another study found that increasing the number of HMOs was associated with an increase in the use of both primary and specialty care physicians in highly competitive markets.[17]

## Competition and Quality of Care

There was little consensus among the studies that examined the relationship between competition in private health insurance markets, predominately HMO competition, and quality of care. Some found that greater competition was associated with lower quality of care, others found an association with higher quality of care, and others found no relationship. For example:

- One study that examined HMO performance on certain quality measures in 1999 found that greater market competition was associated with inferior health plan performance on measures of quality related to women's care, health plan service, and customer satisfaction.[18]
- Using 1997 data, another study found that HMO competition increased the likelihood of gatekeeping—an arrangement in which consumers select a primary care physician who authorizes referrals for other care. The study also found that gatekeeping increased the probability of consumers having a usual source of care, which may improve the quality of care.[19]

## COMPETITION AND EFFICIENCY

Studies that examined the relationship between competition in private health insurance markets and efficiency focused on the effect that different levels of competition or mergers had on costs for health insurers or hospitals. Several studies found that less competition was associated with greater cost savings for insurers or hospitals—although another study we reviewed found the opposite relationship. Other studies examining the effects of mergers found no evidence of decreasing costs as a result of consolidation. For example:

- The results from one study showed that greater HMO market concentration at the state level was positively associated with greater efficiency for hospitals, with the authors concluding that dominant insurers have the ability to promote hospital cost savings by exerting their market power to pressure hospitals to become more cost-efficient.[20]
- Another study that looked at HMO mergers between 1985 and 1997 concluded that, on average, HMO mergers did not provide economies of scale and did not result in either short- or long-term cost savings. However, the authors allowed that certain types of mergers, for example between very small and large HMOs, may result in efficiencies.[21]

## COMPETITION AND INSURER PROFITS

Finally, several studies we reviewed analyzed the relationship between HMO competition and insurer profits or the effect of HMO mergers on profits. Together, these studies suggested that greater competition was associated with lower profits but that mergers do not always result in increased profits. For example:

- One study that examined profit rates in 1994 and 1997 for all HMOs in 259 metropolitan areas found that profits were significantly lower in areas with more competition, as measured by the number of HMOs and their market concentration.[22]
- Another study using 1997 data at the MSA level found that for both local and national HMOs the presence of another HMO with a comparable geographic scope was associated with lower profits while the presence of an HMO with a different scope had no effect on profits.[23]
- A third study that looked at the effects of a sample of 40 mergers that occurred from 1988 to 1994 on an HMO's profitability found that mergers did not improve financial performance, with no significant difference in performance between the pre- and post-merger period.[24]

As arranged with your offices, unless you publicly announce the contents of this chapter earlier, we plan no further distribution of it until 30 days after its issue date. At that time, we will send copies to other interested parties. In addition, the report will be available at no charge on the GAO Web site at http://www.gao.gov. Contact points for our Offices of Congressional Relations and Public Affairs may be found on the last page of this chapter. Please contact me at (202) 512-7114 if you have any questions. Major contributors to this chapter were Kristi Peterson, Assistant Director; Susan Barnidge; Krister Friday; and Nelson Olhero.

Sincerely yours,

John E. Dicken

John E. Dicken
Director, Health Care

Enclosure

**Table 1. Index of Articles by Topic**

| Topic | Article numbers |
|---|---|
| Market concentration | 2, 10, 27, 31 |
| Relationship between competition and: | |
| Premium rates | 11, 20, 33, 35, 36, 37, 39 |
| Provider reimbursement | 9, 31, 40, 41 |
| Utilization of medical services | 2, 9, 14, 38, 39 |
| Quality of care | 1, 4, 5, 13, 18, 19, 21, 22, 25, 26, 28, 29, 30, 32, 34 |
| Efficiency | 2, 3, 8, 11, 16, 33, 35, 37 |
| Insurer profit | 7, 20, 23, 24, 33, 35 |
| Other | 6, 12, 15, 17, 32 |

Source: GAO.

# ENCLOSURE

## ARTICLES IDENTIFIED THROUGH LITERATURE REVIEW

GAO identified 41 articles that included empirical analyses examining concentration of health insurance markets or the relationship between the level of competition in private health insurance markets and other variables, or both. Table 1 identifies articles that address these topics, with the numbers corresponding to the list of articles that follows.

The 41 articles that GAO identified in the literature are as follows:

[1] Baker, L. C., Phillips, K. A., Haas, J. S., Liang, S. Y. & Sonneborn, D. (2004). "The Effect of Area HMO Market Share on Cancer Screening," *Health Services Research*, vol. *39*, no. 6 (December), pt. I, 1751-1772.

[2] Bates, L. J. & Santerre, R. E. (2008). "Do Health Insurers Possess Monopsony Power in the Hospital Services Industry?" *International Journal of Health Care Finance and Economics*, vol. *8*, iss. 1 (March), 1-11.

[3] Bates, L. J., Mukherjee, K. & Santerre, R. E. (2006). "Market Structure and Technical Efficiency in the Hospital Services Industry: A DEA Approach," *Medical Care Research and Review*, vol. *63*, no. 4 (August), 499-524.

[4] Bokhari, F. A. S. (2009). "Managed Care Competition and the Adoption of Hospital Technology: The Case of Cardiac Catheterization," *International Journal of Industrial Organization*, vol. *27*, iss. 2 (March), 223-237.

[5] Bundorf, M. K., Schulman, K. A., Stafford, J. A., Gaskin, D., Jollis, J. G. & Escarce, J. J. (2004). "Impact of Managed Care on the Treatment, Costs, and Outcomes of Fee-for-Service Medicare Patients with Acute Myocardial Infarction," *Health Services Research*, vol. *39*, no. 1 (February), 131-152.

[6] Burns, L. R., Bazzoli, G. J., Dynan, L. & Wholey, D. R. (2000). "Impact of HMO Market Structure on Physician-Hospital Strategic Alliances," *Health Services Research*, vol. *35*, no. 1, pt. 1 (April), 101-132.

[7] Dranove, D., Gron, A. & Mazzeo. M. J. (2003). "Differentiation and Competition in HMO Markets," *The Journal of Industrial Economics*, vol. *51*, no. 4 (December), 433-454.

[8] Engberg, J., Wholey, D., Feldman, R. & Christianson, J. B. (2004). "The Effect of Mergers on Firms' Costs: Evidence from the HMO Industry," *The Quarterly Review of Economics and Finance*, vol. *44*, iss. 4 (September), 574-600.

[9] Feldman, R. & Wholey, D. (2001). "Do HMOs Have Monopsony Power?" *International Journal of Health Care Finance and Economics*, vol. *1*, no. 1 (March), 7-22.

[10] Feldman, R. D., Wholey, D. R. & Christianson. J. B. (1999). "HMO Consolidations: How National Mergers Affect Local Markets," *Health Affairs*, vol. *18*, no. 4 (July/August), 96-104.

[11] Feldman, R., Wholey, D. & Christianson, J. (1996). "Effect of Mergers on Health Maintenance Organization Premiums," *Health Care Financing Review*, vol. *17*, no. 3 (Spring), 171-189.

[12] Frick, K. D. & Powe, N. R. (1998). "HMO Coverage of Cosmetic Procedures: A Response to Market Competition," *International Advances in Economic Research*, vol. *4,* no. 4 (November), 398-410.

[13] Frick, K. D. & Powe, N. R. (2000). "Nonprice Rivalry among Health Insurers and Coverage of New Technologies," *Atlantic Economic Journal*, vol. *28*, no. 4 (December), 450-462.

[14] Gaskin, D. J. (1997). "The Impact of Health Maintenance Organization Penetration on the Use of Hospitals that Serve Minority Communities," *Medical Care*, vol. *35*, no. 12 (December), 1190-1203.

[15] Gaskin, D. J., Escarce, J. J., Schulman, K. & Hadley, J. (2002). "The Determinants of HMOs Contracting with Hospitals for Bypass Surgery,"

*Health Services Research*, vol. *37*, no.4 (August), 963-984.

[16] Given, R. S. (2002). "Economies of Scale and Scope as an Explanation of Merger and Output Diversification Activities in the Health Maintenance Organization Industry," *Journal of Health Economics*, vol. *15*, iss. 6 (December ), 685-713.

[17] Jin, G. Z. (2005). "Competition and Disclosure Incentives: An Empirical Study of HMOs," *Rand Journal of Economics*, vol. *36*, no. 1 (Spring), 93-112.

[18] Kirby, E. G. (2006). "The Impact of Competition on the Importance of Conforming to Social Norms: Strategies for Managed Care Organizations," *Journal of Health Organization and Management*, vol. *20*, no. 2, 115-129.

[19] Liu, H. & Phelps, C. E. (2008). "Nonprice Competition and Quality of Care in Managed Care: The New York SCHIP Market," *Health Services Research*, vol. *43*, no. 3 (June), 971-987.

[20] Maude-Griffin, R., Feldman, R. & Wholey, D. (2004). "Nash Bargaining Model of HMO Premiums," *Applied Economics*, vol. *36*, no. 12 (July), 1329-1336.

[21] Mitchell, S. & Schlesinger, M. (2005). "Managed Care and Gender Disparities in Problematic Health Care Experiences," *Health Services Research*, vol. *40*, no. 5, pt. I (October), 1489-1513.

[22] Mukamel, D. B., Zwanziger, J. & Tomaszewski, K. J. (2001). "HMO Penetration, Competition, and Risk-Adjusted Hospital Mortality," *Health Services Research*, vol. *36*, no. 6 (December), pt. 1, 1019-1035.

[23] Pauly, M. V., Hillman, A. L., Kim, M. S. & Brown, D. R. (2002). "Competitive Behavior in the HMO Market Place," *Health Affairs*, vol. *21*, no. 1 (January/February), 194-202.

[24] Pauly, M. V., Hillman, A. L., Furukawa, M. F. & McCullough, J. S. (2001). "HMO Behavior and Stock Market Valuation: What Does Wall Street Reward and Punish?" *Journal of Health Care Finance*, vol. *28*, no. 1 (Fall), 7-15.

[25] Ponce, N. A., Huh, S. & Bastani, R. (2005). "Do HMO Market Level Factors Lead to Racial/Ethnic Disparities in Colorectal Cancer Screening," *Medical Care*, vol. *43*, no. 11 (November), 1101-1108.

[26] Rivers, P. A. & Fottler, M. D. (2004). "Do HMO Penetration and Hospital Competition Impact Quality of Hospital Care," *Health Services Management Research*, vol. *17*, no. 4 (November), 237-248.

[27] Robinson, J. C. (2004). "Consolidation and the Transformation of Competition in Health Insurance," *Health Affairs*, vol. *23*, no. 6

(November/December), 11-24.

[28] Scanlon, D. P., Swaminathan, S., Chernew, M., Bost, J. E. & Shevock, J. (2005). "Competition and Health Plan Performance: Evidence from Health Maintenance Organization Insurance Markets," *Medical Care*, vol. *43*, no. 4 (April), 338-346.

[29] Scanlon, D. P., Swaminathan, S., Lee, W. & Chernew, M. (2008). "Does Competition Improve Health Care Quality?" *Health Services Research*, vol. *43*, no.6 (December), 1931-1951.

[30] Scanlon, D. P., Swaminathan, S., Chernew, M. & Lee, W. (2006). "Market and Plan Characteristics Related to HMO Quality and Improvement," *Medical Care Research and Review*, vol. *63*, no. 6 supplement (December), 56S-89S.

[31] Schneider, J. E., Li, P., Klesper, D. G., Peterson, N. A., Brown, T. T. & Scheffler. R. M. (2008). "The Effect of Physician and Health Plan Market Concentration on Prices in Commercial Health Insurance Markets," *International Journal of Health Care Finance and Economics*, vol. *8*, no. 1 (March), 13-26.

[32] Sommers, A. R. & Wholey, D. R. (2003). "The Effect of HMO Competition on Gatekeeping, Usual Source of Care, and Evaluations of Physician Thoroughness," *The American Journal of Managed Care*, vol. *9*, no. 9 (September), 618-627.

[33] Town, R. (2001). "The Welfare Impact of HMO Mergers," *Journal of Health Economics*, vol. *20*, iss. 6 (November), 967-990.

[34] Volpp, K. G. M. & Buckley, E. (2004). "The Effect of Increases in HMO Penetration and Changes in Payer Mix on In-Hospital Mortality and Treatment Patterns for Patients with Acute Myocardial Infarction," *The American Journal of Managed Care*, vol. *10*, no. 7 (July), 505-512.

[35] Weech-Maldonado, R. (2002). "The Impact of HMO Mergers and Acquisitions on Financial Performance," *Journal of Health Care Finance*, vol. *29*, no. 2 (Winter), 64-77.

[36] Wholey, D., Feldman, R. & Christianson. J. B. (1995). "The Effect of Market Structure on HMO Premiums," *Journal of Health Economics*, vol. *14*, iss. 1 (May), 81-105.

[37] Wholey, D., Feldman, R., Christianson, J. B. & Engberg, J. (1996). "Scale and Scope Economies among Health Maintenance Organizations," *Journal of Health Economics*, vol. *15*, iss. 6 (December), 657-684.

[38] Wholey, D. R., Burns, L. R. & Lavizzo-Mourey, R. (1998). "Managed Care and the Delivery of Primary Care to the Elderly and the

Chronically Ill," *Health Services Research*, vol. *33*, no. 2 (June), pt. II, 322-353.

[39] Wholey, D. R., Christianson, J. B., Engberg, J. & Bryce, C. (1997). "HMO Market Structure and Performance: 1985-1995," *Health Affairs*, vol. *16*, no. 6 (November/December), 75-84.

[40] Younis, M. Z., Rivers, P. A. & Fottler, M. D. (2005). "The Impact of HMO and Hospital Competition on Hospital Costs," *Journal of Health Care Finance*, vol. *31*, no. 4 (Summer), 60-74.

[41] Zwanzinger, J. (2002). "Physician Fees and Managed Care Plans," *Inquiry-Excellus Health Plan*, vol. *39*, no. 2 (Summer), 184-193.

## End Notes

[1] Health maintenance organizations (HMO) and preferred provider organizations (PPO) are insurance products that generally rely on providers to control service utilization and they provide financial incentives to encourage patients to use network providers who have agreed to accept fee discounts. Under an HMO, patients may be restricted to using only network providers, and they typically require that all specialty care be coordinated through a primary care physician. PPO enrollees face lower cost-sharing requirements when they receive care from network providers, but may choose non-network providers at a higher cost and do not typically need referrals to see a specialist. Other insurance products include, for example, point of service plans, which allow members to decide at the time medical services are needed whether they will seek care from a provider within the plan's network or seek care outside of the network.

[2] Greater concentration rates or fewer insurers may indicate a less competitive market, and lower concentration rates or a greater number of insurers may indicate a more competitive market.

[3] For example, one researcher noted that measuring market concentration generally does not account for the threat of entry of new competitors, which also affects the degree of competition in a market. Other researchers raised concerns that studies on HMO competition assume that HMOs constitute a separate product market though the researchers note that the market for HMO services may not be distinct from other types of non-HMO insurance products. See L. C. Baker, "Measuring Competition in Health Care Markets," *Health Services Research*, vol. 36, no. 1 (April 2001), Part II, 223-251; T. L. Mark and R. M. Coffey, "Studying the Effects of Health Plan Competition: Are Available Data Resources Up to the Task?" *Health Services Research*, vol. 36, no. 1 (April 2001), Part II, 253-275; and D. P. Scanlon, M. Chernew, S. Swaminathan, and W. Lee, "Competition in Health Insurance Markets: Limitations of Current Measures for Policy Analysis," *Medical Care Research and Review*, vol. 63, no. 6 (Supplement to December 2006), 37S-55S.

[4] The 15 other databases included: MEDLINE, SciSearch: A Cited Reference Science Database, EMCare, Elsevier Biobase, EMBASE, NTIS, Dissertation Abstracts, Periodicals Abstracts, Wilson Business Abstracts, Gale Group Business A.R.T.S., ABI/INFORM, Gale Group Legal Resources Index, Wilson Social Sciences Abstracts, Employee Benefits InfoSource, and Insurance Periodicals Index.

[5] We searched the reference databases for all of the following combinations: "health insurance," "managed care," "health maintenance organization," "HMO," "preferred provider

organization," or "PPO;" and "competition," "concentration," "consolidation," "merger," "monopoly," "monopsony," or "antitrust."

[6] For example, some studies examined the relationship between managed-care or HMO penetration rates, which capture the degree to which individuals are enrolled in managed care (often HMOs) relative to other types of plans, and other variables. Though these studies may provide insight on how market structure might affect, for example, premium rates, we determined that they did not meet our criteria unless the study also examined the effects of market concentration or the number of competitors.

[7] R. D. Feldman, D. R. Wholey, and J. B. Christianson, "HMO Consolidations: How National Mergers Affect Local Markets," *Health Affairs*, vol. 18, no. 4 (July/August 1999), 96-104.

[8] GAO work on competition in the small group health insurance market also suggests that the top carriers have increased their market share at the state level in recent years. Specifically, in surveying state insurance regulators, we found that between 2002 and 2008 the median market share of the largest small group carrier has increased to about 47 percent in 2008 from the 33 percent reported by states in 2002. Further, the number of states with a combined market share of the five largest carriers of 75 percent or more also increased during that period, from 19 of 34 states in 2002 to 34 of 39 states in 2008. See GAO, *Private Health Insurance: 2008 Survey Results on Number and Market Share of Carriers in the Small Group Health Insurance Market,* GAO-09-363R (Washington, D.C.: Feb. 27, 2009).

[9] For example, one merger would have increased the Herfindahl/Hirschman Index (HHI), an index of market concentration that accounts for the number of firms in a market and their market share, in the St. Louis metropolitan statistical area from 2,859 to 3,330. According to the study, increases of this magnitude may raise antitrust concerns.

[10] J. C. Robinson, "Consolidation and the Transformation of Competition in Health Insurance," *Health Affairs,* vol. 23, no. 6 (November/December 2004), 11-24.

[11] The study used standards generally applied in the federal review of merger notifications. The Federal Trade Commission and the Department of Justice review notifications pertaining to proposed mergers exceeding a certain size and either agency can take action under the antitrust laws to stop such mergers. See 15 U.S.C. § 18a. As part of such a review, these agencies calculate pre- and post-merger market concentration using the HHI. Depending on the HHI score, the market is categorized as unconcentrated, moderately concentrated, or highly concentrated.

[12] R. Maude-Griffin, R. Feldman, and D. Wholey, "Nash Bargaining Model of HMO Premiums," *Applied Economics*, vol. 36, no. 12 (July 2004), 1329-1336.

[13] R. Weech-Maldonado, "Impact of HMO Mergers and Acquisitions on Financial Performance," *Journal of Health Care Finance*, vol. 29, no. 2 (Winter 2002), 64-77.

[14] J. E. Schneider, P. Li, D. G. Klesper, N. A. Peterson, T. T. Brown, and R. M. Scheffler, "The Effect of Physician and Health Plan Market Concentration on Prices in Commercial Health Insurance Markets," *International Journal of Health Care Finance and Economics*, vol. 8, no. 1 (March 2008), 13-26.

[15] R. Feldman, and D. Wholey, "Do HMOs Have Monopsony Power?" *International Journal of Health Care Finance and Economics*, vol. 1, no. 1 (March 2001), 7-22.

[16] This study found that a 10 percent increase in HMO concentration was associated with about 1.5 to 1.9 percent more inpatient days. See L. J. Bates and R. E. Santerre, "Do Health Insurers Possess Monopsony Power in the Hospital Services Industry?" *International Journal of Health Care Finance and Economics,* vol. 8, no. 1 (March 2008), 1-11.

[17] D. R. Wholey, L. R. Burns, and R. Lavizzo-Mourey, "Managed Care and the Delivery of Primary Care to the Elderly and the Chronically Ill," *Health Services Research*, vol. 33, no. 2 (June 1998), pt. II, 322-353.

[18] D. P. Scanlon, S. Swaminathan, M. Chernew, J.E. Bost, and J. Shevock, "Competition and Health Plan Performance: Evidence from Health Maintenance Organization Insurance Markets," *Medical Care*, vol. 43, no. 4 (April 2005), 338-346.

[19] A. R. Sommers, and D. R. Wholey, "The Effect of HMO Competition on Gatekeeping, Usual Source of Care, and Evaluations of Physician Thoroughness," *The American Journal of Managed Care*, vol. 9, no. 9 (September 2003), 618-627.

[20] L. J. Bates, K. Mukherjee, and R. E. Santerre, "Market Structure and Technical Efficiency in the Hospital Services Industry: A DEA Approach," *Medical Care Research and Review*, vol. 63, no. 4 (August 2004), 499-524.

[21] J. Engberg, D. Wholey, R. Feldman, and J. B. Christianson, "The Effect of Mergers on Firms' Costs: Evidence from the HMO Industry," *The Quarterly Review of Economics and Finance,* vol. 44, iss. 4 (September 2004), 574-600.

[22] M. V. Pauly, A. L. Hillman, M. S. Kim, and D. R. Brown, "Competitive Behavior in the HMO Market Place," *Health Affairs*, vol. 21, no. 1 (January/February 2002), 194-202.

[23] D. Dranove, A. Gron, and M. J. Mazzeo, "Differentiation and Competition in HMO Markets," *The Journal of Industrial Economics*, vol. 51, no. 4 (December 2003), 433-454.

[24] R. Weech-Maldonado, "The Impact of HMO Mergers and Acquisitions on Financial Performance," *Journal of Health Care Finance*, vol. 29, no. 2 (Winter 2002), 64-77.

In: Health Insurance Industry Market… ISBN: 978-1-61761-289-3
Editors: Brent C. Jenner 

*Chapter 4*

# PRIVATE HEALTH INSURANCE: 2008 SURVEY RESULTS ON NUMBER AND MARKET SHARE OF CARRIERS IN THE SMALL GROUP HEALTH INSURANCE MARKET

*United States Government Accountability Office*

February 27, 2009

The Honorable Olympia J. Snowe
Ranking Member
Committee on Small Business and Entrepreneurship
United States Senate

The Honorable Christopher S. Bond
United States Senate

The Honorable Richard J. Durbin
United States Senate

The Honorable Blanche L. Lincoln
United States Senate

Subject: *Private Health Insurance: 2008 Survey Results on Number and Market Share of Carriers in the Small Group Health Insurance Market*

As a follow-up to our 2005 and 2002 reports on the competitiveness of the small group health insurance market, you requested updated information on each state and the District of Columbia.[1] Specifically, this chapter provides information from states and the District of Columbia (hereafter referred to as a state) on the number of carriers licensed in the small group market, the largest carriers, and their market share.[2]

To obtain this information, we sent an electronic survey to the office responsible for regulating insurance, health plans, or both in all 51 states. After following up with nonresponding states by e-mail and telephone, all but 1 state completed the survey. Of the 50 states that responded, however, 3 were unable to provide the requested information on small group carriers and their market share. For the remaining 47 states, not all had the information needed to answer all of the questions. For example, 44 states reported the largest carrier and 39 states provided market share data. Also, the 47 states varied in how they defined the size of a small group. Most—33—defined a small group as 2 to 50 employees; 12 defined a small group as 1 to 50 employees; and 2 had another definition. Finally, states generally reported information as of December 2007, though 6 states were able to provide 2008 numbers, and 3 states were limited to data from 2006. We did not independently validate the information provided by the states. However, in the survey, we asked states to describe the source of the information reported and provide clarifying information about the numbers reported. As a result of this information, we excluded some states' responses from certain market share analysis, e.g., if the state had no way of separating data on small group health insurance from data on all group health insurance. We performed our work from December 2008 through February 2009 in accordance with all sections of GAO's Quality Assurance Framework that are relevant to our objectives. The framework requires that we plan and perform the engagement to obtain sufficient and appropriate evidence to meet our stated objectives and to discuss any limitations in our work. We believe that the information and data obtained, and the analysis conducted, provide a reasonable basis for any findings and conclusions. Because we did not evaluate the policies or operations of any federal agency to develop the information presented in this chapter, we did not seek comments from any agency.

The following summarizes the findings from our 2008 survey:

- The median number of licensed carriers in the small group market per state was 27.
- The median market share of the largest carrier in the small group market was about 47 percent, with a range from about 21 percent in Arizona to about 96 percent in Alabama. In 31 of the 39 states supplying market share information, the top carrier had a market share of a third or more.
- The five largest carriers in the small group market, when combined, represented three-quarters or more of the market in 34 of the 39 states supplying this information, and they represented 90 percent or more in 23 of these states.
- Thirty-six of the 44 states supplying information on the top carrier identified a Blue Cross and Blue Shield (BCBS) carrier as the largest carrier, and in all but 1 of the remaining 8 states, a BCBS carrier was among the five largest carriers.
- The median market share of all the BCBS carriers in the 38 states supplying this information was about 51 percent, with a range of less than 5 percent in Vermont and Wisconsin and more than 90 percent in Alabama and North Dakota.

In comparing what states reported in 2008 to what they previously reported to GAO in 2005 and 2002, we found:

- The median market share of the largest small group carrier has increased to about 47 percent in 2008 from the 43 percent reported in 2005 and the 33 percent reported in 2002. Twenty-four of the 29 states providing information in both 2002 and 2008 saw increases in the market share of the top carrier that ranged from about 2 to 39 percentage points. In contrast, the top carriers in 5 states lost market share with decreases ranging from about 1 to 16 percentage points.
- The number of states with a combined market share of the five largest carriers of 75 percent or more has also increased since our 2002 survey. The combined market share of the five largest small group carriers represented three-quarters or more of the market in 34 of 39 states, compared to 26 of 34 states reported in 2005 and 19 of 34 states reported in 2002.
- Finally, the median market share of all the BCBS carriers in 38 states reporting this information in 2008 was about 51 percent, compared to

the 44 percent reported in 2005 and the 34 percent reported in 2002 for the 34 states supplying information in each of these years.

The enclosure summarizes by state the number of licensed carriers, the largest carrier and its market share, and the market share of the five largest carriers in the small group market. In addition, the enclosure shows the rank of the largest BCBS carrier and the combined market share of all BCBS carriers.

As arranged with your offices, unless you publicly announce the contents of this chapter earlier, we plan no further distribution of it until 30 days after its issue date. Copies will then be sent to other interested parties. In addition, the report will be available at no charge on the GAO Web site at http://www.gao.gov. Contact points for our Offices of Congressional Relations and Public Affairs may be found on the last page of this chapter. Please call me at (202) 512-7114 if you have any questions. Major contributors to this chapter were Kristi Peterson, Assistant Director; Susan Barnidge; Grace Materon; and Nelson Olhero.

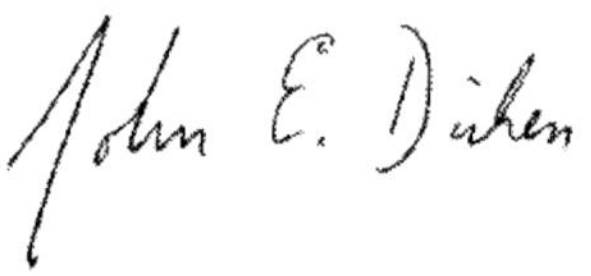

John E. Dicken
Director, Health Care

# ENCLOSURE

## Table 1. Results of 2008 Survey on Number of Carriers, Largest Carrier, and Market Share Data for Small Group Health Insurance Carriers, as Reported by 47 States

| State | Number of Licensed carriers | Largest carrier | Market share of largest carrier (percentage) | Market share of five largest carriers (percentage) | Rank of Largest BCBS carrier | Market share of all BCBS carriers (percentage) |
|---|---|---|---|---|---|---|
| Alabama[a] | 7 | Blue Cross Blue Shield of Alabama | 96 | 100 | 1 | 96 |
| Alaska | 11 | Premera Blue Cross | 77 | 94 | 1 | 77 |
| Arizona | 32[b] | Pacificare Life Assurance Company | 21 | 73 | 2 | 21 |
| California | 28[c] | Kaiser Foundation Health Plan, Inc.[d] | 37[d] | 96[d] | 2[d] | 41[d] |
| Colorado | 21 | Kaiser Permanente | 23 | 79 | 3 | 20 |
| Connecticut | 33[e] | Anthem Health Plans, Inc.[f] | 46[f] | 93[f] | 1[f] | 46[f] |
| Delaware[a] | 14 | Blue Cross Blue Shield of Delaware | 58 | 95 | 1 | 58 |
| District of Columbia | 14 | Group Hospitali-zation & Medical Services, Inc. | NA | NA | 1 | NA |
| Florida | 27 | Blue Cross & Blue Shield of Florida, Inc. | 30 | 87 | 1 | 34 |
| Georgia | 211 | Blue Cross Blue Shield Healthcare Plan of Georgia | NA | NA | 1 | NA |
| Hawaii | 7 | HMSA | NA | NA | 1 | NA |

**(Continued)**

| State | Number of Licensed carriers | Largest carrier | Market share of largest carrier (percentage) | Market share of five largest carriers (percentage) | Rank of Largest BCBS carrier | Market share of all BCBS carriers (percentage) |
|---|---|---|---|---|---|---|
| Idaho | 18 | Regence Blue Shield of Idaho | 49 | 98 | 1 | 90 |
| Illinois | 53 | Health Care Service Corporation[f] | 51[f] | 82[f] | 1[f] | 51[f] |
| Indiana | 328 | NA | NA | NA | NA | NA |
| Iowa[a] | 28 | Wellmark, Inc. | 60 | 90 | 1 | 60 |
| Kansas | 22 | Blue Cross & Blue Shield of Kansas, Inc. | NA | NA | 1 | NA |
| Kentucky[a] | 13 | Anthem Health Plans of KY | 47 | 96 | 1 | 47 |
| Louisiana[a] | 403[g] | Louisiana Health Service & Indemnity Co.[f] | 53[f] | 87[f] | 1[f] | 53[f] |
| Maine | 8 | Anthem BC/BS | 56 | 96 | 1 | 56 |
| Maryland | 16 | CareFirst Blue Choice, Inc. | 51 | 90 | 1 | 71 |
| Massachu-setts | 28 | Blue Cross and Blue Shield of Massach-usetts HMO Blue, Inc. | 44 | 88 | 1 | 52 |
| Michigan | 49 | Blue Cross Blue Shield of Michigan | 47 | 77 | 1 | 58 |
| Minnesota | 17 | Blue Cross and Blue Shield of Minnesota | 42 | 95 | 1 | 42 |
| Missouri | 50 | Health Alliance Life Ins. Co. | 30 | 73 | 3 | 17 |
| Montana | 13 | Blue Cross Blue Shield of Montana | 38 | 91 | 1 | 38 |
| Nebraska | 58 | BlueCross/BlueShield of Nebraska | NA | NA | 1 | NA |
| Nevada | 28 | Health Plan of Nevada | NA | NA | In top 5 | NA |
| New Hampshire | 10 | Anthem-NH | 50 | 99 | 1 | 50 |

(Continued)

| State | Number of Licensed carriers | Largest carrier | Market share of largest carrier (percentage) | Market share of five largest carriers (percentage) | Rank of Largest BCBS carrier | Market share of all BCBS carriers (percentage) |
|---|---|---|---|---|---|---|
| New Jersey | 13 | Horizon Health Care Services Inc. | 28 | 86 | 1 | 46 |
| New York[a] | 31 | Oxford Health Ins-urance and Oxford Health Plans, Inc. | 26 | 74 | 2 | 42 |
| North Carolina | 27 | Blue Cross Blue Shield of North Carolina | 65 | 94 | 1 | 65 |
| North Dakota | 10 | Noridian Mutual Insurance Company dba BlueCrossBlue Shield of North Dakota | 91 | 99 | 1 | 91 |
| Ohio | 180[h] | Anthem Insurance Group | 35 | 85 | 1 | 35 |
| Oklahoma | 25 | Healthcare Services Corp., BC/BS of Oklahoma | 51 | 82 | 1 | 53 |
| Oregon[a] | 15 | Regence Blue Cross Blue Shield | 44 | 79 | 1 | 51 |
| Rhode Island | 4 | Blue Cross & Blue Shield of Rhode Island | 84 | 100 | 1 | 84 |
| South Carolina | 27 | Blue Cross Blue Shield of SC | 47 | 93 | 1 | 56 |
| South Dakota[a] | 15 | Wellmark Blue Cr-oss Blue Shield of SD | 62 | 94 | 1 | 62 |
| Tennessee | 33 | Blue Cross Blue Shield of Tennessee | 68 | 94 | 1 | 68 |
| Texas | 46 | Blue Cross & Blue Shield of Texas | 27 | 68 | 1 | 28 |
| Utah | 31 | NA | 39 | 97 | NA | NA |
| Vermont | 5 | MVP Health Plan, Inc. | 45 | 100 | 5 | 1 |
| Virginia | 36 | NA | NA | NA | NA | NA |
| Washington[i] | 10 | Regence Blue Shield | 45 | 94 | 1 | 79 |

**(Continued)**

| State | Number of Licensed carriers | Largest carrier | Market share of largest carrier (percentage) | Market share of five largest carriers (percentage) | Rank of Largest BCBS carrier | Market share of all BCBS carriers (percentage) |
|---|---|---|---|---|---|---|
| West Virginia | 27[j] | Mountain State BlueCross Blue Shield (Highmark) | 52 | 86 | 1 | 52 |
| Wisconsin | 41 | United HealthCare Insurance Co. | 32 | 56 | Not in top 5 | 4 |
| Wyoming | 12 | Blue Cross Blue Shield of Wyoming[k] | 51[k] | 94[k] | 1[k] | 51[k] |

Source: GAO 2008 survey of state insurance regulators.

Legend: NA = Not available. Notes: Reported data are for December 2007 unless otherwise noted.

Ranking and market share data are based on the number of covered lives unless otherwise noted.

One state did not respond to the survey: Mississippi. In addition, 3 states responding to the survey were unable to provide data on small group carriers and on market share: Arkansas, New Mexico, and Pennsylvania.

[a] Data are as of the following dates: Delaware, December 2008; Alabama, New York, Oregon, South Dakota, and Virginia, June 2008; and Iowa, Kentucky, and Louisiana, December, 2006.

[b] Arizona's data are limited to licensed carriers that had more than $100,000 in annual premiums.

[c] Number represents licensed insurers and licensed managed care plans.

[d] Data reported represent managed health care plans only. California does not have market share data for insurance companies selling small group health insurance.

[e] State clarified that though 33 carriers were licensed, only 19 carriers were marketing small group products.

[f] Ranking and market share data for these states are based on gross premiums.

[g] State clarified that though 403 carriers were licensed to sell small group health insurance, only 28 carriers collected premiums in 2006.

[h] State clarified that though 180 carriers were licensed to sell small group health insurance, 27 carriers were collecting premiums and/or marketing small group products.

[I] Data do not include disability carriers renewing or issuing small group plans. The state, however, reported that the market share of disability carriers is not significant.

[j] State clarified that of the 27 licensed carriers, 25 were renewing existing small group policies and 23 were selling new small group policies.

[k] Ranking and market share data are based on number of covered employees.

## End Notes

[1] GAO, *Private Health Insurance: Number and Market Share of Carriers in the Small Group Health Insurance Market in 2004*, GAO-06-155R (Washington, D.C.: Oct. 13, 2005); and GAO, *Private Health Insurance: Number and Market Share of Carriers in the Small Group Health Insurance Market*, GAO-02-536R (Washington, D.C.: Mar. 25, 2002).

[2] A carrier is generally an entity (either an insurer or managed health care plan) that bears the risk for and administers a range of health benefit offerings.

In: Health Insurance Industry Market... ISBN: 978-1-61761-289-3
Editors: Brent C. Jenner 

*Chapter 5*

# HEALTH CARE AND MARKETS

***D. Andrew Austin***

## SUMMARY

Health care spending is one of the most rapidly growing portions of the federal budget. Projections suggest if the rapid growth in health care costs is not curtailed, governments at all levels will face an uncomfortable choice between significant cuts in other spending priorities or major tax increases. This chapter examines the economic justification for government intervention and involvement in health care markets.

Many analysts claim market-oriented policies, in certain instances, could lower costs and enhance efficiency in health care. This chapter discusses the Invisible Hand Theorem, which states that when certain assumptions hold, market outcomes will be efficient. These assumptions require that no one has an informational advantage over another, that no spillover effects exist in consumption or production, that no one exerts market power, and that no scale economies exist in production.

Many characteristics of health care markets fail to satisfy the assumptions of the Invisible Hand Theorem. Moreover, fundamental characteristics of health care (such as informational asymmetries between patients and health care professionals and between payers and providers, as well as ethical and distributional concerns) complicate efforts to expand the use of market or market-like incentives in health care.

Rising health care costs in part reflect the cost of technological advances, whose benefits exceed their costs, and the aging of the U.S. population. The growing role of third-party reimbursement over the past half century weakened incentives to minimize costs and thus has also led to higher health care costs. Many analysts have called for initiatives which would improve the functioning of health care markets, such as improving consumer information and allowing greater use of bargaining. These initiatives may help reduce or slow the growth of health care costs, but may also have unintended negative consequences. Greater use of market-like incentives can improve the efficiency of the health care system, but only if they take into account the special characteristics of health care.

## INTRODUCTION

Many analysts, policy makers, and politicians argue that the U.S. health care system would perform better if market or market-like institutions played a larger role. This view is based on the belief held by economists that markets generally work most efficiently when left alone, provided that certain conditions are met. These conditions essentially state that consumption or production by one person does not affect others, that no one has a privileged position in the market, and that property rights are well-defined. If those conditions are violated, however, markets may function inefficiently, which is what economists call "market failure." Government intervention may enhance economic efficiency, although in other cases government action may exacerbate market failure. The special characteristics of health care often lead to market failures. The extent of government activity vis-a-vis the health system is seen by many economists and health care analysts as a policy response to the inequalities and inefficiencies associated with such market failures.

Health care professionals often view a market orientation as a threat to their traditions, ethics, and culture. A bottom-line mentality, they argue, cannot deliver the same high quality of care as the so-called traditional approach based on professional ethics and responsibilities. Critics such as Arnold Relman, editor emeritus of the *New England Journal of Medicine*, denounce the "medical-industrial complex" for its dedication to profitability rather than patient well-being.[1] Nevertheless, health care institutions have always cared about their pecuniary interests as well as their patients. As one historian noted, "in many respects [hospitals] have behaved as businesses. But, ... hospitals have simultaneously carried symbolic and social significance as embodiments of American hopes and ideals."[2]

Even if some view market forces and the use of the price system to allocate health care services as an intrusion, consumers and providers of health care are strongly affected by economic incentives. Hospitals cut the average length of an inpatient stay sharply after Medicare switched from cost-based reimbursement to paying a flat diagnosis-related fee.[3] Physicians increased the volume (i.e., number of patient visits) and intensity of patient care (i.e., number or complexity of services provided in an average visit) seen after reductions in Medicare Part B payments.[4] Consumers use less health care when they must pay a larger share of the cost. These behavioral responses, although predicted by economic theory, do not necessarily enhance economic efficiency. The challenge for those who wish to expand the use of market incentives in health care is to design policies that align material incentives facing consumers and providers of health care so that changes in behavior enhance economic efficiency.

Both friends and foes of the expanding role of markets have sometimes relied on crude ideas about what markets can or cannot accomplish. This chapter explains what well-grounded economic theory has to say about the limits and capabilities of the market in the health care sector. These limits and capabilities then outline what the government can or cannot do to improve the health care system's performance. The report provides an overview of efforts to expand the use of market or market-like institutions in health care and considers effects of these initiatives or proposals on the federal budget. Reforms that are designed to address sources of market failure have better chances of enhancing economic performance than those that are not. Nonetheless, improving the performance and efficiency of the health system presents significant policy and political challenges even to well-designed reforms.

## THE U.S. HEALTH CARE SYSTEM

The U.S. health care system is a complex mixture of public and private providers of care, paid for by a mixture of public and private payers, staffed by dozens of health professions, working in clinics, hospitals, nursing homes, private offices, health maintenance organizations, work sites, and home settings, among other venues. This patchwork system provides patients with a broad set of alternatives; gives health professionals in general, and physicians in particular, a substantial degree of autonomy; and assigns separate, if often overlapping, responsibilities among various levels of government. The complexity of the U.S. health system, which gives it considerable flexibility, is also one of the principal causes of its inefficiencies. Dissatisfaction with the performance of the U.S. health care system has spurred wider interest in using market or market- like institutions to generate better results and lower costs.

## International Comparisons

While the United States is a leader in areas of medical technology, outcomes for several key public health indicators, such as average longevity and infant mortality, are among the bottom quarter of the 30 advanced industrial countries that comprise the Organization for Economic Cooperation and Development (OECD).[5] Comparisons of specific conditions or procedures find the U.S. health system does better in some areas and worse in others. An OECD study of ischemic heart care found that the United States used more intensive procedures and had lower mortality rates for older patients, but had higher mortality rates for younger (40-64) patients compared with other OECD countries.[6] Another study used data from Australia, Canada, England, New Zealand, and the United States to compare quality. Twenty-one quality of care indicators were selected on the basis of comparability and importance. These researchers found that each country was best on at least one indicator and worst on at least one indicator. Among these five countries, the United States did worst on kidney transplant survival rates, second worst on liver transplants, and worst on incidence of Hepatitis B, but did best for breast cancer survival, incidence of measles, and the cervical cancer screening rate.[7]

The United States spends far more on health care by any measure than any other country in the world.[8] National health expenditures per capita are expected to reach $7,498 in 2007. One of every six dollars spent in the United States is spent on health care, and by 2016, projections indicate that proportion will rise to one in five.[9] According to the latest OECD figures, U.S. health care spending in 2004 was about a third higher than Switzerland, which had the second highest level of spending.[10] This spending is not due to differences in the proportion of population aged 65 or older nor to higher direct costs of malpractice claims.[11]

While the United States spends more on health care than other countries, fewer health care resources per capita are available compared with many other advanced nations. The number of physicians per capita in the United States is about two-thirds of the OECD average, and the number of hospital beds per capita is lower than the OECD average, so greater availability of medical inputs cannot explain the spending difference between the United States and other OECD countries. Greater intensity and complexity of medical care in the United States may account for some of the difference. A 1996 McKinsey research project found that health care providers in the United States were more efficient, in the sense of producing more outputs for a given amount on inputs, than those in Germany and to some extent than those in the United Kingdom. Many analysts, however, emphasize other explanations for why medical care in the United States costs more than in other advanced countries.

Prices of medical inputs and administrative costs are much higher in the United States than in other OECD countries.[12] For example, average remuneration for medical specialists in the United States, as compared with per capita national income, is higher than for any other OECD country, while the number of specialists per capita in the United States is below the OECD average.[13] A group of Harvard Medical School researchers estimated that administrative costs accounted for about a quarter of health care expenditures in 1999. Administrative costs in Canada and Europe appear to be much lower, although the extent of the difference is subject to controversy.[14] Other factors that help explain differences in health costs between the United States and other countries include differences in payment systems, average national income, average population age as well as other factors.[15]

## Health Care Costs and Public Spending

Health care costs take up a large and growing part of the economy and of public budgets. Medicare, the largest health expenditure in the federal budget, will cost in total $428 billion in FY2007, according to CBO baseline projections, or 3.1% of gross domestic product (GDP), and the federal portion of Medicaid is expected to cost $193 billion, or 1.4% of GDP.[16] Medicare Part A costs per beneficiary grew on average 4.66% a year between 1970 and 2005, and Part B costs grew on average 8.76% a year over the same period.[17] One Congressional Budget Office (CBO) scenario anticipates that in 2050 Medicare spending will take up 8.6% of GDP, with Medicaid taking up another 4.0% of GDP, even aside from state contributions to Medicaid.[18]

Medicaid is one of the largest and fastest growing components of state spending budgets. In FY2004, Medicaid accounted for 22.3% of total state spending, which was slightly larger than the 21.4% spent on elementary and secondary education. The size and rapid growth of Medicaid spending led the National Governors' Association and the National Association of State Budget Officers to call the program "the dominant force in state spending."[19]

Governments in general and the federal government in particular are deeply involved in health care markets. Public spending in 2007 is expected to account for 47% of national health expenditures, up from 38% in 1970. Federal spending alone was expected to reach 34% of national health expenditures in 2007, up from 24% in 1970.[20] Furthermore, federal involvement in health care extends well beyond spending. Health care markets are extensively regulated, and the federal tax code affects health care markets in important ways. In particular, the cost of the federal tax exemption for employer-paid health insurance premiums exceeds that of any federal health program other than Medicare and Medicaid. This exemption will decrease federal revenues by an estimated $100 billion in FY2007.[21]

The pace of health care costs and the expanding public role in health care have stoked interest in using market incentives to slow or limit costs and to improve quality of outcomes. The nature of health care, however, provides some inherent limits to the effectiveness of the market.

## Market Failure and Health Care

Economists' belief in the efficiency of markets is based on the Invisible Hand Theorem, which states that market outcomes are efficient, so long as certain conditions hold.[22] These conditions are:

- **No externalities**. An externality, or spillover effect, exists when one's consumption or production affects the ability of another to consume or produce. Public goods, defined as goods which more than a single person can enjoy at the same time, are a special type of externality.[23]
- **Symmetric information**. Everyone knows the same things. No one has an informational advantage over others.
- **No market power**. No one acts as if he can influence prices through his actions.

- **Voluntary trade**. Property rights are well-defined and individuals can refuse trades that make them worse off.[24]

The Invisible Hand theorem takes the distribution of buying power as given. However, to the extent society cares about fairness or the evenness of distribution, it may wish to use taxes and transfers to alter the distribution of buying power. If transfers and taxes could be made without economic distortions, then society could move to another distribution of buying power, and the economy would run at full efficiency.[25] In practice, however, all taxes and transfers will cause some economic distortions. Thus, society alters the distribution of buying power to a more "fair" allocation, but at some cost of economic efficiency.

## Externalities and Public Goods

An epidemic is a classic example of an externality or spillover effect. Without some form of coordination, individuals will contribute inefficiently small amounts for the prevention of contagious diseases. Therefore, an efficient government can improve public well-being by imposing taxes and spending an appropriate amount on prevention and public health.

Information gained through medical research is an example of a public good, because the same information can benefit many people simultaneously. Individual donations, however, would yield an inefficiently low level of support for medical research. Charging those who benefit from better medical technology or procedures can provide a partial solution; but, to the extent that some patients will be priced out of the market, economic inefficiencies will persist. What economists define as public goods are often financed by private individuals or groups. For example, privately supported basic research is an example of a privately funded public good. Many goods provided by governments are private goods, not public goods. Extending the benefits of police, fire, and municipal trash collection to more people generally requires a proportionate increase in resources, so such services would not be considered a public good by economists.[26]

Redistribution of resources to the poor, according to some economists, can also be considered a public good.[27] In this view, each member of society would benefit by the knowledge that all other members were kept from falling below some minimum standard of living. However, the "warm glow" that each member might feel from redistribution that ensured that minimum standard often falls short of an intensity sufficient to induce opening of one's own pocketbook. Compulsory taxation provides a way to finance redistribution by sharing the cost among all taxpayers. Many people would derive some satisfaction from knowing that a health care system fulfilled the ethical norm that access to medical care was available regardless of ability to pay. Supporting such a system, as a practical matter, requires government intervention.

## Informational Advantages and Market Failure

The lack of symmetric information, which occurs when some have informational advantages over others, is the source of many of the key problems in health care. When consumers know the quality and price of goods, they can search to find higher-quality and lower-priced goods. This puts pressure on firms to increase quality and reduce price. When consumers cannot see prices or quality, however, markets work less well. In general, when one party knows more than another party, market failure can occur. Economists distinguish among several different types of asymmetric information, which are considered as follows.[28]

### *The Principal-Agent Problem*

The principal-agent problem occurs when one person, the principal, must delegate some decision or activity to an agent, who has special knowledge. If the principal can directly assess outcomes and effort, then no problem exists. However, if the principal cannot observe how hard the agent works or if the principal is unable to tell the difference between incompetence and bad luck, then market failure can result. The interaction of a patient and a physician is an example of principal- agent relationship. The patient goes to a physician because the physician has special knowledge. The physician, however, faces different incentives that are not always aligned with the patient's best interests. For example, the physician may be paid more by ordering a test whose costs exceed its benefit. Or the physician may have a patient make additional visits, whose benefits fall short of their costs. Principal-agent problems can be mitigated in several ways.

A physician's reputation can provide one solution to the principal-agent problem. If a good reputation brings benefits to a physician, and if patients occasionally get some information of whether a physician is acting in their best interests or not, then physicians will have an incentive to avoid actions which would damage their reputations. However, if patients rarely obtain information on whether a physician acts in their best interest, or if the penalty of losing a good reputation is too small, then the agents will have weak incentives to be faithful to their principal, and the principal will use physicians less often.

Centralized tracking of physicians is another possible solution. Centralized mechanisms, such as licensure requirements, exist to certify that physicians have received appropriate training. The National Practitioner Data Bank (NPDB) contains information on malpractice claims and disciplinary actions against health care professionals. Governments, hospitals, health plans, and related organizations can access specific records, but individuals cannot. Some consumer groups have attempted to compile their own databases that would allow consumers to assess the quality of different physicians. So far, these databases are fragmentary and limited.

Third-party monitoring can also give incentives for health care providers to maintain and improve quality. Accreditation or certification of health care providers gives consumers and payers a seal of approval for institutions that meet certain standards. The National Committee on Quality Assurance (NCQA) conducts research on managed care plans and performs accreditation audits, and the Joint Commission on Accreditation of Healthcare Organizations (JCAHO) accredits hospitals and related institutions.

### *Adverse Selection and Splintering of Risk Pools*

Adverse selection occurs when some personal *characteristics* which affect health care costs are hidden from others. Pricing of individual insurance contracts can only depend on characteristics that the insurer knows or can discover, and which can be verified by a third party, such as a court or an arbitrator. If sicker and healthier persons are indistinguishable, they will pay the same health insurance premiums. While insurers may not know each individual's characteristics, they will have information, based on claims history and other data, about the aggregate characteristics of various pools of persons seeking insurance. Furthermore, insurers understand that a carefully designed and marketed menu of insurance plans can induce individuals to separate themselves into different risk pools. For instance, a low-premium high-deductible plan is more likely to attract healthier individuals, and a high-premium low-deductible plan is more likely to attract individuals with greater health care needs. Thus, even if insurers cannot observe individual characteristics, they can still achieve some separation of high- and low-risk enrollees.

Insurance companies in a competitive market face strong incentives to attract low-risk customers and avoid high-risk customers, which they can do through underwriting. Underwriting is the process of assessing levels of risk associated with different insurance contracts and setting terms, conditions, and prices for those contracts. Underwriting splinters the insured population into smaller and smaller risk groups, and reduces risk sharing across a broader population. For auto and property insurance this is standard. Adverse selection is less of a problem because insurers can predict risk using observable characteristics of drivers and their claims history. Pooling careful and careless drivers in effect compels careful drivers to subsidize careless drivers. This pooling would be inefficient if such implicit subsidies caused careless drivers to either drive more or drive less well, or if resulting increases in premiums caused careful drivers to buy less insurance. Underwriting by auto insurance companies raises no strong fairness issues to the extent that the risk of having auto insurance claims is linked to personal choices, including the choice of whether to drive or not.

Health care is often viewed differently than other kinds of goods, and health insurance has always worked differently than other lines of insurance. Few would argue that anyone has a right to be a careless driver. On the other hand, differences in health costs are often presumed to stem from factors which are beyond the control of individuals.[29] The idea that access to health care should be equal has had enormous influence on health policy. The need to use health care is typically viewed as a result of bad luck or genetics, rather than carelessness. To the extent that individual demand for health care is unaffected by insurance status, the costs of providing health care can be considered a fixed sum. In this case, the practice of medical underwriting, which consists of offering better prices and conditions to the healthy, rearranges the cost burden of health care but does not affect overall costs. That is, while an individual insurer earns higher profits by attracting a healthier risk pool via medical underwriting, total costs are not reduced. Because underwriting consumes real resources, administrative costs in a system with medical underwriting will be higher than when all risks are in one pool.

Legal or administrative measures can require insurers to charge the same premiums to individuals with differing characteristics, which in the context of health insurance is called "community rating." In a competitive market, community rating may be unsustainable. If sicker and healthier persons face the same premiums, sicker persons face stronger incentives to enroll in insurance plans and to choose more generous health plans. Health plans that attract a higher proportion of sicker enrollees will have higher average costs. If health insurers are unwilling to sustain losses, higher average costs lead to higher premiums, which gives healthier individuals incentive to purchase less insurance relative to a situation in which adverse selection were absent.

A mixed insurance pool may be stable, however, if the proportion of sicker people in a pool is small enough and if economies of scale make larger plans more efficient. If healthier persons remain in the same plans as sicker people, then in effect they subsidize sicker persons. If the proportion of sicker persons is sufficiently large, however, private insurance providers can earn a profit by introducing plans that attract a preponderance of healthier people.[30] As healthier people leave the mixed insurance pools, average costs for remaining enrollees increase, leaving more people unable to afford health insurance. This dynamic is often termed a "death spiral."

The ability to organize large pools of diverse individuals is a central advantage of employer-based health insurance, which has dominated the U.S. health care system for the past half century.[31] Blue Cross/Blue Shield organizations once adhered to the "community rating" principle that spread risks across large, heterogenous pools. Community rating was vulnerable to for-profit insurers' pricing strategies that offered lower rates for firms with healthier employees, which cut Blue Cross's market share. Twelve states still require insurers to use community rating for certain markets.[32] Some see the shift of market share from Blue Cross plans that used community rating to for-profit insurance plans, which offer lower premiums to healthier groups, as an example of a death spiral.[33] Other researchers, however, contend the introduction of community rating need not result in a death spiral.[34] Furthermore, the financial problems of some Blue Cross organizations may have had more to do with administrative problems than with adverse selection.[35]

The tax exemption for employer-provided health care was a major factor in the expansion of employee-based health insurance. While linking health insurance with employment has advantages of low administrative costs and broad pooling of risks, the tax exemption gives the largest subsidies to those with the most generous health plans, and for employees with a choice of plans, encourages the choice of more generous plans. Tying health insurance to employment, which the tax exemption encourages, can discourage employees from switching jobs, a problem know as "job lock." The President's Advisory Panel on Tax Reform recommended capping this tax exemption.[36]

Organizing government-sponsored risk pools is another way to ensure that the risks of incurring major health care costs are spread across a large population. In single-payer systems, such as Canada's, all eligible persons are in the same pool. Putting all Canadians in a single pool and the ban on private health insurance prevents any splintering of the health insurance market that could trigger a death spiral, and ensures that the health care costs of the sickest patients are borne by the whole population.

A more limited approach is to set up risk pools, which allow those with serious medical problems to obtain health insurance.[37] As of 2005, 33 U.S. states had set up risk pools that offer insurance to individuals denied insurance due to an existing medical condition. Despite subsidies from state and federal funds, risk-pool premiums are much more expensive than premiums paid by healthy individuals who have employer-provided insurance.[38] In 2004, state subsidies totaled more than $0.5 billion, and premiums typically cost 125% to 150% of comparable individual market premiums. The number of enrollees in risk pools (about 180,000 in 2004) comprises only a small fraction of the pool of uninsured.[39]

Adjusting payments to plans and providers based on characteristics of enrollees, at least in theory, can provide incentives for private insurers to treat a pool of patients more efficiently rather than to focus on attracting a healthier pool of patients. If insurers were paid less for covering healthy patients and more for covering sicker patients, insurers would have a weaker incentive to attract the healthy and avoid the sick. For instance, Medicare Advantage sets rates for its HMO capitation program based on enrollee characteristics. So far, however, Medicare Advantage (MA) uses crude rules of thumb to set reimbursement adjustments, which do not appear to have changed incentives facing insurers in significant ways. Medicare administrators are currently exploring more sophisticated ways of reimbursing MA providers.

Designing reimbursement schemes to change insurers' incentives is difficult for two reasons. First, health expenditures are highly skewed among the population: 5% of patients account for over 50% of health care costs.[40] Thus to alter insurers' behavior, substantial pricing adjustments would be needed. Second, insurers are likely to have better information about health characteristics of enrollees and potential enrollees, as well as more sophisticated methods of analyzing those characteristics. To the extent that payment adjustments misprice risk, private insurers can profit by medical underwriting.

Providing people with the opportunity to extend or renew their health insurance coverage can provide some protection against the effects of splintering risk pools. If insurance plans are subject to frequent renewal decisions that may depend on past claims history, then insurance becomes less of a shield against financial calamity and more of an installment plan. Congress and several states have enacted reforms intended to preserve enrollees' ability to renew coverage. The Consolidated Omnibus Budget Reconciliation Act of 1985 (COBRA, P.L. 99-272) contains provisions which allow retirees, former employees, and dependents to pay no more than 102% of the full, normal premium to continue coverage. Terminated employees may generally obtain COBRA coverage for 18 months. In some circumstances beneficiaries can obtain COBRA benefits for longer periods. Because employers typically contribute a portion of the cost of premiums, obtaining insurance under COBRA almost always costs former employees much more than what current employees pay for health insurance. COBRA policies, however, cost less than individual health insurance plans, with the possible exception of younger and healthier persons.[41] On average, employees pay 16% of premium costs for individual coverage and 27% for family coverage.[42]

The Health Insurance Portability and Accountability Act of 1996 (HIPAA, P.L. 104-191), also known as the Kassebaum-Kennedy bill, restricted preexisting condition exclusions and limited insurers' ability to deny coverage to people who recently had group coverage. HIPAA also guaranteed eligible employees' ability to renew coverage and to carry over coverage when changing employers, a provision intended to reduce job lock.[43] HIPAA, however, set no limits on premium increases, so insurers could discourage HIPAA-eligible persons from enrolling by setting premiums at high levels.[44]

Almost all state governments have enacted reforms to limit experience rating of small group health insurance, and 21 states limit experience rating for nongroup health insurance. Some states also require insurers to issue policies, and many more have extended COBRA and HIPAA provisions regarding continuation of health insurance coverage.[45]

Despite various federal and state measures intended to limit experience rating and expand health insurance coverage, many people, especially those with preexisting conditions, have trouble finding affordable health insurance.[46] The health insurance trade association reported in 2002 that 71% of applicants were offered standard premiums and 12% were rejected.[47]

### *Moral Hazard*

Moral hazard occurs when a person's *actions* are unobservable, so that changes in behavior cannot be observed.[48] In particular, moral hazard refers to changes in behavior that affect the risks being insured. For example, after a person obtains health insurance she may take less care to remain healthy or may visit her physician more often than necessary. Moral hazard in health insurance may be limited by non-insurable costs. For instance, going to the physician takes time, having procedures performed is painful, and neglecting one's health can cause problems which medical care cannot easily cure.

Copayments and deductibles are standard methods to limit moral hazard. According to economic theory, insurance policies that divide risk-sharing between an insurer and the insured in an efficient way require individuals to pay for relatively small, regularly occurring expenses, such as eyeglasses and routine dental care and require insurers to pay a major part of large, unexpected expenses. The value of insurance is higher for rare or unusual expenses which would cause serious financial disruption for a household. Small and routine costs present lesser financial risks to policyholders, so the benefit of insuring such expenses is minor. Thus economic theory suggests that if consumers are informed and rational then insurance with "doughnut" provisions, which cover small- and high-cost claims, but which fail to cover claims over some intermediate range, is an inefficient means of sharing risks.[49] The Medicare Part D drug coverage is one example of health insurance with a doughnut provision. On the other hand, the Medicare Catastrophic Coverage Act of 1988 (P.L. 100-360), which introduced changes in the Medicare system arguably more in line with standard economic theory, was subsequently repealed in 1990 after vigorous protests by some Medicare beneficiaries.[50]

Empirical evidence shows that patients who do not pay copayments and deductibles receive more health care. The RAND Health Insurance Experiment, which randomly assigned families to insurance plans, found that free care encouraged health care use. Families that paid nothing for their health care were about 10% more likely to use medical care, and incurred about 25% more medical expenses than families with 25% copay plans. Families with 50% and 95% copay plans were less likely to use medical care and incurred fewer medical expenses.[51] Health status for those receiving free care was little different than health status for those in copay plans, with two exceptions. First, low-income people with poor vision and free care had slightly improved vision compared with others. Second, low-income populations with free care had fewer problems with high blood pressure. Within that high-risk group, better control of high blood pressure appeared to lessen mortality risks.[52] Another study, using data from the Medical Outcomes Study, found that older patients with chronic conditions who had zero or low copayments consumed more medical care than those with high copays.[53]

Requiring families to pay a portion of their health care costs, according to the usual theory of supply and demand, reduces demand for low-benefit care. To the extent that costs of some types of care exceed their benefits, excluding such items is a more efficient way to design insurance plans. Demand for health care items whose benefits greatly exceed their costs should be affected to a lesser degree, if patient behavior conformed to standard economic assumptions. There is mixed evidence, however, that higher copayments have different effects on low-benefit and high- benefit care. The RAND Health Insurance Experiment and the Medical Outcomes Study found that higher patient copays and deductibles reduced use of low-benefit items, but also reduced consumption of some high-benefit items as well. That suggests demand for health care responds to monetary incentives, but that patients often have difficulty in distinguishing high-benefit and low-benefit care, or that some portion of the patient pool responds to monetary incentives and another portion does not. In some instances, changes in what patients pay can induce reductions in low-benefit care without significantly affecting high-benefit care. For instance, a 1996 study found that requiring Kaiser-Permanente HMO enrollees to pay $25 to $35 for emergency room visits reduced overall emergency room visits by 15%, while the reduction in emergency room visits for conditions classed as "always an emergency" was small and statistically insignificant.[54]

The extraordinary cost of a major medical intervention presents a difficult dilemma to those who design cost-sharing provisions in health insurance plans. While few patients incur huge charges, that small percentage of cases accounts for a large proportion of total health care costs. On one hand, a health insurance plan has limited value if it does not prevent a health emergency from becoming a financial calamity. Forcing families to pay even a fraction of the costs of an expensive medical episode could strain the finances of most families, even to the point of bankruptcy.[55] On the other hand, if insurance pays all, or nearly all, of the charges associated with a major health episode, then patients, their families, and their physicians have little incentive to control costs, even if the resulting benefits are minimal.[56] One study found no correlation between spending on care for terminal patients and regional mortality rates, suggesting that either higher spending yields little or no benefit in mortality or that data aggregated by region are too crude to identify effects.[57] Many plans have out-of-pocket limits that commit the insurer to pay all charges above a certain level, which provides families with substantial protection against financial calamity at the cost of eliminating monetary incentives to avoid items or procedures with only low or speculative benefits.

In some cases, administrative and financial incentives may induce terminal patients to be treated in high-cost settings, even when patients have expressed a desire to be treated in a low-cost hospice or home setting.[58]

Imposing tighter controls on access to medical care by imposing gatekeeper requirements is another way to limit moral hazard. Most managed care plans require a primary care physician or insurance plan representative to approve hospital visits, procedures, and specialist visits. Managed care plans substantially increased their share of the health insurance market in the late 1980s and early 1990s, a development driven in part by the belief that managed health care and health maintenance plans could control costs. Some research suggested that cost growth moderated in markets where managed care plans had larger market shares.[59] Other evidence suggests that managed care plans do not deliver lower costs.[60] In the late 1990s, consumer dissatisfaction slowed or even reversed the expansion of managed care, although HMO and managed care plans avoided losing market share by loosening controls on access to care and by expanding into the Medicare population.[61]

***Pressures on the Employer-Provided Health Insurance***

Employer-based health benefits, the bulwark of the American health insurance system, is increasingly under strain, threatening the health insurance system's ability to spread the financial risks associated with significant medical problems. The number of people covered by employer- provided health insurance has been dropping since 2000, as insurers have been willing to trade higher margins for lower enrollments. More people are buying individual health plans, but this increase is dwarfed by the decrease in group coverage.[62] Many firms have sought to push a greater share of health cost increases onto employees and retirees, which has become a major source of labor-management conflict.[63] Health benefits remain a standard feature of benefit packages for nearly all businesses with more than 200 employees and for firms that tend to employ high-wage employees.[64] High-wage employees are more likely to fall within higher marginal tax brackets, and therefore gain more from the tax exemption of employer-provided health insurance than low-wage employees. For instance, a high-wage employee whose income puts her in the 35% marginal tax bracket saves 35¢ in taxes for every dollar shifted from post-tax compensation to health insurance paid in pre-tax dollars. A low-wage employee who pays no federal income tax gains no federal income tax advantage from shifting compensation to health benefits.[65] Without some curtailment of the employer-provided health insurance tax exemption, medium and large businesses and firms that tend to hire high-wage individuals will continue to offer health benefits.

Smaller businesses and firms that employ large numbers of low-wage workers, who gain less from tax exemptions, face a stronger temptation to drop or curtail health insurance benefits as health premiums rise. The percentage of small businesses that offer health benefits dropped from 69% in 2000 to 60% in 2005.[66] Low-wage workers may be more willing to take the risk of going without health insurance in exchange for higher take-home pay, although low-wage individuals are more likely to have poor health status.

For example, in 2005 fewer than half of Wal-Mart employees were in its health insurance plan. While some worked too few hours or had not worked long enough to be eligible, many others passed up coverage because of the high cost of benefits relative to their earnings.[67] An internal 2005 Wal-Mart memorandum stated that significant proportion of workers (27%) obtained coverage for their children through public insurance programs such as Medicaid and State Children's Health Insurance Program (SCHIP), and that an additional 19% had children who were uninsured.[68] Walmart employees and their children were less likely to have employer-provided insurance and more likely to be covered by public insurance than the national average for all workers, but were *more* likely to have employer-provided insurance and *less* likely to be covered by public insurance than the average retail worker. In April 2006, in the face of pressure from unions and several state legislatures, Wal-Mart announced changes in its benefits package intended to increase the attractiveness of its health insurance plan, which shortened waiting periods and expanded availability of health benefits.[69]

Public and private health insurance systems do not smoothly conjoin to offer low-income individuals and their families stable and predictable financial protection against medical costs. In addition, the interaction of public and private insurance programs can distort incentives for low- wage individuals and the firms that employ them. Although enrollments in Medicaid and SCHIP increased in the 1990s, in recent years some states have tightened eligibility standards while other states have expanded coverage.[70] Many low-income families lose their eligibility for Medicaid when their incomes rise above state-specific earnings thresholds, which imposes a high implicit marginal tax rate on earnings of those families, serving as a deterrent to work.[71] Some firms that tend to hire low-wage workers have trouble offering insurance plans as attractive to low-income families as public insurance programs supported by tax dollars. Firms that offer low-wage workers health benefits find that through the tax system they pay health insurance costs of their competitors' employees as well as their own. In addition, waiting periods for benefits and other eligibility hurdles impose barriers to insurance benefits and health care access for low-wage workers, who change jobs more frequently and are more subject to economic and social disruptions than workers with greater financial resources.

### *Changing Incentives for Technological Innovation*

Most health economists and practicing physicians, according to one survey, believe that "the primary reason for the increase in the health sector's share of GDP over the past 30 years is technological change in medicine."[72] In other sectors of the economy, most notably those involving computers and information technology, technological advances brought better and cheaper products. Asking why technology causes higher costs in health care but lower costs elsewhere is natural. Part of the answer lies in how incentives facing developers of new medical technologies interact with the structure of health care finance.

The direction and pace of advances in medical technology depend on incentives facing engineers and researchers, which are affected by how health care is financed. Inventors and developers, if motivated by profits, must consider who will pay for new technologies and innovative products. The dominant role of insurers and governments in health care finance implies that converting breakthroughs in medical technology into financial success generally depends on private and public insurers' decisions about what their plans cover. Defining coverage limits of health insurance presents special challenges. While health insurance contracts in a given year specify what is and what is not covered in considerable detail, over time coverage limits evolve as medical practice patterns and medical technology progresses. As medical knowledge and technology advance, what was considered experimental medicine yesterday becomes standard today.[73] The knowledge that what health insurance covers shifts over time has an important effect on incentives facing those working to develop new drugs, devices, and procedures.

Because health insurance makes patients and physicians less sensitive to price, developers have stronger incentives to invent new treatments or technologies which do something new or better, rather than invent cheaper ways of doing existing things. Innovation in computer hardware technology is mainly focused on making cheaper computers that run faster. If firms and individuals had "computer insurance," computers might perform more esoteric tasks, but at a much higher price.

One proposed strategy is to design health insurance plans that will pay an amount equivalent to the cost of an existing technology. If a patient wanted a newer and better technology, then the patient would have to pay out of her pocket. If the new technology's benefits warranted its higher costs, then presumably the patient would be willing to pay the extra amount. For example, an insurer could set reimbursement for pharmaceuticals aimed at a specific condition equal to the cost of an existing drug of known efficacy. If a drug company developed a more effective drug for that condition that was more expensive, then the patient would pay the difference. If the gain in efficacy was large compared to the increase in price the consumer would presumably be more willing to choose that drug. This reimbursement policy would provide developers of new medical technologies with a powerful incentive to make newer products better and cheaper.

While fixing reimbursement levels for new pharmaceuticals at the level of existing approved drugs would give drug developers strong incentives to consider the costs and prices during the R&D process, it could also create pricing anomalies in the short run. For instance, a study based on data from the Clinical Antipsychotic Trials in Intervention Effectiveness (CATIE) found no significant differences in quality-of-life measures for second-generation drugs and a first- generation drug (perphenazine), even though newer drugs cost \$300 to \$600 more per month.[74] Thus, for some patients, switching to an older antipsychotic could yield large cost savings. However, different patients with the same condition often respond differently to the same drug, and patients with schizophrenia often must try several different drugs to find one that is clinically effective and does not create serious side effects. Some patients will do better with a second- generation drug, while other patients with the same condition will do better with a first-generation drug. If reimbursement levels of second-generation drugs were set at the level of first-generation drugs, either some patients would pay substantially more (or someone would pay more on their behalf). for their treatment using a second-generation drug, or they would have to use a first- generation drug which, for them, works less well.

### *Market Power*

Health care providers often have substantial market power. Shopping around for the most attractive health provider when sick or injured is difficult or impossible. Switching physicians or health plans is costly and inconvenient for patients, and changing health insurers is costly and time-consuming for businesses. Prices for individual health services are difficult to find. Drug and device manufacturers have legal monopoly powers due to patent protection.

While major buyers, such as governments, have bargaining power which can allow them to buy at lower prices, individuals have little or no bargaining power.

In other markets consumers can, in effect, hire a firm or organization to bargain on their behalf. A Wal-Mart shopper enjoys the benefits of the company's bargaining power with manufacturers. A union member enjoys the benefits of collective bargaining, such as better working conditions and higher pay. Similarly, a patient benefits from the bargaining power of his employer with his insurer, as well as from the insurer's bargaining power with health care providers.[75] Likewise, a retiree can benefit from the government's bargaining power. Lower prices for health care in other OECD countries are, to a large extent, due to the willingness of governments to use their bargaining power with providers.[76] If consumers have a wide choice of organizations or firms that can negotiate on their behalf, then competition will ensure that consumers will reap most of the benefits. If consumers cannot easily choose or switch among such organizations, however, then the middlemen will capture a larger portion of those bargaining benefits for themselves. Moreover, while the bargaining power of employers, insurers, and governments benefits consumers, as compared to a situation in which consumers face providers directly, bargaining interactions among employers, insurers, and providers create economic distortions which can reduce efficiency.[77]

## Efficiency and Redistribution in Health Care

Economists tend to separate questions of efficiency from questions of redistribution. If market failure occurs, market outcomes are inefficient in the sense that other outcomes exist that would make some people better off without making anyone else worse off. Even if markets are efficient, society may decide to redistribute resources, despite efficiency losses. Designing policy, according to mainstream view of public economics, is a matter of achieving a given set of distributional goals with minimal loss of efficiency.[78]

The concept of social insurance, which is embedded in the design of Social Security and much of federal health policy, provides a way to redefine the distinction between efficiency and redistribution. For instance, Social Security benefits resemble annuities offered by private insurers. A retiree who purchases an annuity pays for the right to receive regular payments until death. Annuities therefore, insure retirees against the risk of having their assets run out before they die, and allow retirees to reallocate income to match over time financial resources to needs. An actuarially fair annuity (i.e., one whose expected benefits match its cost for each category of risk) cannot be properly said to redistribute income, even though annuity holders who live longer receive more benefits than those who do not.

Unlike private annuities, Social Security payments are determined by a progressive benefit schedule, so that retirees who had low wages receive more relative to the payroll taxes they paid than what retirees who had high wages receive. Thus, the progressive structure of Social Security benefits tends to transfer income from richer to poorer retirees, in a way that a private insurer would not. While this could be viewed as pure redistribution, the progressive structure of Social Security benefits can be seen as implicitly providing insurance against the risk of having low earnings. To the extent that this socially provided insurance reduces the riskiness of individuals' incomes over their lives, economic efficiency is enhanced.[79]

A broader interpretation of the social insurance concept would be that redistributional programs aimed at the poor, act as an insurance program that all members of society join before birth. Some part of regular taxes constitutes the premium for this social insurance, and individuals collect benefits if they suffer bad luck of some sort that makes them poor. Social insurance provides protection against some consequences of becoming poor, at the cost of higher taxes for others.

The introduction of Medicare and Medicaid in 1965 reflected both social insurance and more purely distributional concerns. Medicare, which reduced the share of the elderly living in poverty, added medical benefits to the Social Security program. By including nearly all of the working population in Medicare, its original proponents sought to distinguish it from more redistributive "welfare" programs and emphasize its social insurance aspects. In contrast, while Medicaid also provides substantial social insurance benefits, its design continues to reflect its origin as a redistributive program. Medicaid stemmed from various poor-relief programs aimed at low- income groups and those impoverished by poor health, which were extended and consolidated in a multi-billion-dollar federal-state program.[80]

## THE FEDERAL BUDGET AND MARKET-ORIENTED HEALTH CARE REFORM

The rapid rise in health care costs is straining public budgets at all levels of government, and projected increases in health care costs promise to intensify pressures on public budgets.[81] If health care costs continue to grow at past rates, cutbacks in other types of consumption will be inevitable. Even if health care costs moderate, a substantial portion of the gains from economic growth will be directed towards the health care system. Rising costs have stemmed in part from the introduction of medical advances, which have increased longevity and reduced morbidity.[82] The increasing proportion of the elderly population is another cause of rising medical costs. Finally, third-party reimbursement, by shielding consumers from health care costs, makes consumers less sensitive to price signals. This, in turn, gives providers incentives to expand the supply of health care and to change practice patterns to a more complex and intensive style of medicine.[83]

Rising health care costs have cut into the *growth* of other types of consumption for most households. In the decades following World War II, productivity and incomes grew fast enough relative to health care costs to allow steady increases in health and non-health spending. In more recent decades, real incomes for most households grew more slowly while health costs continued to rise rapidly and cut into the growth of non-health expenditures. Since 1972, real incomes for the lower 99% of household grew on average only 1.2% per year to 2002. Over the same period real national health expenditures rose 4.9% a year.[84] Had health care spending in the U.S. been held to 10% of GDP, a proportion similar that in Canada, France, Germany, and Switzerland, non- health consumption would have grown about 25% faster.[85]

To the extent that choices of rational consumers, or of rational voters and politicians, drive this expansion of the health care system, rising health costs are not necessarily a cause for concern. In all advanced industrial countries the fraction of the economy devoted to health care has been rising. If consumers prefer to buy more technologically advanced medical care rather than more advanced cars or refrigerators, then higher medical costs are a natural consequence of rising standards of living. A 2001 review of studies regarding medical technology for heart attacks, lowbirthweight babies, depression, and cataracts indicated that increased benefits of better treatment options far outweigh costs. For breast cancer, according to that review, increased costs and benefits of new technologies were roughly of the same magnitude.[86]

Rising medical costs threaten to price a growing number of Americans out of the insurance market. In the past few decades, the number of uninsured has hovered around 40-46 million. Depending on the definitions used, tens of millions more are underinsured against the risk of having a health emergency become a financial catastrophe. As health care becomes more expensive, the logic of supply and demand suggests the pool of uninsured persons will grow. Two health economists projected that the number of uninsured persons will grow from 45 million in 2003 to 56 million by 2013, largely due to the continually rising costs of health care.[87]

Absent the political will to increase taxes significantly, rising federal health care expenditures will force major cuts in benefits or fundamental changes in the health delivery system.[88] Economic theory suggests that addressing the root causes of market failure provides the best chance for enhancing system performance. The following discussion examines the potential of market-based solutions, which address sources of market failure noted above, to help transform the health care system in ways that would lead to better performance and lower costs.

## Improve Health Consumer Information

Consumers shopping for cars have many sources of information on quality and price of various models. To the contrary, consumers shopping for health care have trouble finding basic information about quality and price. Certainly comparing health care alternatives, given their complexity, uncertainty, made-to-order nature, will be harder than comparing mass-produced goods. However, providing health care consumers with better information can stimulate competition, which in turn can deliver better performance and prices.

### *Information on Pricing*

More transparent pricing of health care could help consumers make better decisions. However, transparent pricing is likely to be effective only when combined with other measures. Often, price information is of little value without accompanying information on quality.[89] In addition, consumers will be sensitive to prices only if they share a non-trivial portion of their health care costs. However, the bulk of medical costs stem from a small proportion of high-cost episodes, often occurring in the last few days of life.[90] Insured patients in those episodes are well above out-of-pocket limits, above which the insurance plan pays until some very high limit of coverage is reached. For this reason, insurance plans—not consumers—will be in the best position to put pressure on providers to lower prices and improve quality for the most expensive types of health care. That is, better price information for consumers can spur competition among providers of eyeglasses, teeth cleaning, and routine check-ups, but better price information is unlikely to sharpen competition among heart surgeons.

Hospitals, in general, have been reluctant to provide a transparent set of prices for their services. In part, this is a consequence of their cost structure. Hospitals, for their part, must pay large fixed costs for items such as buildings, maintenance, equipment, and computer systems. At the same time, hospitals provide a perishable service: an empty hospital bed cannot be saved for tomorrow. Economic theory suggests that industries that have high fixed costs, and which sell perishable goods or services, face strong pressures to charge different customers different prices and compete in markets subject to unstable prices.[91] In addition, many hospitals provide services, such as indigent care and graduate medical education, for which they may not be not wholly compensated. Such hospitals must find other ways to finance these services, which often involves cross-subsidies. In these conditions, a simple flat-rate price system may not be a viable strategy for hospitals. Therefore, imposing greater transparency of health care prices may require closer attention to cross-subsidies and uncompensated training and care.

### *Information on Quality*

Health care consumers have access to little useful information about quality. In part this is due to the inherent complexity of medical care and the difficulty of defining and measuring quality. However, the development of large electronic databases has opened the possibility of creating quality indices based on sophisticated statistical methods. Large corporations, insurance companies, and government agencies have developed extensive databases which contain information reflecting the quality of health care. These data, aside from some limited exceptions, are unavailable to consumers.

Medicare pays an average of more than $400 million per year to run 53 Quality Improvement Organizations (QIOs), which work with hospitals, physicians, nursing homes and other providers to improve quality of care. Research by academics and the Institute of Medicine has cast doubt on the efficacy of QIOs.[92] Other research, however, suggests that interventions by QIOs are associated with quality improvements.[93] Hospital professional organizations in 2002 created the Hospital Quality Alliance, which provides comparative data. For each hospital, 20 indicators measuring the proportion of patients who receive specific treatments recognized to constitute "best practice" in the areas of heart attacks, heart failure, pneumonia, and prevention of surgical infections are reported.[94] For example, one item reports what percentage of heart attack victims received aspirin upon arrival at the hospital. Critics say this type of reporting focuses on what a hospital *did*, rather than what happened to patients. They note that if food critics operated according to similar principles, perhaps their reviews would report which restaurants remembered to include important ingredients of meals or how sophisticated the restaurant stoves were, while failing to report how meals tasted.

Traditional approaches to quality monitoring in health care focused on "zero/one" indicators that provide no information on gradations of ability or competence. Physicians were licensed, and hospitals were accredited, and those who were not could not legally engage in medical care. Providers were certified for Medicare reimbursement. Such measures, however, only served to set lower bounds. The board certification of physicians is a partial exception, which provides consumers an opportunity to select physicians who have passed a more rigorous set of standards.

Providing consumers with more useful data on outcomes can improve health care quality.[95] Of course, outcome data must include risk adjustments, so that statistics reflect the fact that healthier patients will on average have better outcomes. For example, the United Network for Organ Sharing, established by Congress in 1984, collects data on all transplant operations in the United States. Risk-adjusted outcome data for each transplant center are available at http://www.unos.org. Public availability of risk-adjusted outcome data puts pressure on surgeons and transplant centers to improve performance. New York State has published risk-adjusted average mortality rates for cardiac surgery since 1991. After starting this program, the mortality rate among cardiac patients treated in top-performing hospitals or by top-performing surgeons was about half the mortality rate for patients treated by a hospital or surgeon rated in the bottom 25% of the rankings.[96] A 2003 study, however, contended that publication of performance data gave providers incentives to avoid difficult cases, leading to worse health outcomes for sicker patients and higher resource usage.[97]

In the absence of effective quality-control programs, malpractice and the tort system act as a rough substitute for quality control.[98] Expanding consumer access to useful medical outcome data would take pressure off the tort system. For instance, once New York State started publishing cardiac outcome data, surgeons with high reported risk-adjusted average mortality rates were more likely to retire or stop performing operations. Giving patients information that allows them to avoid surgeons with high mortality rates is preferable to having their estates sue.

## Make Extras Cost Extra

One strategy for slowing the growth of health care is to make patients pay more when they choose health care which is more expensive to provide. For example, many employers tie their contribution to an employee's health insurance plan to the cost of the cheapest plan. Employees then face a choice of paying for the incremental cost of a more generous insurance plan out of their own pocket or spending that money on other things. However, some employees can pay for more generous insurance out of pre-tax income via premium conversion plans, so that the tax exemption for employer-provided health care still tilts those employees towards buying more health insurance.[99]

Limiting the income tax exemption for employer-provided health care at some fixed level would help ensure that those who benefit from more generous health plans pay for their added cost themselves.[100] To the extent that consumers make rational decisions between health and non- health expenditures, the tax exemption creates an economic distortion that lowers allocational efficiency. Limiting this exemption would make employees with more generous health plans more sensitive to the cost of health insurance, which would put downward pressure on health care costs. As noted above, the President's Advisory Panel on Tax Reform called for capping this exemption for those reasons.

The Weisbrod proposal, described above, which would tie reimbursement for new drugs to the level of an existing drug of recognized efficacy, is another application of the "make extras cost extra" principle.[101] Providing drug developers with a strong incentive to find new drugs that would be cheaper but just as effective as currently available drugs could help constrain the growth of health care costs. In effect, some insurers have partially implemented this approach in their efforts to promote use of generic drugs by waiving copays or deductibles that would apply for non-generic drugs.[102] Patients who want more expensive drugs, rather than cheaper generics, must pay some portion of the difference themselves.

The same "pay more for extras" approach appears in various forms in several health care reform proposals. For example, this idea is central to the rationale for the favorable tax treatment of high- deductible insurance plans linked to health savings accounts (HSAs), which have been an important part of the President's health reform agenda. Those who choose these plans pay for routine expenses from HSAs, or beyond some point, out of pocket, but retain insurance protection against the financial risks connected to health care.

## Expand Use of Information Technology

Many health analysts contend that more extensive use of information technology (IT) could improve quality and increase efficiency of medical care. The Veterans' Health Administration (VHA), which treats about 5 million patients per year, began an organizational transformation in 1995 that featured a centralized health information system. This system not only simplified record keeping, giving physicians instant access to records on all previous visits made by a patient, but also provided researchers and managers access to treatment and outcome data that provided hard evidence on clinical effectiveness.[103] The VHA is now considered a leader in the application of IT to health care administration.[104] Several studies have concluded that quality of care in the VHA exceeds that in comparable private health care providers.[105]

Centralized clinical IT systems can also allow payers to link physician reimbursement with measures of quality of care. The British National Health Service (NHS) initiated pay-forperformance contracts with family practitioners in 2004, which tied physician payments to 146 indicators of the quality of clinical care for 10 chronic diseases.[106] In the first year of this program, almost 97% of U.K. physicians met quality targets. While analysis of these initial data cannot determine whether initial clinical quality targets were set too low or whether clinical quality improved, the information collected on quality indicators provides the NHS with a powerful tool to monitor the quality of patient care and to push for further improvements.

The federal government has taken preliminary steps in the same direction. The federal government has funded demonstration projects that make extra payments to physicians and hospitals that report certain quality indicators.[107] The Medicare Prescription Drug, Improvement, and Modernization Act of 2003 (P.L. 108-173) cuts payments by 0.4% to hospitals which do not report on 10 quality indicators for acute myocardial infarction, congestive heart failure, and pneumonia. The Deficit Reduction Act of 2005 (P.L. 109-171) increased that penalty to 2% of payments and authorized the Department of Health and Human Services to modify the set of quality indicators. The Tax Relief and Health Care Act of 2006 (P.L. 109-432) ties increases in physician reimbursement under Medicare Part B to reporting of quality measures selected by the Centers for Medicare and Medicaid Services' Physician Voluntary Reporting Program. At present, this program collects data on 16 quality measures. In future years, the Secretary of Health and Human Services may select other quality measures. While the data supplied by U.S. hospitals and physicians is much less detailed than information supplied by U.K. physicians participating in pay-for-performance programs, U.S. efforts to collect a basic set of quality indicators in a systematic way could underpin future efforts to link payments to quality of care.

## Concluding Thoughts

Market competition has brought rapid technological change, higher quality, and lower prices to many parts of the economy, leading many to ask why broader application of market principles to the health care system could not reduce costs and improve performance. As many have noted, health care is not a standard commodity. Unless institutions and reforms are designed to reflect the unique characteristics of the health care market, failures will continue to be the norm. Certainly past experience indicates that patients, insurers, and providers all react to financial incentives. Unfortunately, designing incentives that align behavior of consumers and health care payers and providers is difficult because of the nature of medical care. Broadening financial protection against unexpected health care costs, enhancing access to routine and preventative care, constraining costs, and setting up economic incentives that induce efficient behavior among individuals and firms are all worthwhile goals. Designing policies with a reasonable expectation of reaching each of those goals is difficult.

Information asymmetries between patients and physicians as well as between providers and payers stem from the unavoidable need for highly specialized roles. The specialized expertise of medical personnel gives patients access to sophisticated therapeutic measures, many of which could hardly have been imagined a generation ago. This specialization of expertise also necessitates an informational asymmetry that requires patients to depend on their physicians to guide them through the system. Thus, the principal-agent relationship lies at the heart of the health care experience. Similarly, because physicians see *patient*s while payers only see *paper claims*, physicians possess an important informational advantage over third-party payers. Expanded use of performance measurements and information technology has the potential to reduce these problems.

The health insurance system's ability to spread risks across a broad pool of beneficiaries will continue to face challenges as insurers seek to avoid losses through medical underwriting and related practices. Extending coverage to individuals in poor health, from the point of view of an insurer, is more akin to providing a subsidy than insuring a risk. Insuring such individuals may require either subsidies or pricing schemes that induce private insurers to compete on grounds of efficiency of service rather than ability to avoid those with greater needs for health care. Alternatively, health insurance for those in poorer health could be guaranteed by policies that would create larger and broader pools, such as the Canadian single-payer system. Another alternative is the United Kingdom's two-tier system, in which all residents are enrolled in the National Health Service, but those who wish access to more convenient services may buy supplemental policies, such as provided by the British United Provident Association (BUPA). This system gives all U.K. residents access to a reasonable standard of care, although this may involve some level of inconvenience and waiting in some cases, and restricted access to some care regarded by health planning authorities as of low benefit. Those wishing to bypass such inconveniences can pay for access to more extensive and comfortable care.

Some state governments have introduced other reform strategies. After July 2007, Massachusetts will require all residents to obtain health insurance. This approach parallels the typical automobile insurance system, which requires citizens to have insurance, but allows them to choose among many approved and regulated insurance providers. Low-income individuals will be eligible for subsidized access to insurance on a sliding scale.[108] Governor Schwarzenegger has proposed a health insurance reform plan that also includes a requirement that all individuals obtain health insurance.[109]

Even if the design of health care policy requires balancing of goals that present conflicting requirements, policy innovations can deliver better results. Policies that harness market incentives and recognize the nature of health care can enhance efficiency and improve performance. Because asymmetric information is a cause of market failure, policies that provide better information to patients and payers may improve performance. Because market power often serves as a cause of market failure, policies that either reduce or counterbalance market power can help improve performance. Policies that either fail to reflect the nature of the health care or that fail to address causes of market failure are unlikely to lead to lasting improvements.

## End Notes

[1] Arnold S. Relman, "The New Medical-Industrial Complex," *New England Journal of Medicine*, vol. 303 (October 1980), pp. 963-970.

[2] Rosemary Stevens, *In Sickness and Wealth* (New York: Basic Books, 1989), p. 6.

[3] Louise B. Russell, *Medicare's New Hospital Payment System: Is It Working?* (Washington, DC: Brookings, 1989), pp. 25-46.

[4] Centers for Medicare and Medicaid Services, "Physician Volume and Intensity Response," memorandum from Volume-and-Intensity Response Team, Office of the Actuary, HCFA, to Richard S. Foster, Chief Actuary, August 13, 1998; available at http://www.cms.hhs.gov/ActuarialStudies/downloads/PhysicianResponse.pdf.

[5] Uwe E. Reinhardt, Peter S. Hussey, and Gerard F. Anderson, "Cross-national Comparisons of Health Systems Using OECD Data, 1999," *Health Affairs*, vol. 21, no. 3 (May/June 2002), pp. 169-181.

[6] Pierre Moise, Stéphane Jacobzone, et al., *OECD Study of Cross-national Differences in the Treatment, Costs and Outcomes of Ischaemic Heart Disease*, (Paris: OECD, May 2003), p. 8.

[7] Peter S. Hussey et al., "How Does The Quality Of Care Compare In Five Countries?" *Health Affairs*, vol. 23, no. 3 (May/June 2004), pp. 89-99.

[8] Gerard F. Anderson, Peter S. Hussey, Bianca K. Frogner and Hugh R. Waters, "Health Spending In The United States And The Rest Of The Industrialized World," *Health Affairs*, vol. 24, no. 4 (July/August 2005), pp. 903-914.

[9] These projections were calculated by the Centers for Medicare and Medicaid Services. For details, see John A. Poisal, et al., "Health Spending Projections Through 2016: Modest Changes Obscure Part D's Impact," *Health Affairs Web Exclusive*, February 21, 2007, available at [content.healthaffairs.org/cgi/reprint/hlthaff.26.2.w242v1].

[10] The city-state Luxembourg, which spent $5,089 per person, is excluded. These data were obtained from OECD, "OECD in Figures 2006-2007 - Health spending and resources from the OECD" (OECD: Paris, February 6, 2007), available at [ocde.p4.siteinternet.com/publications/doifiles/012006061T02.xls]. Figures computed in U.S. dollars using purchasing power parity (PPP).

[11] Gerard F. Anderson et al., "Health Spending In The United States And The Rest Of The Industrialized World," *Health Affairs*, 24, no. 4 (July/August 2005), pp. 903-914 and Uwe E. Reinhardt, Peter S. Hussey, and Gerard F. Anderson, "U.S. Health Care Spending In An International Context," *Health Affairs*, vol. 23, no. 3 (May/June 2004), pp. 10-25.

[12] McKinsey Global Institute, *Healthcare Productivity*, October 1996, available at http://www.mckinsey.com/mgi/ publications/healthcare.asp.

[13] OECD, *Health at a Glance - OECD Indicators 2005*, (Paris, March 7, 2006), Chart 2.10, available at http://dx.doi.org/10.1787/753873300856.

[14] S. Woolhandler, T. Campbell, and David U. Himmelstein, "Costs of Health Care Administration in the United States and Canada," *New England Journal of Medicine*, vol. 349, no. 8 (Aug 21, 2003), pp. 768-775. On the other hand, some argue that the research by

Woolhandler and colleagues overstates the magnitude of the difference in administrative costs between the U.S. and Canada. See Henry Aaron, "The costs of health care administration in the United States and Canada—questionable answers to a questionable question," *New England Journal of Medicine*, vol. 349, no. 8 (August 21, 2003), pp. 801-803.

[15] For one analysis, see McKinsey&Company,"Accounting for the Cost of Health Care in the United States," 2003 available at http://www.mckinsey.com/mgi/publications/healthcare/images

[16] Congressional Budget Office, *The Budget and Economic Outlook: Fiscal Years 2007 to 2016*," January 2006, p. 52 et seq. Medicare figures exclude offsetting receipts, which are expected to total $60 billion in FY2007.

[17] Author's calculation using data from Table V.B1, "HI and SMI Average per Beneficiary Costs" in the *2006 Annual Report of the Boards of Trustees of the Federal Hospital Insurance Trust Fund and the Federal Supplementary Medical Insurance Trust Fund* and GDP deflator data from the Bureau of Economic Analysis.

[18] See the discussion of the intermediate spending/lower revenues scenario in the CBO Report, *The Long Term Outlook*, December 2005.

[19] National Governors Association and the National Association of State Budget Officers, *The Fiscal Survey of States*, June 2006, pp.vii and 10.

[20] Poisal, et al., op. cit.

[21] U.S. Congress, Senate Committee on the Budget, *Tax Expenditures: Compendium of Background Material on Individual Provisions*, committee print, 109th Cong., 2nd sess., S. Prt. 109-072, p. 661. For a comprehensive discussion of tax benefits for health spending, see CRS Report RL33505, *Tax Benefits for Health Insurance and Expenses: Overview of Current Law and Legislation*, by Bob Lyke and Julie M. Whittaker.

[22] Among economists, the Invisible Hand Theorem is called the First Welfare Theorem. See Gerard Debreu, *Theory of Value*, (New Haven: Yale, 1959), pp. 94-96 for a proof.

[23] More precisely, a good is considered a pure public good if the cost of allowing one more person to enjoy its benefits is zero. For example, a radio broadcast can be considered a pure public good because the cost of adding one listener is zero.

[24] A technical condition on consumer preferences (non-satiation) that rules out "bliss points," is also required. This discussion uses the assumption of symmetric information, rather that the assumption that individuals possess perfect information used in standard proofs. A proof of the First Welfare theorem with symmetric information requires slightly stronger conditions on consumer tastes.

[25] This is the Second Welfare Theorem.

[26] Tom Means and Stephen Mehay, "Estimating the Publicness of Local Government Services: Alternate Congestion Function Specifications," *Southern Economic Journal*, vol. 61, no. 3 (January 1995), pp. 614-627.

[27] Mark V. Pauly, "Income Distribution as a Local Public Good," *Journal of Public Economics*, vol. 2 (1973), pp. 35- 58.

[28] This discussion follows Kenneth Arrow, "Uncertainty and the Welfare Economics of Medical Care," *American Economic Review*, vol. 53, no. 5 (1963). For a modern analysis of market failure in health care markets see Peter Zweifel and Friedrich Breyer, *Health Economics*, (New York: Oxford Univ. Press, 1997), ch. 5.

[29] For example, few employers offer plans which charge non-smokers lower premiums than smokers, suggesting a strong reluctance to use experience rating within groups even when cost differences are strongly associated with behavioral choices.

[30] For a presentation of the economic theory of insurance in the presence of information asymmetries, see Michael Rothschild and Joseph E. Stiglitz, "Equilibrium in Competitive Insurance Markets: An Essay on the Economics of Imperfect Information," *Quarterly Journal of Economics*, vol. 90, no. 4(1976), pp. 630-49.

[31] For an overview of the U.S. health insurance market, see CRS Report RL32237, *Health Insurance: A Primer*, by Bernadette Fernandez.

[32] Mila Kofman and Karen Pollitz, "Health Insurance Regulation by States and the Federal Government: A Review of Current Approaches and Proposals for Change," March 2006, Health Policy Institute working paper, Georgetown University, p.3.

[33] Paul Starr, *The Social Transformation of American Medicine* (New York: Basic, 1983), pp. 327-33 1.

[34] Thomas C. Buchmueller and John E. DiNardo, "Did Community Rating Induce an Adverse Selection Death Spiral? Evidence from New York, Pennsylvania and Connecticut," *American Economic Review*, vol. 92, no. 1. (March 2002), pp. 280-294.

[35] James C. Robinson, "The Curious Conversion of Empire Blue Cross," *Health Affairs*, vol. 22, no. 4 (July/August 2003), pp. 100-118.

[36] President's Advisory Panel on Tax Reform, *Simple, Fair, and Pro-Growth: Proposals to Fix America's Tax System: Report of the President's Advisory Panel on Federal Tax Reform*, November 2005, pp.80-81. In particular, both the "Simplified Income Tax Plan" and the "Growth and Investment Tax Plan" recommend that this exemption be capped at the average health premium, which the Panel estimated at $5,000 for individuals and $11,500 for families.

[37] For state-level details, see CRS Report RL3 1745, *Health Insurance: State High Risk Pools*, by Bernadette Fernandez.

[38] Mark Merlis, "Fundamentals of Underwriting in the Nongroup Health Insurance Market: Access to Coverage and Options for Reform," National Health Policy Forum Background Paper, April 13, 2005, pp. 19-21. A list of state risk pools is available at http://www.healthinsurance.org/riskpoolinfo.html.

[39] Bruce Abbe, "Overview—State High Risk Health Insurance Pools Today," available at http://www.selfemployedcountry.org/riskpools/overview.html.

[40] M. L. Berk and Alan C. Monheit, "The Concentration of Health Care Expenditures, Revisited," *Health Affairs*, vol. 20, no. 2 (March/April 2001), pp. 9-18.

[41] U.S. Dept of Labor, Employee Benefits Security Administration, "FAQs About COBRA Continuation Health Coverage," available at http://www.dol.gov/ebsa/faqs/faq_consumer_cobra.html.

[42] Kaiser Family Foundation, *Employer Health Benefits 2006 Annual Survey*, September 2006, sec 6.

[43] For an account of the passage of this bill, see Brian K. Atchinson and Daniel M. Fox, "The Politics Of The Health Insurance Portability and Accountability Act," *Health Affairs*, vol. 16, no. 3 (May/June 1997).

[44] Merlis, op. cit., pp. 13-14.

[45] Merlis, op. cit., pp. 15-16.

[46] Merlis, op. cit., pp. 10-12.

[47] Thomas Musco and Thomas Wildsmith, "Individual Health Insurance: Access and Affordability," Health Insurance Assoc. of America Brief Analysis, October 2002, available at http://www.heartland.org/Article.cfm?artId=15320.

[48] Mark V. Pauly, "Overinsurance and Public Provision of Insurance: The Roles of Moral Hazard and Adverse Selection." *Quarterly Journal of Economics*, vol. 88 (1974), pp. 44-62.

[49] Arrow (1963), op. cit., Appendix. Price distortions introduced by the tax exemption for employer-provided health insurance or the impression that individuals are unable to compare accurately the costs and benefits of health care may explain why many policies cover routine or preventative care.

[50] Thomas Rice, Katherine Desmond, and Jon Gabel, "The Medicare Catastrophic Coverage Act: a Post-mortem," *Health Affairs*, vol. 9, no. 3(Fall 1990), pp. 75-87. The act ensured that all costs of a hospital stay beyond an initial deductible of about $500 and all reasonable physicians' bills beyond an annual limit of about $1,400 would be covered for Medicare beneficiaries.

[51] W. G. Manning et al, "Health Insurance and the Demand for Medical Care," *American Economic Review*, vol. 77, no. 3 (June 1987).

[52] R.H. Brook et al., "Does Free Health Care Improve Adults Health?" *New England Journal of Medicine*, vol. 309 (1983), pp. 1426-34.

[53] Mitchel D. Wong et al., "Effects of Cost Sharing on Care Seeking and Health Status: Results from the Medical Outcomes Study," *American Journal of Public Health*, vol. 91, no.11 (November 2001), pp. 1889-1894.

[54] Joe V. Selby et al., "Effect of a Copayment on Use of the Emergency Department in a Health Maintenance Organization." *New England Journal of Medicine*, vol. 334, no. 10 (March 7, 1996), pp. 635-642.

[55] David Himmelstein, Elizabeth Warren, Deborah Thorne, and Steffie Woolhandler, "Illness and Injury As Contributors To Bankruptcy," *Health Affairs, vol.* 24 (2005), pp. 63-73.

[56] One solution that preserves the value of insurance while introducing price incentives would be to allow families to receive cash in lieu of aggressive treatment. See Margaret M. Byrne and Peter Thompson, "Death and Dignity: Terminal Illness and the Market for Non-treatment," *Journal of Public Economics*, vol. 76, no. 2 (May 2000), pp. 263- 294.

[57] J. Skinner and John E. Wennberg, "How Much is Enough? Efficiency and Medicare Spending in the Last Six Months of Life," National Bureau of Economic Research Working paper 6513, 1998.

[58] Melinda Beeuwkes Buntin and Haiden Huskamp, "What Is Known About the Economics of End-of-Life Care for Medicare Beneficiaries?" *The Gerontologist*, vol. 42, special issue III (2002), pp. 40-48.

[59] Jack Zwanziger and Glenn A. Melnick, "Can Managed Care Plans Control Health Care Costs?" *Health Affairs*, vol. 15, no. 2 (summer 1996), pp. 185-199.

[60] J. Sung, M. Wessel, S.F. Gallagher, J. Marcet, M.M. Murr. "Failure of Medicare Health Maintenance Organizations to Control the Cost of Colon Resections in Elderly Patients," *Archives of Surgery*, vol. 139, no. 12 (December 2004), pp. 1366-1370.

[61] M. Susan Marquis, Jeannette A. Rogowski, and José J. Escarce, "The Managed Care Backlash: Did Consumers Vote with Their Feet?" *Inquiry*, vol. 41, no. 4, pp. 376-390.

[62] James C. Robinson, "The Commercial Health Insurance Industry in an Era of Eroding Employer Coverage," *Health Affairs*, vol. 25, no. 6 (November-December 2006), pp. 1475-1486.

[63] Margaret Ann Cross, "Rising Costs Strike Unions As Being Cause for Unrest," *Managed Care*, May 2003.

[64] Kaiser Family Foundation/Health Research and Educational Trust 2005 Annual Employer Health Benefits Survey (Kaiser/HRET) available at http://www.kff.org/insurance/chcm091405nr.cfm.

[65] Shifting compensation from take-home pay to employer-provided health care would reduce payroll taxes for Social Security and Medicare, but would also reduce future Social Security benefits in most cases.

[66] Ibid.

[67] Steven Greenhouse and Michael Barbaro, "Wal-Mart Memo Suggests Ways to Cut Employee Benefit Costs," *New York Times*, October 26, 2005. See "Wal-Mart Announces Additional Health Benefits Improvements and Timeline," available at http://www.walmartfacts.com/articles/1650.aspx. Under Wal-Mart's benefit plan introduced in April 2006, full-time associates become eligible for health benefits in six months, and part-time associates becomes eligible in one year.

[68] Susan Chambers, "Reviewing and Revising Wal-Mart's Benefits: Strategy Memorandum to the Board of Directors," 2006, Exhibit 3, available at http://www.nytimes.com/packages/pdf/business/26walmart.pdf. Wal-Mart claims that about 80% of their employees have health insurance coverage, either through family members or public insurance programs such as Medicaid or Veterans' Health Administration. See http://www.walmartfacts.com/FactSheets/ *832006*_Health_Care.pdf.

[69] Wal-Mart Fact Sheet, "What's the Story about Wal-Mart Health Care Benefits?" available at http://www.walmartfacts.com/FactSheets/832006_Health_Care.pdf.

[70] Donna C. Ross and Laura Cox, "In a Time of Growing Need: State Choices Influence Health Coverage Access for Children and Families," Kaiser Commission on Medicaid and the Uninsured Report, October 2005, available at http://www.kff.org/medicaid/upload/In-a-Time-of-Growing-Need-State-Choices-Influence-Health-Coverage-Accessfor-Children-and-Families-Report.pdf.

[71] Medicaid eligibility rules are complex and vary among states. For a description of Medicaid eligibility rules for the non-elderly, see CRS Report RL33019, *Medicaid Eligibility for Adults and Children*, by Jean Hearne.

[72] Victor R. Fuchs, "Economics, Values and Health Care Reform," *American Economic Review*, vol. 86, no.1 (March 1996), p. 8. A minority of economic theorists, however, believed technological change was to blame for increasing medical costs.

[73] Burton A. Weisbrod, "The Health Care Quadrilemma: An Essay on Technological Change, Insurance, Quality of Care, and Cost Containment," *Journal of Economic Literature*, vol. 29, no. 2 (June 1991), pp. 523-552.

[74] Robert A. Rosenheck, Douglas L. Leslie, Jody Sindelar, et al., "Cost-Effectiveness of Second-Generation Antipsychotics and Perphenazine in a Randomized Trial of Treatment for Chronic Schizophrenia," *American Journal of Psychiatry*, vol. 163 (December 2006), pp. 2080-2089.

[75] Henry J. Aaron, "A Funny Thing Happened on the Way to Managed Competition," *Journal of Health Politics, Policy and Law*, vol. 27, no. 1, February 2002.

[76] Gerard F. Anderson, Uwe E. Reinhardt, Peter S. Hussey, and Varduhi Petrosyan, "It's The Prices, Stupid: Why The United States Is So Different From Other Countries," *Health Affairs*, vol. 22, no. 3 (May/June 2003), pp. 89-105.

[77] Mark V. Pauly, "Managed Care, Market Power, and Monopsony—Examining the Role of Regulation in an Evolving Healthcare Marketplace," *Health Services Research*, vol. 33, no. 5 pt. 2 (December 1998), pp. 1439-1460.

[78] In some cases, treating individuals more equally may enhance economic efficiency. If incomes depend in some part on luck or other random causes, then a social insurance policy that reduces income inequalities can enhance economic efficiency. For details see Gareth D. Myles, *Public Economics* (New York: Cambridge), pp. 6-7, 470-484.

[79] For a detailed analysis of the social insurance character of Social Security, see Peter Diamond, "Social Security," *American Economic Review*, vol. 94, no. 1 (March 2004), pp. 1-24.

[80] See Paul Starr, *The Social Transformation of American Medicine* (New York: Basic Books, 1983) for a description of the enactment of Medicare and Medicaid.

[81] See point 10 of the *United States ofAmerica—2006 Article IV Consultation, Concluding Statement of the IMF Mission*, May 31, 2006, available at http://www.imf.org/external/np/ms/2006/053106.htm and the GAO report, *21st Century: Addressing Long-Term Fiscal Challenges Must Include a Re-examination of Mandatory Spending*, GAO-06- 456T, February 15, 2006.

[82] David M. Cutler, *Your Money or Your Life*, (New York: Oxford Univ. Press, 2004).

[83] Amy Finkelstein, "The Aggregate Effects of Health Insurance: Evidence from the Introduction of Medicare" *Quarterly Journal of Economics*, vol. 122, no. 1 (2007).

[84] Income data from Table A1 in the April 2006 update of tables for Emmanuel Saez and Thomas Piketty, "Income Inequality in the United States, 1913-1998," *Quarterly Journal of Economics*, vol. 118, no. 1 (2003), pp. 1-39, available at http://elsa.berkeley.edu/~saez/TabFig2004prel.xls. According to the Saez and Piketty data, real gross income (i.e., income before individual income taxes and individual payroll taxes but after employers' payroll taxes and corporate income taxes and excluding transfers) per tax unit was roughly the same in 1972 and in 2002. However, the number of tax units per household rose, the Consumer Price Index (CPI) used to adjust for inflation overstates price changes, and transfers to households rose. Combining these effects gives a 40% increase in

real consumption per household over this period. National health expenditures from the Centers for Medicare & Medicaid Services, Office of the Actuary. Prices adjusted using the Bureau of Economic Analysis's implicit GDP price deflator, which is less subject to the biases of the CPI.

[85] Calculations based on the following data: real income growth for households outside of the top 1% was 40% between 1972 and 2002, according to Piketty and Saez, and the proportion of national health care was 7.5% in 1972 and 15.3% in 2002, according to the Centers for Medicare and Medicaid Services.

[86] David M. Cutler and Mark McClellan, "Is Technological Change in Medicine Worth It?" *Health Affairs*, vol. 20, no. 5 (September/October 2001), pp. 11-29.

[87] Todd Gilmer and Richard Kronick, "It's The Premiums, Stupid: Projections of the Uninsured Through 2013," *Health Affairs,* Web Exclusive, April 5, 2005.

[88] For an analysis of the role of health care spending in the federal government's future fiscal situation, see CRS Report RL33623, *Long-Term Measures of Fiscal Imbalance*, by D. Andrew Austin.

[89] Testimony of Sara R. Collins and Karen Davis entitled "Transparency in Health Care: the Time Has Come," in U.S. Congress, House Committee on Energy and Commerce, Subcommittee on Health, "What's The Cost? Proposals to Provide Consumers with Better Information About Healthcare Service Costs," hearings, 109th Cong., 2nd sess., March 15, 2006.

[90] Of course, at the beginning of an episode of care, whether a patient will survive is usually unknown. Therefore, distinguishing between life-saving care that saves a patient and futile care for a patient in his last days is difficult.

[91] Lester G. Telser, "Competition and the Core." *Journal of Political Economy*, 1996, vol. 104, no. 1, pp. 85-107.

[92] Claire Snyder and Gerard Anderson, "Do Quality Improvement Organizations Improve the Quality of Hospital Care for Medicare Beneficiaries?" *Journal of the American Medical Association*, vol. 293, no. 23 (June 15, 2005), pp. 2900- 2907; and the Institute of Medicine of the National Academies, *Medicare's Quality Improvement Organization Program: Maximizing Potential*, March 2006.

[93] William Rollow, et al., "Assessment of the Medicare Quality Improvement Organization Program," *Annals of Internal Medicine*, vol. 145, no. 5 (September 5, 2006), pp. 342-353. For the period analyzed by this study QIOs were allowed to select which providers they would work with. It is difficult, therefore, to infer whether QIOs were good at helping providers improve quality of care or whether QIOs were good at selecting providers with higher potential for quality improvement. Future studies by these authors promise more careful controls.

[94] These data are available at http://www.hospitalcompare.hhs.gov/.

[95] For a more extensive analysis of the potential of providing consumers with useful outcome data see Michael E. Porter and Elizabeth O. Teisberg, *Redefining Health Care: Creating Value-Based Competition on Results* (Allston, Mass: Harvard Business School Publishing, May 2006).

[96] Ashish K. Jha and Arnold M. Epstein, "The Predictive Accuracy of the New York State Coronary Artery Bypass Surgery Report-Card System," *Health Affairs*, vol. 25, no. 3 (2006), pp. 844-855.

[97] David Dranove, Daniel Kessler, Mark McClellan, and Mark Satterthwaite, "Is More Information Better? The Effects of 'Report Cards,'" *Journal of Political Economy*, vol. 111 (2003), pp. 555-588.

[98] Michelle Mello and Troyen Brennan, "Deterrence of Medical Errors: Theory and Evidence for Malpractice Reform," *Texas Law Review*, vol. 80 (2002), pp. 1595-1637.

[99] Mark V. Pauly, "Taxation, Health Insurance, and Market Failure in the Medical Economy," *Journal of Economic Literature*, vol. 24, no. 2 (June 1986), pp. 629-75.

[100] Ibid.

[101] Burton A. Weisbrod, "The Health Care Quadrilemma: An Essay on Technological Change, Insurance, Quality of Care, and Cost Containment," *Journal of Economic Literature*, vol. 29, no. 2 (June 1991), pp. 523-552.

[102] Henry Kaiser Family Foundation, "Insurance Companies Promote Use of Generic Drugs in Effort To Cut Costs," *Daily Health Policy Report*, September 19, 2006.

[103] Kenneth W. Kizer, John G. Demakis, John R. Feussner, "Reinventing VA Health Care: Systematizing Quality Improvement and Quality Innovation: VA's Quality Enhancement Research Initiative," *Medical Care* 38(6), Supplement I:I-7-I-16, June 2000.

[104] M.W. Morgan, "The VA Advantage: The Gold Standard in Clinical Informatics," *Healthcare Papers*, vol.5, no. 4 (2005), pp. 26-9.

[105] Steven M. Asch, et al., "Comparison of Quality of Care for Patients in the Veterans Health Administration and Patients in a National Sample," *Annals of Internal Medicine*, vol. 141, no. 12 (December 2004), pp. 938-945.

[106] T. Doran, C. Fullwood, H. Gravelle, et al., "Pay-for-Performance Programs in Family Practices in the United Kingdom," *New England Journal of Medicine*, vol. 355 (July 27, 2006), pp. 375-384.

[107] Arnold M. Epstein, "Paying for Performance in the United States and Abroad," *New England Journal of Medicine*, vol. 355, no. 4 (July 27, 2006), pp. 406-408.

[108] Henry J. Kaiser Foundation, "*Massachusetts Health Care Reform Plan - Fact Sheet*," April 2006, available at http://www.kff.org/uninsured

[109] For details, see Arnold Schwarzenegger, "*Governor's Health Care Proposal*," press release, available at http://gov.ca.gov/pdf/press/Governors_HC_Proposal.pdf.

# CHAPTER SOURCES

The following chapters have been previously published:

Chapter 1 – This is an edited, reformatted and augmented version of Congressional Research Service publication, Report R40834, dated May 11, 2010.

Chapter 2 – This is an edited, reformatted and augmented version of Congressional Research Service publication, Report RL32237, dated March 17, 2009.

Chapter 3 – This is an edited, reformatted and augmented version of United States Government Accountability Office publication GAO-09-864R, dated July 31 2009

Chapter 4 – This is an edited, reformatted and augmented version of United States Government Accountability Office publication GAO-09-363R, dated February 27, 2009.

Chapter 5 – This is an edited, reformatted and augmented version of Congressional Research Service publication, Report RL33759, dated March 9, 2007.

# INDEX

## D



## E

## F



## G



## H



## I